THE MAKING OF A
POKER
PLAYER

THE MAKING OF A
POKER
PLAYER

How an Ivy League Math Geek Learned to Play Championship Poker

Matt Matros

LYLE STUART
Kensington Publishing Corp.
www.kensingtonbooks.com

FOR PETER FABRIZIO, JR.,
1979–2002

Contents

Foreword
by Ben McGrath

My most vivid poker memory: I am maybe twelve years old, and on summer vacation with my family. We have finished dinner, and my mom, my dad, and I are sitting around the living room table (my sister has wisely chosen to slink off and read), playing seven-card stud, five-card draw, and, when it is my turn to deal, baseball stud (threes and nines wild; four buys another card). I am at that stage of adolescence where beating one's parents, especially in games of cunning and skill, seems vitally important. And yet I am not winning, not at all. My father has been bluffing quite successfully, or else getting very lucky, and then using his tall stacks of chips to chase us from contending for most pots, by raising—early and often. Finally, I've had it. Good cards or not, *I am going to win the next hand*. The cards, as it happens, don't exactly comply, but no matter; when my turn to bet comes I throw all of my remaining chips in the pot with gusto. All in! My mother, cautious and maybe a little sympathetic, folds. My father smiles, matches my contribution without hesitation, and says, "Whaddya got?" (He has three of a kind.) I'm not particularly proud of what happens next, but, well, here it is: I take my mug of hot tea, half full, and I toss it at my father's chest. We've never played poker as a family since.

Matt Matros had a different kind of formative poker-playing experience, not least because he seems to have had better control of his temper than I had. (And perhaps, I'd like to think, because he had better beginner's luck.) Nonetheless, we have several things in common, Matt and I. We went to college together. We both spent an inordinate amount of time while there playing video games. (He played computer poker, of course; I played Sega hockey.) And we both, on occasion, went to the library. To be honest, I didn't get much work done in the library (I took many naps), but, then, neither did Matt. He played poker in the library. He organized full, lengthy games, with seven or eight people, to be played there—during exam time, no less. And when that didn't work—when other students, furiously reading and cramming, had claimed all of the library's best real estate—he found empty classrooms in which to hold his poker games.

I played in a couple of those games, but not memorably. I think I may have been distracted by the constant, nagging urge to refill my beer (this being college, after all). Mostly, I suspect, I suffered from that same impatience I'd demonstrated at the living room table long ago. After sitting out a few hands, I'd manage to convince myself that a pair of twos is only a strong-willed bluff away from winning the pot. Alas, it typically isn't—and wasn't. I gave the game up. I'm therefore grateful that Matt has chosen not to include me in this book, as he has many of his more regular opponents. (There is, you'll notice, a character whose first name is the same as mine, but do not be fooled; that Ben is no doubt a far better poker player.) Because, despite my forgettable performances, I'm fairly sure that Matt *does* remember my tendencies and tics, my missed opportunities and even my strengths, such as they are. This, more than anything else, is what makes Matt such a good poker player: he watches, he notices, he remembers—everything.

It's also what makes Matt an ideal teacher, and what makes this book such an engaging guide. Odds charts and hypothetical scenarios can teach you, as any good instructor must, that winning at poker requires folding your cards far more often than you'd like. They can't cure you, however, of the boredom that begets impatience that results in, um, *losing at poker*, when you try to put this advice into practice. (I trust that I am speaking not only for myself, here.) Matt Matros's detailed narration of countless real matches, and the lessons he's learned from them, the tips he's picked up in progression along the way, quickly becomes part of your own poker-playing story. (If only I could remember, as Matt would have, what cards I was holding when I tossed that teacup . . .) His perceptiveness about seemingly unimportant moments and decisions, in fact, teaches that most valuable lesson—that, whether you're in or you're out, there's never a boring moment in a poker match as long as you know what to look for.

I was at a bachelor party in Las Vegas with Matt not long ago. He played poker most of the time, and I'm sure he did fine; he almost always does. I stuck with roulette, where the odds are mediocre but unchanging. That way, I reasoned, I couldn't make things any worse than they were apt already to be. I started off slowly, but I hung in there, and soon my fortune changed: I came away an $800 winner at the end of the weekend. So now I've got luck back on my side. And I've read the book. I don't much want to play against Matt, but I think I might, at least, be ready to play poker again.

Introduction

The Mohegan Sun poker room was a welcoming place. Anyone with $30 in his pocket could sit down among the bamboo and the TV monitors and receive his very own poker hand, along with a warm smile from the dealer. My friends had told me how great it was, how much fun they'd had losing their money over a green felt table. I had a problem, though—I hated losing money.

So before I made the trip to Uncasville, Connecticut, I did some studying. I read a book. And I was silly enough to think that would give me an advantage over people who'd been playing the game for years.

That's how I convinced myself to make the one-hour trip from my dorm room in New Haven; and that's how I found myself in the middle of a hand, peering at three cards sitting faceup on the table. There were two fours and a queen. These were community cards, part of every player's hand. If they helped someone else's hand, chances were they didn't help mine. In front of me, facedown, were my two hole cards: an ace and a queen. In most of the hands until now, I had been throwing away my hole cards before any others were dealt, not wanting to pay even $3 to continue. The book told me to do this.

Finally involved in a hand, I tried my best not to be nervous. Most people get uncomfortable when real money that can buy real things in the real world is on the line. That book I'd read, *Winner's Guide to Texas Hold'em Poker* by Ken Warren, said if you thought of $6 in poker chips as a ticket to a matinee, or a personal pizza, or anything that six bucks could buy away from the table, then you had already lost. I was supposed to forget the money. The only thing that mattered was whether to bet, call, raise, or fold.

I had bet my hand aggressively, the correct play according to the book. I was betting chips, not money—a red chip and a white chip, not six bucks, I told myself. But my opponent, a quiet blond lady, wouldn't fold her hand. Did she think I was just a young punk and probably bluffing? Or did she have a four in the hole, meaning my two pair would lose to her three of a kind? I didn't think she had a four, but then I had no idea how much to trust my instincts. I was playing this game for the first time.

The betting finished and, since neither of us had folded, it was time to show the hands. I exposed my ace–queen. The blond woman reached for her cards to turn them over. Despite my newness to Hold'em, I knew from my other poker experience that this gesture meant trouble. Most players don't show their hands unless they hold a winner. I was still wondering how she had managed to beat me when the woman flipped up her cards. An ace . . . and a queen. We had the same hand, and we would each get half the pot. Although this was an unlikely result—the odds against someone else at the table having ace–queen, given the queen on board, were 17.7 to 1—it fit perfectly with my assessment of her hand: strong, but not too strong.

The woman and I smiled at each other as the dealer split the chips into equal-sized stacks and gave me my share.

"I thought one of you had the four!" said an obnoxious player at the end of the table, looking sketchy in his mostly unbuttoned shirt. It was the fall of 1998, and for the first time in my life, someone was pushing me chips after a hand of Texas Hold'em poker.

I somehow did leave the Mohegan Sun a winner that night. More important, I left feeling this victory was something I could repeat. I had won money in casinos before, from slot machines, but I knew I couldn't play slot machines forever and expect similar results. I thought I had a shot to win at poker.

Amid school, a job, and now more school, poker has been the one constant in my adult life. Most of the friends I've met since my days as a Yale undergrad I've met through poker. I've used poker to get through failed relationships and bad situations at work, and I've used it to celebrate my minor and major successes. It's an all-purpose drug—a drug that helps pay the bills. When I quit my job in the summer of 2002 to pursue an M.F.A., I subsidized my tuition with poker winnings. Poker is now one of my main sources of income.

My passion for poker has allowed me to make money and travel the country meeting intelligent players of all kinds—old and young, fat and skinny, geeky and suave. This book tries to create the same passion for the reader, and allow him or her to become a winning player.

Readers who know no poker will start where I started, as a high school kid playing dealer's choice with his buddies on a Friday night. I explain all games, and you'll learn everything the same way I did. You'll relish my wins and suffer my losses. You'll see my brilliant bluffs and stupid calls, my stupid bluffs and brilliant calls. You'll meet my poker buddies and my poker enemies.

This book, however, is a strategy book above all else. The first five chapters teach the basics. I begin with the rules, of poker generally and Texas Hold'em specifically, and quickly get into guidelines for how a beginner should approach the game. I explain how a tournament works and how new players can enter them without feeling overmatched. I discuss the popular variants called No Limit and Pot Limit Hold'em. I show the reader how to set up a home game. I explain how to interpret the body language of opponents. I do all these things by looking back at my own experiences with the game.

Chapters 6 through 10 teach intermediate-level strategy through stories of the sessions and tournaments I played as I evolved as a player. The final ten chapters cover more advanced material—game theory, the power of suggestion, high limit tournaments, thorough hand analysis, online poker, and how to profit from losing. Veteran players should look forward to the second half of the book.

My journey to becoming a successful poker player is about to become your journey. Enjoy learning poker with me.

THE MAKING OF A
POKER PLAYER

1

♠ ♣ ♦ ♥

Learning to Play

Fifteen-year-olds love an excuse to stay up all night. I was no different. Even if I didn't really want to get drunk or stoned, I still wanted to rebel in some way. An all-night poker game seemed just illicit and interesting enough to be acceptable. The only problem was I had almost no idea how to play. I knew the rules of what beat what, and not much else. Still, one night when a friend and I were crashing at another friend's house, a poker game emerged. We didn't quite play all night, as most "all night" activities fail to meet the literal definition, but we did play safely into the A.M. hours, learning new games along the way. I found joy in betting and calling with those plastic chips, stacking them up after winning a pot, flipping over the cards, and staring at opponents' faces.

We were so intoxicated with poker that my friends and I started getting together for regular games. Once, as many as ten guys from Westhampton Beach High School played (never girls, except for the one night we tried a game of strip poker and everyone showed up wearing five layers). I had been around card games since I was a little kid, when my great aunt Julia taught me something called Dirty Dog. Poker was in another class. Every hand was a different adventure, even though we always used those same fifty-two cards.

For the new players reading this book, here are poker's basic rules:

- Poker is played from one (never more, unlike blackjack) standard deck of fifty-two cards.
- A poker hand is made up of five cards.
- The hands are ranked, in order of best to worst, as follows:

  - *Straight flush*—Five consecutive cards in the same suit. An ace-high straight flush, called a **royal flush**, is the best hand in poker.
  - *Four of a kind*—A hand containing four cards of the same rank, such as four sevens and an ace.
  - *Full house*—Three cards of the same rank and two matched cards of another rank, such as three nines and two fours (nines full of fours).
  - *Flush*—Five nonconsecutive cards in the same suit.
  - *Straight*—Five consecutive cards not all in one suit.
  - *Three of a kind*—Three cards of the same rank and two other unmatched cards.
  - *Two pair*—Two cards of the same rank, two matched cards of another rank, and one unrelated card.
  - *One pair*—Two cards of the same rank and three unrelated cards.
  - *High card*—Five nonconsecutive cards of different ranks, not all of the same suit.

- When two hands are the same, higher cards beat lower cards. So four queens beat four tens, an ace-high flush beats a jack-high flush, and a seven-high straight beats a six-high straight. A full house is bigger than another if the three matched cards are of a higher rank, so kings full of threes beats queens full of aces. With two pair, the highest paired card is the winner—aces and fours beats kings and queens.

A poker hand contains several rounds of betting. On each round, every player gets the chance to "act" on his hand. When the "action" is on a player, he has these choices:

Check—Pass rather than bet. This costs nothing. If another player has already bet, checking is not an option.

Bet—Put chips into the pot. Every other player must at least match the bet if he wants to remain in the hand. A player can only bet if no other player has bet when the action gets to him.

Fold—Throw your cards in the muck, conceding the pot to one of the other players.

Call—Match a bet that another player has made.

Raise—Increase the amount it costs to stay in the hand by putting even more chips in the pot after someone has bet (this is my favorite option, and should be yours too). Doing this after having checked earlier is called *check-raising,* a powerful play that some consider unethical but is certainly not. It is merely another weapon at a poker player's disposal.

A betting round ends when each player who hasn't folded has put the same amount of money in the pot. After the last betting round, if more than one player is left in the hand, the cards are exposed and the best hand wins. Many times in casino poker a player will win a pot without ever showing his hand. This result is only possible if everyone else folds.

During a deal of five-card draw (where everyone gets five cards and is given the opportunity to exchange some of them), a goofy player looked over his hand and said, "Tally Ho." Tally-Ho is a brand of playing cards, and as with most decks, the brand name appeared on one specific card. A quiet player looked at the goofy player and said, "Evan, do you have the ace of spades?" Evan nodded and, realizing his mistake, removed the ace of spades from his hand and showed it to us (remember, revealing cards in poker is bad). Really, he had shown us already.

One night we played Indian Poker. In this incredibly stupid variant, four cards are dealt to each player, *all faceup*, and then each player puts the fifth and final card on his forehead, so that everyone except him knows what he has. After four cards, I had four spades and Chris, my lone opponent, had a pair. As I put the fifth card to my forehead the entire table gasped, and my opponent cowered in fear in his seat. "Um, uh, I uh, bet," he said. I called, meaning I matched the money he had bet, more sure that I had the flush than if I had seen the card myself. Of course the ace of spades was on my head, and I raked in the pot. "You practically told me what you had," I said. His response? "I was scared, seeing that ace up there!"

These were my first experiences in guessing my opponents' hands without knowing what they were. We call this **reading** a player. When Evan said "Tally-Ho," everyone at the table read him for having the ace of spades in his hand. When Chris bet and I had the ace of spades on my forehead, I read it as a bluff—an attempt to win the pot by betting with a lousy hand, hoping I would fold. Reading opponents is essential to poker success, and it is a topic we will return to throughout the book.

My high school friends all had fun playing, but most of them didn't win. In fact one particular player, Jeremy, seemed to be the only one consistently coming out ahead. He didn't talk much and almost never lost. I suspected him of cheating—not big-time stuff, but at least dealing himself a good hand every once in a while. I mean, I was the class nerd, and I was spending time away from the table thinking about when to fold and why. How could someone else have been the big winner? Now I know. He was the only one who would bet the maximum. He would fold earlier than everyone else. He didn't chase hands in wild-card games. Jeremy was playing well, and the rest of us were playing miserably. This fact still makes me shake my head.

I'm sure many readers will enter the poker universe through kitchen table games like the ones I played, so let's examine some of the reasons I didn't do well in them.

1. *I played too many hands.* It is virtually impossible to be a winning poker player if you're committed to playing every hand "at least for the first few cards." Even players considered gamblers, maniacs, **loose** (in poker-ese), usually fold more than half their hands at the first opportunity. The reason is simple: to win a pot, your hand has to be the best, not second or third, but the best. Opponents generally don't fold often enough to allow you to play

weak hands hoping to win without a showdown. You have to play only strong hands to win, at least when you're first learning the game. For example, in draw poker you should only play big pairs, and sometimes hands with four to a straight or flush (you would never draw more than one card hoping to hit those monsters). You'll see later in the book how much experience I had before I started playing less-than-premium hands.

2. *I never bet the maximum.* Our game had a minimum bet of a dime and a maximum bet of $1.25. I would usually bet a quarter or so, since it was a friendly game. Being friendly is not the way to win. Earning the maximum with your good hands and minimizing the losses on your bad hands is the way to win. Furthermore, there is nothing unfriendly about playing your best game. To me, everyone playing his best and discussing hands after they're over is the friendliest game possible. There is a poker adage that says if you can't check-raise your grandmother, you shouldn't be playing.

3. *I chased and chased and chased.* I would never fold a hand unless I had absolutely no way to win the pot. I had no idea there was a very specific way to determine whether to call a bet looking to improve, or to fold and give up (I'll discuss this in detail later). I never thought to fold if there were cards in the deck that could win it for me.

The above comments apply to all forms of poker. As I mentioned, however, some of the games we played were wacky. These wacky games require a few guidelines that are all their own. You won't see Doyle Brunson and Chip Reese discussing these points over the $1,500–$3,000 table at the Bellagio.

1. In a game featuring wild cards—that is, a game where one card, like a deuce, can be used as any card in the deck—it is of paramount importance to have a wild card in your hand. Let's say, for example, that you have three fours, but no wild cards. In a "real" poker game, you'd have a reasonably strong hand. But if we're playing deuces wild, and I have just one deuce in my hand, then I will win even if I only have a pair of fives to go with it. God for-

bid I get two wild cards—then a single natural pair gives me four of a kind! Natural hands only make you money in wild-card games when your opponents play them.

2. It takes a much stronger hand to win in a game with wild cards. Really, this is just another way of making my first point, but it's so essential that I make it again. If eight or more cards in the deck are wild, it's not uncommon to see five of a kind versus a straight flush at the showdown, which usually leads to an argument over who gets the pot (most would say five of a kind beats all other hands). Even if just deuces are wild, four of a kind is a fairly typical winning hand. Do not draw to straights and flushes in wild-card games—they will only get you broke. Holding wild cards with pairs is the only way to show down a winning hand consistently.

3. Don't be afraid to fold without looking at your hand. Sound stupid? One of our variants was called Seven-Card No Peek. Each player got dealt seven cards facedown but could not look at any of them. When all the cards were dealt, the first player turned over one card, and there was a round of betting. Then the next player had to turn over cards until he could beat the first player's hand. So if the first player turned over an ace, the next player had to turn over cards until he found a pair. Let's say the second player eventually turned over a pair of tens, and after the next round of betting, the third player turned over his cards one at a time, and they were seven, seven, seven. He now has trips already, and there is another round of betting. If he's smart, he'll bet the maximum. You haven't seen any of your cards yet, but of course you shouldn't call! Your opponent has trips in three cards, and he is a huge statistical favorite. How can you fold a hand where you haven't even seen any cards? Simple, take your hand, throw it in the muck, and count all the money you saved as everyone else keeps dumping chips in the pot.

None of the points I just made, about general strategy or wacky-game strategy, were obvious to me in my high school days. But poor intuition notwithstanding, I was smitten with the game. I chose to write a poker-playing program as my end-of-semester project for a mathematical computing class. Programming is essentially logic. If this happens, then do that. If not this, then do something else. Poker can be approached the same way. Should I bet? If there is x amount in the pot, then yes. If there is less than x, then is there a chance your opponent will fold? If not, should I check and then fold, or check and then call? You could carry out these "if-thens" forever, which is what makes the game so intriguing.

My program didn't know any strategy and made all betting decisions at random (oh, to have a player like this in my games today). If I were to take up this project again, I would try to make it execute all of the strategy described in this book. But back in high school, I had trouble getting the computer to even print playing cards on the screen. I never had a finished product, but I had the beginnings of a lifelong curiosity.

At 5 A.M. on Christmas morning, 1995, I was an eighteen-year-old in the backseat of the family station wagon on my way to Long Island–McArthur Airport. My father had reasoned no one else would be flying at that time (correct!), so what better time to head out for a winter vacation in sunny Phoenix, Arizona.

I didn't want to go on the trip to begin with. I had a girlfriend at home whom I hadn't seen much during my first semester in New Haven, and instead of being with her for the next six days, I would be doing God-knows-what with my family in the middle of the desert.

After reaching our condo, getting fed, calling my girlfriend to wish her Merry Christmas, and taking a nap, I found one thing to like about Arizona. The legal age for gambling was eighteen. By seven and a half months, I was permitted to enter a casino and make wagers however I chose. I only wanted to play poker.

My father is an action junkie, so he gladly took me out for a night at Fort McDowell Casino, located just outside Phoenix on a Native American reservation. The only poker game being spread that I'd played back home was Seven-Card Stud. With $11 in my pocket, I walked to the ATM to withdraw a hundred bucks. I had expected to receive more than one bill. Welcome to the world of casinos, where hundreds play, twenties cannot be found, and fifties are just annoying.

The dealer did have three twenties in change for me when I bought in to the $1–$3 Stud game for forty bucks. I didn't have much strategy going in, or rather, the strategy I had was dreadful. In Seven-Card Stud, players are dealt two cards facedown and one card faceup. There is a round of betting and then a second up-card is dealt. In all, four cards are dealt faceup, with a round of betting after each. The seventh and final card is dealt facedown, followed by the final round of betting and then a showdown. In $1–$3 Stud, players can bet anywhere between $1 and $3 at any time. I never folded after the third card (you've only seen three cards, how could you fold?), and never folded if I still had the potential to make the best hand, no matter how much of a long-shot it might have been. Any poker player reading this should have a good idea how the session turned out. As I explained earlier, you just can't play everything that gets dealt to you.

On my first hand I had some **rag** as my up-card—maybe a deuce or a trey. "One dollar to you, sir," the dealer said.

"What?" I said.

"That's a forced bet, sir," the dealer said. I threw in a dollar, wondering if I had just been suckered. At home, the highest card showing always had the action, and no one was ever forced to bet. I learned after watching a couple of hands that it doesn't work this way in casinos. On third street (after the first three cards have been dealt) the lowest card showing is forced to bet some minimum amount. On all the other rounds, the highest hand showing has the action and can bet or check.

Early in the session I had a seven, eight, ten, and jack in my hand, and was facing a $3 bet on sixth street (that is, with one card to come). Using my strategy of never folding when I had potential to win, I called. I peered down at my final card—nine! It had hit me right in the gut. I don't even think I raised on the final betting round, that's how bad I was playing. (Remember, it's important to win the maximum with your good hands.) Even as I raked in the pot, I shook my head, mumbling something about how lucky I had been. "Yeah, but you have to have the balls to stay in," said the guy next to me. I still shook my head. The casino was starting to teach me lessons I hadn't learned in dozens of home games. Balls have their place in poker, but only when used in conjunction with the brain.

I won't pretend I learned this lesson in real time, because I didn't deviate from my strategy. Even after winning that nice pot with the straight, I soon lost the $40 I had started with. I bought another forty in chips from the dealer, and that went much faster than the first forty. I used the final $20 bill in my wallet to buy some more chips. They went up and down as I won a hand, then lost a hand. Finally I lost a few hands in a row, and my chips were gone. It had taken about three hours, but the inevitable did occur. I lost all the money I had allowed myself to lose on poker, playing an awful, awful strategy. Time to try the roulette wheel. Why not? The most I could lose was eleven bucks, which seemed like nothing after dropping a hundred.

Instead of placing chips on a number, roulette bets at Fort McDowell were somehow made electronically. I had to fight my way through the crowd to put $5 in the machine and bet on number ten. I would make a quick $175 if it hit, and all my poker woes would be forgotten with interest. The wheel spun round and round with the ball seeming to pass every number at least twice a second. The ball came down into the slots, bounced, and landed right next to ten. But not *in* ten. Sunk, I left the frenzied roulette area with $6 in my pocket.

I told Dad the story, arguably the first **bad beat** story I ever told. A bad beat in poker is when a hand that was heavily favored to win ends up a loser after all the cards are dealt because another hand improved to beat it. People love to complain when their big hands lose. They'll tell a bad beat story to anyone who will listen. In the literal sense, no loss at the roulette wheel could ever be considered a bad beat, because every bet in roulette has negative expectation. The house is the only one that should show a profit when I bet $5 on number ten (a profit of 26.3¢, in the long run). When I finished telling the story, I told Dad I would go lose my last six bucks and then be done. This is a strange phenomenon, the throwing away of one's last few dollars. You try so hard to win with your first six bucks, why just rid yourself of your last six? People do it all the time, though. It's especially common among gambling addicts and other compulsives. For me, I was disgusted with the place. I guess I wanted my disgust to be complete. It was so obvious there was no way to make easy money there, and I couldn't believe I had bought into this gambling hysteria for as much as I had.

I tried to get back to the roulette area to give it another shot, but it was so mobbed I gave up. I wandered around, not sure where I was going, when I saw an open slot machine. That seemed perfect, and I sat down next to it and loaded it up with my final $6. The machine gave me the option to bet either $2 or $1. In the spirit of trying to lose my money as fast as possible, I bet $2 and pushed the button. Cherry, seven, blank. No money. I made another $2 bet. Blank, cherry, orange. No money. I tried to bet my last $2, but the machine wouldn't let me. I almost screamed. I tried to bet $1 instead, and this time the machine went in motion. Again, I lost. With my final dollar in the machine, I made my last bet of the night. The columns started spinning, and again they each stopped in turn. Then something different happened. The middle column remained still and the two outer columns started spinning for a second time. They stopped in turn, and then the light on top of the machine started flashing. It kept making this ringing sound, but no coins were coming out. Trying to get permission to leave, I turned to the person next to me.

"What's going on?" I said.

"Oh, you won," he said.

"Huh?"

"You won, you won a thousand dollars."

I just stared.

"That's if you bet two dollars," said some jealous old lady. "If you bet one dollar, you won five hundred dollars."

"Excuse me?"

A woman in a business suit came by and said, "Congratulations, sir," and told me I just needed to put another dollar into the machine to make it official.

"I don't have another dollar," I said.

"Oh, that's fine," she said, and she pressed some buttons on the machine to make it spin another time. It spun around and stopped just like it had the first three times. The instant it finished she said, "Congratulations, sir, I'll be right back with five hundred dollars for you."

"Okay," I said, still not believing I would receive money. I waited at the slot machine for what seemed like an hour but was probably around ten minutes. The woman did come back, and when she did she handed me a mixture of hundreds, twenties, and tens that added up to five hundred smackers.

I went back to Dad's table to tell the good beat story. I had six dollars, then four, then two, then one, and on my last dollar . . .

"You won twenty," Dad said.

"I won five hundred," I said. Dad made one of his grunting sounds that is a cross between "What?" "Huh?" "Uhh," "Ahhh," and "Ehhh." Then he said, "Really? Hey that's great! Hey, my son won five hundred dollars!" he said to everybody at his table. Then he asked me what I was going to play next. Nothing, I told him. I wasn't falling for their trap anymore. I had defied the odds and had $389 profit in my pocket. I was not about to give it right back. I would never enter a casino again. I just couldn't see the point in playing games where I always figured to lose.

I should have known a lot of things before entering a casino for the first time. I should have known that poker is one of the only games where you can win money. The best roulette, craps, and slot players in the world cannot expect to make a living at these games. Except in rare cases, there is no strategy a player can use to make him a long-term winner. Blackjack is beatable by experts, but the money a player wins comes from the house, and casino management never likes to lose. Because of this, blackjack experts often find themselves unwelcome at gaming establishments. Poker is different. The house makes money in poker by taking a small piece out of every pot (usually no more than $4), so no matter what happens the house always wins. The house doesn't care if a poker player is an expert—the other players are paying him. The first rule of poker then, is: do not use your poker bankroll to gamble on anything else. Many top tournament players give back their poker winnings at the craps tables, or the sports book, or at the racetrack. Don't fall prey to any of these **leaks**.

I also should have known some basic poker strategy. I made the same mistakes I made in my high school games, only this time they cost a lot more. After Arizona, I had a few years before my next casino experience, as it's twenty-one or over to play on the East Coast. It was enough time for me to forget my desire never to gamble again.

I still didn't win on either of my trips to the Connecticut casinos during the summer of 1998. I still didn't understand poker strategy, I still didn't understand that poker was beatable, and I still hated losing.

I told my friend after the second trip that the odds are always against us, that we're never supposed to win. My friend asked why, then, did we bother going? It was tough to answer.

The next day I told myself, "I'm even today. And I'm going to be even every day from now on, because I'm not going back to any of those stupid places." I meant it that time.

I needed poker knowledge to talk me out of it.

2

♠ ♣ ♦ ♥

Texas Hold'em

"You're right, I don't have spades," John Malkovich says through a thick Russian accent in the first scene of *Rounders*. Malkovich is Teddy KGB, a ruthless mobster/poker player running a New York City card room from some seedy, unadvertised location. KGB's opponent is Mike McDermott, played to perfection by Matt Damon, himself a real-life participant in the 1998 World Series of Poker main event.

Mike has just risked all his chips on a full house, nines full of aces, and goads Teddy by saying, "I don't think you have the spades." Mike actually wants Teddy to have the spades—an ace-high spade flush, that is—a hand Mike beats if Teddy calls the $33,000 raise. Unfortunately for our hero (if you haven't guessed, the character named "KGB" is the bad guy), Teddy has a bigger full house, aces full of nines, and cleans Mike out. Mike then suffers the torment of playing no poker for the next nine months, all the while living off his girlfriend Jo (portrayed, in possibly the worst performance ever by a modern-day actress, by Gretchen Mol).

I saw this landmark poker film for the first time in September 1998. Only weeks earlier my father had described to me the game Mike and Teddy were playing, a game called Texas Hold'em. Dad had tried this game during his most recent visit to Foxwoods, a casino in Ledyard, Connecticut, and come out a $150 winner. He called me that same night and giddily described the basic rules.

1. Each player is dealt two cards facedown. These are the only cards unique to his hand.

2. Five additional cards are dealt faceup, but they are community cards every player can use.
3. A player can use any combination of his two hole cards and the five community cards to make his five-card hand.

This is all the information you need to understand the first scene of *Rounders*. In that devastating hand for Mike McD, Teddy's hole cards are two red aces (the ace of diamonds and the ace of hearts), while Mike's are the ace and nine of clubs. The community cards, or **board**, are A♠9♠8♣9♥3♠ (where the small letters represent suits). As you can see, Mike's five-card hand of 999AA gives him a full house, but Teddy has an even bigger one with AAA99. One reason Mike lost all his chips on this hand is because he thought Teddy had a flush—a possibility only because there were three cards of the same suit on board. Did Mike play his hand well? Was he just unlucky to go broke on this hand? Or was there a way Mike could have lost less than the $50,600 he ended up forking over to KGB? These are questions not for simple moviegoers but for serious poker players, and we will return to them throughout the book.

When I first saw the movie I was certainly not qualified to judge Mike's play—I was lucky to understand what was going on at all. But I still loved the film, and so did two of the Yalies I saw it with, Burke and Fabian. Both of these guys were entrepreneurial types and fellow staffers at *The Yale Herald*, Yale's weekly newspaper (Fabian was the publisher). Fabian was the fiscally responsible, watch-every-penny member of our team. Burke, once the editor-in-chief, would push for spending everything the paper earned on end-of-semester parties. Ironically, they took on the exact opposite style of their personalities at the poker table. But more on that later.

Burke and Fabian loved *Rounders* so much they immediately took a trip to the Mohegan Sun, a casino less than an hour away with a poker room. They had little success on their first excursion but came back even more determined to play this game and play it well. Meanwhile, I had called my father and told him to go see this new movie all about his new game. I mentioned that some of my friends had already tried their luck at the Hold'em tables, and that through fate, or coincidence, or whatever, these same friends would be joining my father and me at my childhood home in Westhampton, New York, in just a few days because I had volunteered my house for an upcoming *Herald*er getaway. Upon hearing this, Dad, a high school math teacher, quickly offered to organize a basic Hold'em strategy session when we got there. He had just read Ken Warren's book and planned to use it as the basis for discussion. Burke and Fabian were excited. Dad was delirious in his babbling anticipation. I probably should have been looking forward to it as well.

But remember that, following my hugely unsuccessful trips that summer, I had vowed to never again set foot in a casino. *Rounders* showed me I still loved the game, but did not show me I could be any good at it. I had it in my head that casino games were losers—traps set by the house in such a way that no player could beat them. Dad's win at Foxwoods, and the fact of his upcoming strategy session, were not enough to convince me otherwise.

The day came, and the *Herald*ers descended on Westhampton. We were an eclectic group—five men and five women: a playwright, a pre-med, a math major (yours truly), a future Rhodes scholar, a future elementary school teacher, a history major with near-perfect LSAT scores, an award-winning short story writer, a future graduate of Harvard Business School, a future real-estate lawyer, and a Manhattanite who went on to work for ESPN. It was the kind of crowd parents loved, especially mine. We enjoyed Mom's chicken parmigiano dinner before the boys and girls went to separate parts of the house. It was time for the men to talk poker, and for the women to . . . do whatever it is women do.

My father, in his zeal, had written a three-page pamphlet and made photocopies for everyone. He passed them out as we gathered around the kitchen table, the same table on which I had played so many zany forms of poker with my high school buddies years earlier. Reading from his notes, Dad described the game play for the form of Hold'em spread in almost all casinos—Limit Hold'em with structured betting. This game has a **small bet** and a **big bet**, for which the different limits are named: $1–$2 Hold'em, $3–$6 Hold'em, $10–$20 Hold'em, and $400–$800 Hold'em, among many others. Here's how the betting works.

1. Hold'em does not use antes—in other words, players are not forced to put money in the pot every single hand. Instead of antes, Hold'em uses **blinds**.

2. A small, flat disk that says DEALER is placed in front of one player, the theoretical dealer for that hand (a nonplaying, casino-employed dealer actually deals the cards). This disk is called the **button**.

3. The two players to the left of the button must put money in the pot before the cards are dealt—in effect, making bets without seeing their hands. Starting from the button and moving left, these players are called the **small blind** and **big blind**. In a $3–$6 Hold'em game, the small blind **posts** $1 and the big blind posts $3 at the start of a hand. Also, the first time any player sits down at a casino table he must post a $3 blind in order to get cards. His other option is to wait until it's his big blind (not receiving a hand until then).

4. After the first two cards are dealt, the action is on the player to the big blind's immediate left. We call this player **under the gun (UTG)**. He has three options—fold, call, or raise. He cannot check; he must at least match the big blind if he wants to remain in the hand.

5. If UTG chooses to raise, he must raise the exact amount of the big blind. In a $3–$6 game, an UTG raise costs $6, doubling the $3 big blind.

6. After UTG acts on his hand, play proceeds to the left. Each player must at least match the highest bet or fold. Raises must be in increments of the small bet; for example, in a $3–$6 game, the first raise is to $6, the second to $9, and the third to $12.

7. Once the action gets to the big blind, he has the **option** to raise if no one has raised yet, or he can choose to check.

8. We call the betting on the first two cards **preflop** action. When the preflop action is complete, the first three community cards are dealt all at the same time. These three cards are called the **flop**.

9. Betting on the flop starts with the first active player to the left of the button. He can either check or bet exactly the amount of the small bet (which is also the amount of the big blind).

10. When the flop action is finished, the fourth community card, the **turn**, is dealt. Betting again starts to the left of the button, but this time any bets and raises must be in increments of the big bet ($6 in a $3–$6 game).
11. After the turn action, the **river**, the fifth and final community card, is dealt. Action proceeds in the same way as on the turn. If two or more players are left after the river betting, there is a showdown and the best hand wins.
12. When the hand is finished, the button moves one seat to the left, and the next hand begins.

That's it. That's the glorious game that has expanded beyond any Texan's wildest imagination. Don't worry if it sounds complicated. The mechanics of the game are actually very simple. Deal two to everyone, facedown, bet. Deal three faceup in the middle, bet. Deal another faceup in the middle, bet with doubled stakes. Deal a final card faceup in the middle, bet one last time. Not so hard, right? The only somewhat tricky parts are the blinds and the structured betting. I promise the game will feel natural after a short time at the table.

After dealing a few sample hands to the college journalists around him, my father started to explain some of the game's most basic strategic concepts.

Strategic Concept #1: Play good starting hands.

A friend of mine, after hearing the rules of Hold'em, said to me, "Well, obviously you wouldn't fold after the first two cards." He's not the only one who thinks this way, and it's easy to see why. After two cards, you've only received two-sevenths of your hand. Wouldn't it make sense at least to look at the next three cards, which conveniently come all at once via the flop?

Well, if you remember the number one reason I was a poor player in high school, you'll know that this line of thinking makes no sense at all. Those first two cards in Hold'em are the only cards that differentiate your hand from everyone else's. If your hole cards are weak, it's asking quite a lot to expect five community cards to help your hand more than everyone else's (as I explained last chapter, improving to the second or third best hand doesn't get you anywhere).

No, the primary way to show down the best hand is to start with a strong hand. Consider a full, ten-handed $3–$6 Hold'em game at your local casino, where bluffing rarely works and almost every hand goes to a showdown. Here are some starting hands a beginner should never play unless he is in the big blind: an ace and seven of different suits, a six and a five of different suits, the king–four of hearts, the jack–six of diamonds. For different reasons, each of these hands is a potential disaster for an inexperienced player. So what hands should a beginner play? Well, as my father explained, it depends a lot on your **position** relative to the blinds. If you're sitting UTG, or to UTG's immediate left, you're in **early position**. Moving left, the next three seats are considered **middle position**. The button, and the two players to his right, are in **late position**.

Position is a hugely important factor in deciding whether to play a hand. The reason is simple—the later your position, the more information you'll have over the course of a hand. This is because early position players act *before* late position players on every betting round, or **street**. The late players, then, know more about the other players' hands when it's their turn to act; and in poker, information is money.

Here's a quick example. Let's say I have the A♠T♦ UTG. Six players see the flop, which comes A♥Q♥4♦. The big blind bets, and now it's up to me. Well, my pair of aces figures to be a pretty strong hand, so I raise. Except the next player reraises, and the button raises yet again, making it four small bets total to see the turn. When the action gets back to me, I know I'm in deep trouble. Against sane players, I'm probably up against a hand like A♦Q♦, which leaves me pretty much **drawing dead** (this occurs when not a single card or combination of cards can win a hand for a player; in the example I gave, I could still catch two running cards to make a straight or full house, so I would not be drawing totally dead against A♦Q♦). So I fold. I lose two small bets on the flop action.

Now, say I have the same A♠T♦ with the same flop but this time on the button. The big blind bets, the next player raises, and the player to my right—the **cutoff**—reraises. My pair of aces doesn't look so good anymore, especially because my **kicker** is a ten. Against hands like

A♦K♦ and A♣J♣, my *best* hope of winning is to catch one of three remaining tens in the deck. This is quite a longshot, and that's if I even have a shot at all. So I fold. But this time I don't lose any money on the flop action. I was able to save two small bets because I learned something about my opponents' hands before the action got to me. In a $3–$6 game, my position would have made a $6 difference.

This example of the importance of position also illustrates another major factor in deciding whether to play hands before the flop—**domination**. A♦Q♦ is a very strong Hold'em hand, but not against A♠K♠. This is because of the shared ace between the two hands. Barring a straight or flush (which A♠K♠ is about as likely to make as A♦Q♦), the only way for A♦Q♦ to win is to make a pair with one of the three remaining queens in the deck. Pairing the ace will not help, as the pair of aces with a king kicker is still the best hand. Although 2♥3♠ is not a hand you'd ever want to play voluntarily, it will defeat A♠K♠ on far more boards than A♦Q♦ will because pairing either the deuce or the three could make 2♥3♠ the winner. Kickers really matter. It is for this reason that I declared hands like A♠7♣ unplayable. Any ace with a bigger kicker crushes this hand, and may well cost you money if an ace flops.

With these concepts in mind, here are a beginner's guidelines for choosing starting hands in Hold'em. These guidelines assume no one has raised in front of you, but one or more players may have called. If no one has entered the pot at all when the action gets to you, you should pretty much raise whenever you have a playable hand for your position (i.e., you should raise or fold, never call). If there is a raise in front of you, a beginner should fold everything except AA, KK, QQ, and AK. Remember, position saves you money, and part of the way it does is by giving you the chance to fold to a raise. But if no one has raised, here's a suggested course of action.

Notation

"T" means ten.

A little "s" denotes that both cards in the hand must be of the same suit—a **suited** hand.

A little "o" denotes two cards of different suits—an **offsuit** hand.

Guidelines

Early Position
Raise—AA, KK, QQ, AK
Call—JJ, AQ, KQs
Fold—Everything else

Middle Position
Raise—Early position raising hands plus JJ, AQ, KQs
Call—TT, 99, 88, 77, AJ, ATs, KJs, QJs, KQo, KTs
Fold—Everything else

Late Position
Raise—Middle position raising hands plus TT, 99, AJ, ATs
Call—88, 77, 66, 55, 44, AT, A9, Axs (where x is any small card), KJ, KT, K9, K8s, QJ, QT, Q9s, JT, J9s, T9, T8, 98, 97s, 87s
Fold—Everything else

Notice a few things about these guidelines.

1. *Small and medium pocket pairs are not as strong as most people think.* In a low limit game, where almost every hand is shown down and many players are in every flop, pocket pairs of tens or lower will rarely win unimproved. Pairs below jacks should be thought of as drawing hands, for when they make three of a kind (*sets*) they are very strong hands indeed. But they are *never* very strong until then.

2. *Pocket aces and pocket kings should almost always be played for a raise.* Yes, aces and kings are the two strongest preflop hands by far. So why in the world would you not want to raise with them in a low limit game where players love to call? Low limit players who try to trap their opponents by just calling before the flop with aces or kings usually end up trapping themselves. Aces and kings are strong, but they still give you only one pair. Besides, you want *more* money in the pot preflop when you hold these hands.

3. *Most suited hands are UNplayable.* The possibility of making a flush should be thought of as a bonus for a Hold'em hand, be-

cause that's really all it is. Given two suited cards, the chances of making a flush are about 6.4 percent. Players who play any two suited cards are sure to go broke quickly.

4. *Position, position, position.* Just look at how many more hands I recommend playing in late position than in early position, and how few hands I do recommend playing in early position. Trust me, the information gap warrants this difference.

5. *Play tight.* This means fold early and often. The biggest mistake beginners make is to call when they should fold. When you start out, I want your biggest mistake to be that you fold too often preflop. In **loose** games, where every hand has many players calling preflop, a **tight** but predictable player will make a lot of money simply by playing only premium hands. You'll have plenty of chances to play trash as you evolve as a player. Try to win some money playing real hands first.

Dad threw all this material at us and we tried to absorb it. Fold around 90 percent of our hands, pay a lot of attention to position, don't overvalue suited cards or pocket pairs. It seemed like a palatable amount of information, but we were to be given more. We had learned about preflop play, now we needed to know what to do on the flop.

If you follow the starting hand guidelines above, you will have a fairly strong hand most of the time you see the flop. If you improve on the flop, you should have a very strong hand indeed. A pair of the highest card on the flop is called **top pair**. A top pair with the highest possible kicker (for example, AK on a flop of K42, or AQ on a flop of AK3) is called, simply, **top pair–top kicker**. A pocket pair higher than any card on the flop is called an **overpair**. Top pair–top kicker or better is very strong. Against the type of opponents you'll face in low limit games, namely opponents who call a lot, you want to bet, raise, and reraise with these hands. This advice follows a more general strategic principle.

Strategic Concept #2: Play aggressively.

There are two ways to win a pot in poker—show down the best hand, or get everyone else to fold. The only way everyone else can fold is if you bet or raise, so failing to play aggressively removes one of your two chances to win the hand. Unfortunately, as I've mentioned several times, low limit players rarely fold, so the above is not a major reason to be aggressive in these games. Betting and raising your good hands is still, however, the best strategy, and I'll tell you why.

An old poker maxim is the best players win the most with their good hands, and lose the least with their bad hands. This maxim is a good one, so how can we use it? Well, to win the most with your good hands, you have to get money into the pot with them. Bet and raise with your strong hands, don't expect someone else to do it for you. Low limit players are **passive**, not aggressive. If you check, they will check right along with you, and your top pair will win less money—or worse, lose to a hand that got to see more cards for free. Yes, *sometimes* you will lose more money with good hands by playing them aggressively. But in the long run, aggressive play will earn far more than passive play, and the long run is all that matters.

An example. Let's say you have A♦Q♥ in a six-way pot. If the flop comes A♠T♥4♦, you want to bet, raise, and reraise, trying to get as much money in the pot as you can. Yes, at some point you have to back down, and when your opponents happen to hold hands like AK, AT, or A4 you will lose money. But that's poker. If you never bet with your good hands, you won't win enough with them. And God help you if you call bets with marginal hands. Checking and calling is a great way to go broke in this game. If you don't have a strong hand, fold at the first sign of interest in the pot from another player. If you do have a strong hand, bet and raise with it; on the flop, turn, and river. It's more fun and more profitable that way.

Other strategic concepts are important, but the first two I listed stand apart from the rest. Tight-aggressive poker is what makes a new player profitable, in all forms of the game. Other strategies tweak the basic concepts to grind out a little more profit, but you should never forget that tight-aggressive play is the basis for winning.

Now, I said that most of the time you're involved, it will be because you have the probable best hand. This is true. But here comes another, more ugly, truth—there will be many times you don't have the best hand but will have to call, hoping to improve to the best hand. This is called **drawing**. The most common draws in Hold'em (and indeed most forms of poker) are straight draws (four cards to a straight) and flush draws (four cards to a flush). If I hold Q♠J♥ and the flop comes T♥9♣2♠, I have an **open-ended straight draw**, so named because I can hit cards on both ends (an eight or a king) to complete my straight. If I hold the same Q♠J♥ on a flop of 9♣8♥2♠, I have a *gutshot* or **inside straight draw**, as only a ten will make my hand. **Flush draws** are easier to spot, as they occur when two or more of one suit hits the flop (this will happen more than 60 percent of the time). The best flush draws are **nut** flush draws, or draws to the best possible flush. A player holding the ace of spades with any other spade would have the nut flush draw on a flop of 9♠6♣2♠. On a flop of 9♠6♣2♦, there are no flush draws, but there are **backdoor** flush draws, which require the turn and river to both match one of the suits on the flop, for hands like A♠4♠ and A♣4♣. The odds against hitting a backdoor flush draw are roughly 23 to 1.

Draws are a different animal than **made hands** like top pair or three of a kind. When you are first learning poker, playing draws aggressively is usually a mistake. It takes experience to know when drawing hands want to get as much money in the pot as possible, and when they want to see the next card cheaply. For now, you only need to understand when it is worth at least calling with a draw. For this, I'll introduce a new strategic concept.

Strategic Concept #3: Make sure the pot is big enough to pay for your draw.

Explaining this requires a little math. Don't be scared, math-phobes, it doesn't require much. When drawing, the first thing you do is count your **outs**, the number of cards in the deck that make your hand. An open-ended straight draw has eight outs, while a flush draw has nine. Let's say you have a flush draw after the flop. There are forty-seven unseen cards—fifty-two minus the three on the flop and the two in your hand. This means that, on the turn, thirty-eight cards are bad for you and nine are good. These numbers might sound strange. After all, twenty cards were dealt before the flop, the dealer **burned** a card after the preflop action (meaning she mucked the first card off the deck before dealing the flop), three cards were flopped, and another card will be burned before the turn. So there are only twenty-five cards that could actually appear on the turn. *But*, you've only seen five cards, the ones in your hand and on the flop. The odds of making our hand on the turn must be calculated based on the number of *unseen* cards. Knowing that other cards have been dealt only helps us if we know exactly what they are. Think of it this way: if the dealer throws all but one of the cards in the trash, and then deals his one remaining card as the turn, this of course would not change the odds of making our flush. And neither does the existence of cards in the muck or in other players' hands.

So thirty-eight cards are bad for you, and nine are good, which means the **odds** against making a flush on the next card are 38 to 9. To keep it simple, let's say this is approximately 4 to 1 (to be perfectly accurate 38/9 = 4.22, so the correct odds would be 4.22 to 1), meaning for every four times you miss your hand, you'll hit your hand once.

After you know the odds of making your hand, the next step is to figure the size of the pot. Let's say we're playing $3–$6 Hold'em, six people have taken the flop including the two blinds, and there's a bet and two calls when the action gets to you. There are nine small bets in the pot, for a total of $27. In other words, if you call, you are getting 9 to 1 **pot odds** on the small bet you invest (neglecting the **rake**, the cut the house takes out of every pot). That is, if there is no more betting you make $27 when you win, and lose just $3 when you lose; 9 to 1 pot odds. Many new players get confused by this. They think that because they invested $3 before the flop, they can only win $24, or that it costs them $6 to call on the flop, or both. Both these ideas are wrong. Once you put money into the pot, that money is not yours anymore. I can prove it. If you fold, is someone going to give that money back to you? No. So it's not yours. It belongs to the pot now.

Now that we know the pot odds and the odds of making our hand, we have enough information to say whether we should call the bet with our flush draw. We said that our pot odds are 9 to 1, and the odds of hitting are 4 to 1. So, if we call, over the long run we'll miss four out of every five times. Over five hands, we'll lose $3 x 4 = $12 during the times we miss, and we'll win $27 the time we hit, for a net profit of $15, or $15/5 = $3 per hand. (Again, this is over the long run. You could easily miss five or even hit five flush draws in a row.) Therefore, we should call. The numbers work out this way because the pot odds are *bigger* than our odds of hitting. If the pot were only offering 2 to 1, then calling would've shown a *loss* of $1.20 per hand. If the pot had been offering 4 to 1, calling would have been equivalent to folding.

The long-run profit or loss of a given play is called the **expected value (EV)**. In poker, EV is everything. EV is God. If you make a positive EV play, then it doesn't matter if you win or lose on a particular hand, you've still made money overall. This concept can be extended to every stage of the hand. The question "Should I call preflop?" is equivalent to asking "Does calling with this hand have positive EV in this situation?" How the cards fall is beyond our control. The only thing we can do as players is put our chips in with positive EV ("Getting the best of it," as players like to say). Do that often enough, and the cards will take care of themselves.

It would be asking a lot to calculate your EV on the fly every time you play poker. The good news is you don't have to. A flush draw will always be nine outs, an open-ended straight draw will always be eight outs, and there will always be forty-seven unseen cards after the flop. The odds against hitting a flush draw in one card will always be 4.22 to 1, and an open-ended straight draw 4.88 to 1. It gets better. In almost every low limit Hold'em game you play, the pot odds will be there to draw at open-ended straights and flushes, even after the betting doubles on the turn (provided you're **drawing live**).

Some players like to calculate their chances of making their hand with two cards to come (we've only been calculating the odds for making your draw on the next card). A shortcut estimation is to multiply your number of outs on the flop by four to get the percent chance of making your hand. So, with a flush draw on the flop, you have about a $9 \times 4 = 36$ percent chance of improving to a flush by the river (actual number 35 percent). Notice that this is the **probability** of improving, and not the odds against improving. To convert probabilities to odds, compare the chance of missing to the chance of hitting. In the above example, there is a $100 - 35 = 65$ percent chance of missing our flush after two more cards. So the odds against hitting the flush with two cards to come are roughly 65 to 35, or 1.86 to 1. Be careful about calculating odds for draws with two cards to come, though, as it will often cost far more than one small bet to play a hand to the river. And yes, there is a similar trick for estimating probabilities with one card to come—multiply your number of outs by 2.2 (not quite as convenient, I know).

I've said that it's almost always correct to at least call with flush draws and straight draws in low limit Hold'em games. Let's look at one situation where it might be even better to raise with these draws. Say you're on the button in a $3–$6 Hold'em game and have flopped a flush draw. The big blind bets, four people call, and the action is on you. If you call $3, the big blind will very likely bet the turn and you'll have to call again, even if you miss, for another $6. Drawing at your flush will cost you $9. But what happens if you raise? Low limit players are passive. They don't like to bet and raise without very strong hands. If you raise, most of the time the big blind will just call (along with everyone else) and check to you on the turn (along with everyone else). People love to "check to the raiser." Watch closely the scene in *Rounders* when Mike goes to the judges' game. Mike makes exactly this play, raising with a draw (although he does it on behalf of the professor played by Martin Landau), and one of his opponents says on the next betting round, "Check to the raiser." If you've missed your flush, you can check after everyone checks to you and see the river card without paying another bet. By raising on the flop, drawing for the flush costs only $6, a savings of $3 over flat-calling. And if you hit your flush, you may very well make more money than you would have by just calling the flop. Raising to reduce the price of your draw is a great low limit play.

A not-so-great low limit play is everyone's favorite play—the **bluff**. A bluff is a bet by a player holding a hand that can't possibly win a showdown. Bluffing is largely ineffective at low stakes poker because people love to call, and a bluff only works when your opponent folds. That said, even low limit players will fold when they have absolutely nothing, and there will be plenty of times when you've missed a draw and have no hand yourself after all the cards have been dealt. In these cases, you should consider a bluff.

The first factor to think about is the number of opponents. If there is more than one, forget it. It's hard enough to make one low limit player fold, and it's twice as hard to make two of them fold. Three opponents and you'd be an absolute fool to try a bluff. So say you've got it narrowed down to one opponent after the last card (it is unwise to bluff before then in a low limit game, because so many people call just to see what the last card is), and your hand is very weak. First ask yourself what the chances are of your opponent folding a better hand if you bet. Take, as an example, a board of T♠8♣4♥A♣2♦. You were in the big blind, holding 6♠5♠, and flopped a flush draw plus a gutshot straight draw. None of your cards came in, and now you're at the river holding a six-high against a lone opponent. There are certainly better hands he might fold. Maybe he has J♠Q♠ and missed a draw himself. Or maybe he has K♥J♦ and decided to bet the flop with just **overcards**. Or maybe he had a straight draw like J9, 97, or 76. All these hands are weak, but they're better than yours. Your low limit opponent is unlikely to fold a pair, but he'll fold a jack-high. So let's say the chances that your opponent will fold if he has a better hand than yours are 10 percent. Translating that means the odds against your bluff working are 9 to 1. So should you invest $6 on your bluff? The answer is yes if the pot has more than $54 in it, and no if it has less. Again, it comes back to pot odds. We need them to be more than 9 to 1, and $6 x 9 = $54. Notice that even a 10 percent chance of success can sometimes be enough to make a bluff the right play. If you feel there is a 20 percent chance or higher that your opponent will fold with a better hand, then bluffing will be the right play whenever there are just four big bets in the pot!

What about the other side of bluffing—what about calling a bet on the river with a medium-strength hand? Once more, the key question is how big the pot is. If your opponent bets $6 into a $30 pot, you are getting 6 to 1 odds to call him (risking $6 to win $36). So if in your estimation there is better than 1 in 7 chance you have the best hand, you should call. Be careful, however, if another player has already called the $6 in front of you. In this case, you must beat *both* of your opponents more than one time in eight to make calling correct. Unless the caller is an extremely loose player, you should **overcall** (call after someone has called already) with far less frequency than you would call the bettor alone.

A cute play that often works in low limit Hold'em is to try to entice an overcall when you have a strong hand. Say someone has bet on the river, you have a monster and are next to act. If there are many players left to act behind you, you probably don't want to raise. You want to call and bring in as many callers (or maybe even raisers) behind you as you can. You go for the overcall. This is an especially good play when the pot is large, and your opponents will be sorely tempted to call with garbage for just one more bet.

The pot size is an enormous consideration in poker. One of the first skills new players should practice is counting the number of bets in the pot. You can work on this during all the hands you're not involved in, which if you follow my advice should be plenty. Don't worry, counting bets comes naturally after not too much time.

Yes, we did cover all this material over the course of Dad's seminar. No, it didn't all stick right away. But I found it fun to think about, and I realized that what I'd been doing at the kitchen tables, and at the casinos in Arizona and Connecticut, wasn't playing poker. Calling every hand, every time I had even the faintest chance of winning, wasn't ballsy persistence, it was throwing money away. Someone had finally turned on the lights. I finally saw the game as it was meant to be seen.

I've given you the approach that made me a winner as a new Hold'em player. There are certainly other approaches, but this book is the story of how *I* learned to play poker—and I learned by playing ultratight and predictable in my earliest days at the tables. If you have read and understood the material in this chapter, and if you apply it to your game, you will already be a winning low limit casino player.

I had that first fateful Mohegan Sun session with the blond opponent a few days after Dad's lesson, though not before I read Ken Warren's book to the end. From that point on, trips to Mohegan Sun and Foxwoods were a regular part of my senior year at Yale. I had rediscovered the game, and discovered for the first time that I could actually play it.

3

♠ ♣ ♦ ♥

Introduction to Tournaments and Connecticut Poker

If you've ever heard someone referred to as a world champion poker player, I'll let you in on a secret—he didn't earn this title playing poker. He earned it in a **poker tournament**. I'll grant that tournament poker looks like poker, uses chips like poker, has the same betting structure and almost all the same rules as poker; but it is not poker.

In a tournament, when you lose all the chips in front of you, you're out and you can't come back. In regular **ring-game** poker, players are welcome (and encouraged) to buy more chips at any time. But it gets better. In tournaments, players can *make* money when they lose all their chips. The reason is simple. In a tournament, all players start with the same number of chips, and the tournament continues until one player has them all. These chips are not redeemable at the cashier's desk for real money—their only value is in relation to the other tournament chips. For this reason, it doesn't matter if everyone starts with 10,000 in tournament chips (T10,000 for short) or 500. (This is also why, when you see players betting $2 million at the final table of the World Series of Poker main event, they are not *really* risking these amounts of money.) As players get eliminated the tournament directors move players around, gradually reducing the number of tables until it gets down to one. Well, it would be pretty brutal to a hold a tournament with a few hundred people and only give prize money to the winner. The other final tableists would be distraught, to put it lightly. So tournaments typically reward the top 10 percent of the field with cash. If I lose all my chips, but 95 percent of the tournament entrants have already lost theirs, I get paid when I go broke. You won't see that in your local $3–$6 Hold'em game.

There are many subtle strategic differences between tournament poker and real poker. Rather than bog down new players with these differences now, let me explain how I got my virgin poker tournament experience.

On one of my visits to the Mohegan Sun, I learned about the Early Bird Hold'em Tournament held every Saturday at 10 A.M. My poker buddies and I would need to leave at 8:30 A.M. if we wanted to get there for the complimentary breakfast. The earliest class I took senior year started at 9:30 A.M., and even though it was a Probability class, I always dreaded going. But I always felt a surge of adrenaline when the alarm went off on a Saturday morning, knowing I was about to hit I–95 for another Early Bird Tournament.

I had learned some things about Limit Hold'em since those first few sessions following the *Herald* retreat. Much of it came from reading my second book on the game—*Winning Low-Limit Hold'em* by Lee Jones. Jones had two rules of thumb I found particularly helpful. The first was, *don't* usually continue past the flop with just overcards unless you have something else going for you, like a backdoor flush draw. The next was, *do* draw to a gutshot straight on the flop if the pot is offering you 6 to 1 or more. These were important ideas for me to think about, because at the time I was routinely folding hands like overcards and gutshot straight draws. Jones made me realize that although I would often lose with longshot draws like gutshots and overcards, I was probably costing myself money by folding them *every* time. I said you don't have to worry about calculating odds on the fly, and I stand by that. Jones's simple rules of thumb gave me a good way to decide whether to continue with some tricky draws.

I thought about Mr. Jones and Mr. Warren as Burke, Fabian, and I pulled into Mohegan Sun for our very first Early Bird tournament. I loved the place, and I continued to love it until their poker room closed in the fall of 2003. There was something about walking in, seeing the clashing colors on the carpet, hearing the pleasant rings of slot machine noise, and noticing the blackjack dealers smile at us as we walked by. And the temperature inside was always perfect. People say rain is good poker weather. But when I was on my way to Mohegan Sun, 75 degrees and sunny was good poker weather.

The breakfast we got with our $20 tournament entry was a full all-you-can-eat buffet. I was generally displeased with the food served in the Yale dining halls. So at the casino, I feasted on the sausage links, waffles, bagels, scrambled eggs, croissants, and just about everything else they put out there. My grandfather once told me, after an enormous Thanksgiving dinner, that the sleep-inducing effect a large meal has on the body is called the "alkaline tide" because of the increase in the body's pH level. I experienced the alkaline tide as I entered the poker room, trying just to stay awake as I prepared for my first ever poker tournament.

I eventually found my table, but before I had a chance to examine the mostly wrinkled faces around me, I heard someone announce "get the cards in the air" (a new expression to me). Our dealer spread the deck facedown across the table and mixed it up by moving her hands through it in *Karate Kid* wax-on/wax-off fashion before collecting the cards into a single stack in front of her.

As she started dealing, I knew immediately this tournament would be different from the low limit ring games I was used to. I could tell from the players' faces. These bulky men sitting around me weren't looking at their cards as they floated in from the dealer; these guys were looking at the other players. I had read about this in my books and tried to do it myself. The idea is that you can look at your cards any time. You can only watch your opponents react to *their* cards once. For the same reason, it is best not to look at the flop as it is being dealt. Instead, you should watch your opponents react to the flop. In the games I was used to, no one ever did this. People couldn't wait to see what cards they had. Some even looked at them one at a time as they arrived from the dealer's hands. But the people at this tournament were different. They seemed to understand a few more things about Texas Hold'em.

I don't want to say I went into a panic at this point. I prefer to think of it as being aware of my situation. These people seemed to know more than I did; and if they didn't, they certainly had played the game a few decades longer. So I decided, either consciously or subconsciously, that I was going to have to play better than I was used to playing. The only problem was I had no idea how to do it.

In the first hand I remember playing, I held an unimproved ace–king after all the cards had been dealt—meaning my hand was just an ace-high. I was down to a lone opponent at this point, not surprisingly an elderly male. He checked and I bet. He called and I flipped my hand over. He started nodding his head repeatedly. He kept nodding and nodding and nodding . . . and finally mucked his hand without show-ing it. Remember, I didn't even have a pair. Usually when a player bets without a pair and gets called, it means disaster. It didn't happen that way in this case.

A few hands later I held the ace–jack of hearts in a seven-way pot (that is, a pot where seven people saw the flop). The flop came with what I thought were two hearts. So when the action got to me I just called, as was my usual strategy for playing draws. The turn brought another red card, a diamond. At first I was annoyed, but then I realized this red card looked different from the three red cards that had come before it. I rechecked the flop, and it contained not two, but three hearts. I had flopped the **nuts**—the best possible hand—and not real-ized it. I must have been nervous because I haven't done that in Hold'em since (sadly, I have made a similar mistake in Omaha, but more on that game later). This time when the action got to me, you better believe I raised. Only the original bettor called. When the last card was turned up, I still had the nuts. My opponent checked, and I was actually un-sure of the correct play! Thankfully I bet, and my opponent called. As I flipped my cards up, the old guy sitting next to me said, "Beautiful!" The man who lost the pot chose not to say anything.

Even though I won the pots, my play and my thought process on these two hands were mediocre at best. Yes, I was nervous, but I had a more fundamental problem. I didn't understand what it meant to **value bet**.

When all the cards are dealt, there are generally only two reasons to bet: to get someone to call with a worse hand, or to get someone to fold a better hand. Bets made for the first reason are called value bets. Bets made for the second reason are called bluffs, as you already know.

Let's look closer at those two hands from my first tournament. First, I bet an unimproved ace–king on the river. Was that a value bet or a bluff? If this sounds like a difficult question, it is. Did I think my opponent would fold a pair? If not, did I think he would call with a hand worse than mine? The fact is, I didn't really think at all. I had forgotten one of the most important points of Lee Jones's book: only value bet the river if you're a favorite *when called*.

This takes some explanation—after all, if you think you have the best hand, why shouldn't you bet? Well, let's suppose, in an extreme example, that you will *only* be called by a better hand, and all worse hands will fold. Then betting can only cost you money, because you're going to win the pot (and no more than the pot) whether your opponent folds or you show down the best hand. But you're always going to lose when you bet and get called—and you'll lose one bet more than you would have if it had been checked down! This hypothetical situation is actually relevant because if you think your opponent was on a draw, and you are right, then he's always going to fold when he misses his draw. But when he hits his draw . . . betting will get you into serious trouble. It's almost exactly the same situation as our "extreme" hypothetical, because if you're called you're usually beaten.

When I bet the unimproved ace–king, it was either a bad value bet (because I'll almost never win when called) or a bad bluff (because very few players in small tournaments will fold a pair for one bet on the river). In this particular circumstance, I somehow did get called by a worse hand (maybe he had ace–queen?), and my value bet was successful. I use it here as an example of what not to do. An unimproved ace–king is usually *not* a hand you want to bet on the river.

What about when I had the nuts with my ace–jack of hearts? Was I correct to bet the river then? If you said, "Of course!" you're right. I had a hand that couldn't be beaten, so obviously it was correct to bet. I win the pot every time, whether my opponent calls or not. What would be the point in checking? I would have turned my cards over and won, but I was going to win no matter what. So why not try to win an extra bet? In poker there are some beautiful situations, like this one, where you can put money in the pot, knowing with 100 percent certainty you'll get the money back, and you could possibly get more. When these situations arise, make sure you put that money in.

After winning those two pots, I had enough chips to last longer than I should have in my first tournament. I continued, however, to make aggressive-but-unwise plays that ended up costing me. In one pot, I bluffed at every opportunity only to have my opponent call me down. When I turned my cards over, my somewhat surprised opponent turned up his and dragged the pot. The guy next to me, the same one who had complimented my flush, turned to me and said, "I believed you." The end came when I had ace–eight suited and couldn't get it to win. I went **all-in** with that hand, meaning I bet all the chips I had left. When a player goes all-in, he can see the rest of the cards without committing any more chips; so an all-in player never folds. The only way to get eliminated from a poker tournament is for another player to turn up a better hand than yours, and this fact gives every tournament player hope. The other side is that very few things are more painful for a player than busting out of a tournament—and only the eventual winner doesn't bust out.

My ace-eight suited was not the best hand when all the cards were turned over, and I got up from the table after wishing the surviving players luck. I had low expectations at the time, and the sinking feeling—the one I typically get these days when I bust out—wasn't there. I shook off the defeat (something I still do—a vital skill for any serious player) and returned to Mohegan Sun a few weeks later. I still made some aggressive plays, like check-raising the flop with a straight draw, but this time my opponents were folding. I got to the final table and ended up finishing sixth. Ordinarily this result would've made me a hero among my poker buddies, except that my fellow poker buddy Fabian finished third! He bet, raised, and reraised with nothing, and somehow it worked for him. This was the same guy who wouldn't spend more than $20 on snacks for the *Herald* staff when we worked through the night until 7 or 8 A.M. How did his maniacal style get him the money? Keep reading, we'll get to it.

I got knocked out of the tournament when I called all-in preflop with two jacks against a raise and a **cold-caller** (a player who called the raise without having previously put any money in the pot). The cold-caller had two kings, and I didn't improve. Back then, I wondered if I really needed to put my last chips in with two jacks in that situation. Now I realize that I had a very strong hand, and my decision wasn't really close.

This example illustrates one of the key points about tournament poker and ring-game poker—the same hands can have different values. I won't get into too many specifics at this stage, but here is the basic idea. In a tournament, unlike a ring game, you can't reach into your wallet and buy more chips. This means most of your opponents play much tighter. As a result, you will sometimes have to play tighter yourself. Hands I suggested calling with in late position, like ten–eight and nine–seven suited, will have to be thrown in the muck. There just won't be enough loose action to make these hands profitable (although you might try **stealing** with them).

All this changes, however, at the final table. At that point **stack sizes**, or the amount of chips players have in front of them, become the single biggest factor in determining how to play. A big stack can play very many hands, knowing that small stacks will not want to risk elimination from the tournament. Similarly, small stacks should take extra care of their last few chips, especially if knocking out just one other player will be worth a lot of money. The overriding concept is that the more chips a player accumulates in a tournament, the less each one is worth. A $10 chip, for example, is far more valuable to a player with T10 than a player with T45,000.

I didn't match the success from my second-ever Early Bird Tournament in any of the six or seven Early Bird tournaments that followed. I did, however, have other successes in my first year of casino poker. I soon learned that Foxwoods, the largest resort casino in the world, is just down the road from Mohegan Sun (although "down the road" is not quite an appropriate phrase, as the route from Mohegan Sun to Foxwoods consists of twists and turns down tree-lined streets boasting antique homes and the occasional karaoke bar). The best part of driving to "The Woods" is, of course, getting there, but not only because poker lies in wait. The final approach to the casino, from any direction, has a view of an open field for the last mile or so, until Foxwoods appears, rising out of the plain like Emerald City in *The Wizard of Oz*. It is usually puffing smoke from its chimneys, and soon takes up the entire skyline. If Mohegan Sun feels like home, Foxwoods feels like Space Camp. The poker room, when we finally found it, was just as impressive, featuring seventy-plus tables (they've since knocked a bunch out) and a ceiling so high a local bird makes his home there (really).

As I sat down for my first $3–$6 Hold'em game in this palace, I noticed the game had a more animated feel than I was used to. Though
there were more younger players than I had expected, I soon realized it
went beyond this. On some hands the pot started with more money in
it, and the betting was not $3–$6, but $5–$10. Someone had to explain
that I was in a **kill** game. In this type of game, the occasional hand is
played at $5–$10, even though it is technically a $3–$6 table. The way
it works at Foxwoods is, when a pot gets bigger than a certain amount
(say, $50), the winner of the pot posts a $5 blind for the next hand (in
addition to the usual small and large blinds posted in their usual spots),
which is played at $5–$10.

I wasn't quite prepared for these higher stakes. It might not sound
that much different, but when the kill kicks in the stakes usually stay
raised for a while. It is much easier to make a $50 pot playing $5–$10
than $3–$6. And it didn't help that there were gamboolers raising their
hands **dark**, that is without looking, to make sure the game stayed at
$5–$10.

One person happy to play the higher limits (if this guy was ever
happy about anything) was a fellow we'll call Adam. I learned his
name because everyone else seemed to know it, and they had reason to
speak to him often. Adam continuously rattled off his gambling strategies for football betting, keno, blackjack, and, of course, poker as we
played. Here are some examples:

"What did you have—seventeen, nineteen outs? You should've
been raising!"

"Parlays are a scam, just like anything else, but if you're sure one
team can't possibly win you *might* be getting the right odds. But
you've gotta be really sure."

"That guy in the one seat is so slow, watching paint dry would be
an improvement."

"It might have worked out in this situation, but in the long term it's
the wrong play."

Adam was one of those thirtyish guys who wore shirts out of a
Charlie Brown cartoon (you know, the ones with one or two orange or
red stripes), had greasy hair he probably never washed, enunciated
every word to the point of annoyance, and got very, very irritated
when something went even slightly wrong. It was probable he lived

with his parents. But he wasn't like all the others whiners I had met. I could tell, even with my limited experience, that Adam knew what he was talking about. He had clearly thought about when to make certain sports bets and when not to, about when to raise for value in poker and when not to. He was not **results-oriented**, as is illustrated in his last quote above. Adam knew it didn't matter whether he won the pot, it only mattered if he played his hand correctly. Knowing this didn't stop him from bitching; nevertheless, his understanding went way beyond that of a typical low limit player.

So I was in over my head, playing stakes that were too high against at least one opponent with superior knowledge. I still found some success in the game—usually enough to make up for the $35 I had lost at the Mohegan Sun tournament ($20 for the initial buy-in and $15 more for a **rebuy**, a purchase of additional tournament chips that is allowed during the early stages of some events). Looking back, only two hands from those Foxwoods tables really stick out. In both, Adam was sitting to my right and the rest of the table was the usual low limit loose-passive types. The first hand was a five-way pot. I had just a king-high on the river and was still in the hand only because no one had bet. It had been **checked around** on both the flop and the turn. On the river, Adam decided to bet . . . and I felt very strongly that he had nothing. I couldn't say for sure why I felt this. Maybe it was because Adam almost never **slowplayed**. When he had a good hand, he didn't try to fool people by checking, he just bet. Since he hadn't bet until the last possible chance, and since the river card looked harmless, I figured he was bluffing. But as I had nothing myself, I had to raise if I wanted to win this pot. So I did. A few people behind me had their $6 ready to call Adam's bet. But when the dealer announced my raise, they promptly restacked their chips and folded. When the action got to Adam, he too mucked his cards and said, "You win." Adam must have thought no one had anything and decided to try a bluff. Ironically, the only way for Adam or me to win the pot was for Adam to bet and me to raise, because even with "nothing," players were going to call behind us for $6, probably with hands like ace-high. So I made a successful bluff-raise in a five-way pot in a $3–$6 game. It's one of those things that doesn't ever happen.

Although I'd made a very strong play, I had no thoughts whatsoever of turning my cards over and showing off my bluff. Why infuriate the rest of the table and get them gunning for me? And why give them any information for no cost? I wanted to maintain the *status quo*—a loose, passive game where no one really knew what to make of my play.

In my second memorable hand, a kill hand, I raised seven or eight other players with two jacks in late position. Everyone called (of course), and the flop came with two threes and another low card. A few players checked until the action was on a petite, youngish, blond woman. Her options were, of course, to check or bet $5. I should point out that this woman had not bet or raised the entire time we'd been playing, and was clearly new to Texas Hold'em (even by my standards). Before she acted she spoke up and asked, "I just want to know, can I bet ten?" The dealer informed her she could only bet five, and she did.

"Can I bet ten, huh?" I said.

Adam turned to me and said, "You believe that chatter?" indicating that he didn't believe it. This disbelief was a manifestation of Adam's greater problem. Adam thought everyone was out to get him, including this woman who was probably playing poker for the first time. Of course, she was not trying to be deceptive when she asked if she could bet $10. She wanted to bet $10 because she had an extremely strong hand. I realized this, and I folded my pocket jacks. The woman ended up winning the hand . . . with four threes.

Notice that I mucked a reasonably strong hand for the very first bet after the flop in a big pot. This is not something I advised doing last chapter. So why did I do it? Well, even though I might not have been able to articulate it at the time, I did it because I had a **tell** on my opponent. A tell is something a player does that gives away the strength of his or her hand. Some tells can be extremely subtle and hard to interpret (what did it mean when Teddy KGB ate his Oreos in *Rounders* anyway?). Others, like the one the woman with the quad threes gave off, should be obvious (even if our friend Adam couldn't see them). Spotting tells is a fun and profitable part of this game. We'll discuss the science of tells in more detail later. For now, new players should just watch out when they hear things like, "How much can I bet?" or

"Whose turn is it?" When low limit players say these things, they almost always have a strong hand.

My earliest days of real poker, at the Early Bird Tournaments at Mohegan Sun, and at the colorful low limit tables of Foxwoods, are still some of my happiest. Whether it was Burke and I spouting off Adamisms on our drive back from Foxwoods, or waking up to an alarm on Saturday morning with thoughts of the breakfast buffet in my head, I loved almost every minute of it.

After I graduated I moved to the Washington, D.C., area, whose closest card rooms are in Atlantic City, with Connecticut a distant second. But I returned in February 2001 to Mohegan Sun to play one more Early Bird Tournament—almost two years after my last appearance there. It was a miserable experience. The blinds went up so fast it removed almost all the skill, and the players were so atrocious it wasn't even fun. I couldn't believe this event was once something I looked forward to all week. I realized my game had moved way beyond 10 A.M. $20 tournaments.

It wasn't only, however, the absurdity of the tournament structure (the schedule of when the blinds and limits will increase) that got to me. Limit Hold'em had long since ceased to be my favorite poker game. A much more fierce, more taxing, and yes, more difficult version of Hold'em was my passion by the time I returned to Mohegan Sun, and it is still my passion now. Experienced players know, I'm sure, that I'm referring to No Limit Hold'em—the Cadillac of poker games.

4

♠ ♣ ♦ ♥

Introduction to No Limit Hold'em

I raced home from the library in the middle of the afternoon. It was finals time, and I had plenty of studying left to do, but I had a certain hour earmarked for a break. It wasn't to call my girlfriend, or check on an ill family member, or work on a job application, or any other such nonsense. When I burst into my dorm room I asked Burke, "Did it start yet?"

"Nope," he said. "And I'm taping it anyway."

We settled in to watch an ESPN broadcast of the 1994 World Series of Poker (WSOP).

Our obsession started when we stumbled across an airing of Scotty Nguyen's (last name pronounced "win") triumph over Kevin McBride at the 1998 WSOP. I was so taken in by the drama, and so impressed by Nguyen's play, I wrote an article about it for *The Yale Herald* (I'd been working at the paper long enough for this to fly). Here's an excerpt in which I think my infatuation comes through:

> In the final twosome of the Series, bad boy Scotty Nguyen, sporting a white jogging suit, gold chains, sunglasses, and moussed hair, has the edge over rookie Kevin McBride, who has chosen to go with a slightly tamer look—black shirt, jeans, glasses, and a goatee. Two nines and an eight appear as the first three cards on the table. McBride bets, and Nguyen—reluctantly, it seems—sticks around. A second eight appears as the fourth card, and McBride continues to bet. Nguyen calls, and the crowd can't figure out why he doesn't fold and finish off

McBride later. The final card is turned . . . and it's an eight! A full house on the table for both players to use!

Nguyen pushes all his chips into the pot, and now McBride has to put the rest of his money on the line to try to win. Nguyen looks him over and grabs a Michelob. Before taking a swig, he says, "You call this one it's all over, baby." McBride stares at the pot. With dreams of a $1 million purse dancing in his head he says, "Call, I play the board." But Nguyen wasn't lying. He pulls a nine from his hand, giving him a full house, nines full of eights, beating McBride's eights full of nines. The million bucks goes to Scotty. He calls it a dream come true.

After witnessing Nguyen's performance, Burke and I scanned the listings for other poker tournaments. We were lucky—three other events from three different years would be shown over the next week. At the time, we had no idea how much of a coup this was. Those next three tournaments were the only poker of any kind slated for broadcast in the next several months. Present-day readers may be surprised by this, as nowadays a new World Poker Tour (WPT) event gets aired every week, and ESPN seems to have poker on every hour of the day. Poker really did take off in just five years.

The game played in most tournaments shown on television is No Limit Texas Hold'em. The cards are dealt in the exact same way as Limit Hold'em; the only difference is in the betting. But what a difference. In Limit, as you know, players are obligated to bet and raise in predetermined increments. In No Limit, a player can bet as many chips as he has in front of him at any time. This change may not seem extraordinary to a new player, but I assure you it is enormous. In my view, Limit Hold'em is more similar to limit games like Seven-Card Stud or even Omaha Eight-or-Better than it is to No Limit Hold'em.

Most Hold'em books go on for many pages, exhausting everything they have to say about Limit Hold'em before discussing No Limit strategy (if they even broach the subject at all). But, as promised, readers of this book will learn as I learned—and I learned No Limit only a few months after learning the simpler Limit game.

Before I confuse too many new players, let me explain that not *every* high-stakes event is a No Limit event; it's just that the very biggest usually are. Almost all major tournaments, including the WSOP, are actually a series of tournaments covering many different games (the winner of *any* WSOP event gets a coveted gold bracelet). The series culminates in a championship event, which has the biggest buy-in and the most prestigious title. The championship event of most tournaments, again including the WSOP, is a No Limit Hold'em tournament. For years, the WSOP championship event was poker's undisputed world championship. Many still consider it our world championship, though I consider the $25,000 buy-in WPT final the true championship (and many of the top players agree with me).

The first thing I learned watching the WSOP, and the first thing many people learn upon tuning in to any WPT event, is that all-in is a popular play. As in Limit Hold'em, a player who is all-in has the right to see all remaining cards and can only lose in a showdown. The big difference is that in Limit, an all-in player has usually been forced to throw in his last few chips in desperation, and he virtually always gets called because his bet is so small. In No Limit, an all-in is often a big raise where a player risks all his chips. This is unlike some $3–$6 Hold'em game where a player bets $3, his opponent goes all-in for $5, and the bettor calls for $2 more. In No Limit, if my opponent bets $100, I can raise all-in for $1000 (if I have that much on the table). Not such an automatic call for my opponent, is it? The all-in bet or raise is a key weapon in No Limit Hold'em, because your opponent has no way to make you fold. His only options are to call and hope to win a showdown, or to muck.

It is no surprise, then, that Burke and I saw many players shoving all their chips in as we watched No Limit on television—particularly in the 1996 U.S. Poker Championship (USPC). The USPC is held at the Taj Mahal in Atlantic City, and 1996 happened to be one of the years it received coverage from ESPN. It also happened to feature the most memorable final table of any televised tournament I've seen to this day. This was almost entirely because of the outbursts of one Phil Hellmuth, Jr. In the early stages of my poker career I had no idea who Hellmuth was. Now even many nonplayers would probably recognize him, by reputation if nothing else. Hellmuth is known for being loud, talkative, openly critical of opponents' play, and given to fits of rage at the table. In short, he's a poker brat, and he's the first to admit it. He was also a world champion at age twenty-four, and is still the youngest player ever to win the WSOP Main Event.

Hellmuth lived up to his nickname at the Taj in 1996. First, his opponent Paul McKinney reraised and Hellmuth re-reraised all-in. McKinney called almost instantly, holding ace–seven. Hellmuth had ace–queen, making him about a 3 to 1 favorite to win the pot. But McKinney got lucky and won, so Hellmuth berated him. "He's playing so bad! Playing so bad! How could you call the reraise? Call the reraise with an ace and a seven?" he said. History repeated itself when Hellmuth lost a pot to Surinder Sunar. "Calling raises with seven-high!" Hellmuth shouted. It was a beautiful ending for Hellmuth-haters everywhere when he made an all-in bet on a pure bluff and the late Ken "Skyhawk" Flaton called with two pair to eliminate him. Hellmuth had gone **on tilt**, playing too many hands too aggressively because he let his emotions influence his game, and ceded his entire stack to Flaton.

Eager to learn the secrets of this game capable of causing so much fury in a human being, Burke purchased World Series of Poker Deluxe Casino Pak for his computer. Masque's software isn't just poker, it is a complete simulation of a trip to Vegas. It starts by showing a plane landing at McCarron International Airport, and you, the player, catching a cab to Binion's Horseshoe (site of the WSOP). Once there, you can take the $5,000 in your pocket and buy in to ring games, or even one-table **satellites**, smaller tournaments whose prizes were entries into the $10,000 buy-in championship event. You can also drop by the famous Gambler's Book Shop and buy a copy of Doyle Brunson's now classic tome *Super/System*. I didn't own *Super/System* in real life until after I graduated from college. But I did read the computer game version (which, not surprisingly, only contained excerpts of the six-hundred-page epic) on Burke's monitor.

Reading a pseudo-manual from a fake digital bookstore probably wasn't the typical player's introduction to No Limit strategy, but then again there was no textbook or course available for an aspiring poker professional (and there still isn't), and everyone had to start somewhere. A miniature *Super/System* seemed as good a place as any. The actual hard copy of Brunson's book contains six sections, each written by a different poker expert, and each discussing in-depth strategies for a specific game. But *Super/System*, first published in 1978, is still popular only because of the No Limit Hold'em chapter, written by Doyle himself. Doyle is a two-time world champion, and widely considered the best high stakes player ever. Knowing this, I paid special attention to the slim portion of his writing to which I had access. I still remember his basic points, which I will summarize for you now.

Doyle divides No Limit starting hands into six categories:

1. *Pocket aces and pocket kings.* As in Limit Hold'em, these are the premiere starting hands. You want to get your opponents to put as much money into the pot as possible when you hold these hands; but ideally you want this money to go in before the flop. Doyle does not believe in slowplaying these hands, in acting weak before the flop to lure opponents in. The big pocket pairs are nice to have, but you only have one pair with them after most flops, so they are hardly invulnerable. Don't let opponents see the flop cheap, as your hand will be very tough to get away from should someone flop a **set** (three of a kind). Oh, and don't worry too much about running into pocket aces when you're holding pocket kings. If it happens, it happens, but it's better not to try to outguess yourself. If you never fold two kings before the flop you're probably not making much of a mistake. (I have never in my life made this fold.)

2. *Ace–king.* Doyle's favorite hand. He says he prefers AK to AA, because he wins more when he wins and he loses less when he loses. Ace–king is a good hand to raise with before the flop, but not necessarily a good hand to call with. AK should be used to put small pairs to the test. Make them pay to see the flop. And if you do get an opponent to take the flop with you, AK is relatively easy to play—fold when you miss the flop, play aggressive when you flop a pair or better. That said, do be careful of opponents who flop a set. You don't always have to go broke when you flop a pair with AK.

3. *Pocket queens.* This hand is in its own class because it's a very special hand that is played differently from all others. It's not a big pair, but it's not a small pair either. There are times when this hand should be folded preflop, and there are times when it should

get all the money in preflop. Play of QQ is extremely situation dependent. When first learning the game, you should probably treat two queens like a small pair, and get more creative with it as you gain experience.

4. *Small pairs.* By small pairs, Doyle means pairs smaller than queens (yes, even jacks). You should at least call the first bet and probably the first raise with these hands. This is because the potential to win a big pot is great when you flop a set. Sets are well disguised, so opponents will have trouble reading your hand. The ideal situation for a small pair is for an opponent to have AA, and for that opponent to slowplay AA before the flop. When you flop a set in that scenario, you have a fantastic opportunity to take all of your opponent's chips. And when you do flop a set, don't worry about someone else holding a bigger set. If he does, he'll take all your chips, but you can't go around playing small pairs only to fold when you flop trips. Just as with kings preflop, you're probably not making much of a mistake if you never fold a set on the flop.

5. *Suited connectors.* Hands like 7♠6♠ or 9♥8♥. Doyle loves these hands. He will *limp* (call the first bet to see the flop) with them in any position and might even raise with them in late position. Just as with the small pairs, Doyle is looking to win a big pot against a big pocket pair when he flops small trips, or a small two pair, or a straight, or even flush. He will also, however, play aggressive when he flops a draw.

6. *Suited aces.* These hands are similar to the suited connectors in that they could win a big pot when they flop small trips or a flush. The difference is that they can't flop a straight, and they are difficult to play when they flop a pair of aces.

Any hand not listed above Doyle considers trash. This includes hands like AQo (especially AQo, in fact), KQs, Kxs, and QJo. If Doyle would ever play hands like these it would be in late position for the first bet, and he would be sure to play them very carefully.

Finally, Doyle's overriding piece of advice for No Limit Hold'em is to be aggressive, aggressive, aggressive. Doyle plays most of his draws, particularly his straight draws, which are hard to read, the same way he plays a set—he bets and raises with them. He also raises a lot preflop, looking to take the blinds. If he gets called, he fires away again at the flop. By playing this way, Doyle wins a lot of small pots. When he finally plays a big pot, he either has a big hand and busts his opponent, or he has a draw, and still busts his opponent some of the time. Winning the small pots, though, is Doyle's "secret." His aggressive play wins him the chips to enter a big pot, so that when he does, he's freerolling.

This advice made sense to me at the time, and regardless it was all I had to go on. Some may say that as an intelligent person well versed in mathematics and probability, I should've been able to come up with my own theoretical strategic approach to No Limit Hold'em before I even played my first hand. These people do not understand the level of complexity involved in poker. To analyze the game without having played it would be akin to deriving calculus with no formal mathematical training, or writing a Beethoven sonata without knowing how to play the piano. I'm not saying these things are impossible, but they would require a true genius—not just an intelligent person.

I did have other sources of information besides Doyle. I had picked up a few things from the television broadcasts. Specifically, the ESPN tournaments taught me about all-in matchups. As I mentioned, all-in is a popular No Limit move, and at the final tables of tournaments, two players all-in preflop is a common scenario. It became apparent listening to the announcers, watching the action, and doing a little math, that a pair against two higher cards—**overcards**—is a small favorite, usually around 57 to 43, and that a pair against a higher pair is a big underdog, about 4.5 to 1. But I also learned that a dominated hand is a big underdog. As explained earlier, a hand can dominate another when both hands contain one card of the same rank, but have different kickers. For example, AK dominates AQ, KT dominates K9, and T9 dominates T7. For this reason, a hand like AQ is often in danger, even though it is a reasonably strong hand. If it runs into AK, suddenly AQ is a 3–1 underdog. These three basic matchups—pair versus overcards, pair versus pair, and dominated versus dominating—are important for any No Limit player to know, even a beginner.

I took Doyle's advice, and my knowledge of matchups, and used them to start thrashing the computer game. Actually, Burke was the first one to have success, winning a satellite into the championship event. He called me while I was at a happy hour in another student's apartment just to tell me about it. I was also not the first person to go deep in the computer championship. That distinction went to Fabian. He made the final table, with Burke and I **sweating** (watching) him.

Pretty soon I got in on the triumphs. It didn't take me long to figure out that the computer opponents all played the same way. And soon after making that discovery, I realized they all folded *way* too much. By applying Doyle's hyperaggressive approach, I found I could easily build up my chips while the rest of my artificially intelligent foes busted one by one. When I won the computer WSOP championship for the first time, and saw my winning cards displayed on the table surrounded by cash (as is done in the actual World Series), I admit I was pretty psyched. But it quickly got to the point where I was winning the tournament more often than not. Let me put that in perspective. If there were 399 computer players in the tournament with me, I should expect to win once every 400 times if I were of average skill. Yet I was winning a majority of the time. In real life this level of success is impossible, as no player is anywhere near good enough to win this often. The very best players are only about three to four times as likely as the average player to win a given tournament. So what accounts for my spectacular win rate on the computer game? Well, when opponents fold, they have no way to win the pot. When my opponents continually folded, I had almost no risk. All I had to do was play very aggressive, and win maybe one or two showdowns along the way (when I was against an all-in player, for example) to accumulate chips. This approach wasn't enough to guarantee victory, but it was enough so that I won an inordinate amount of the time.

Even at that time I understood I couldn't expect live human beings to play anything like what I was used to on the Masque game. But I was still confident when I learned that Foxwoods hosted a No Limit Hold'em tournament every Tuesday night. I was eager to play this fascinating game for money, instead of just running up the fake bank account into the tens of millions.

I often hear stories from tournament players about how they won their first-ever No Limit tournament. I do not have such a story. In fact, my first outright win in a No Limit tournament played for money came four years after my first attempt. This statistic doesn't disturb me, though, as most of the people who win their first tournament think they are much better players than they actually are, and end up making tournaments profitable for the rest of us. My first few Foxwoods tournaments, all played in the second semester of my senior year, were unsuccessful. But I learned a lot, and I got to watch some truly great play. The following hands are from my initial foray into real-world No Limit Hold'em.

I had been watching all the body language, and listening to all the comments from each opponent at my first table in this No Limit tournament. I'd heard enough to know that the middle-aged guy two seats to my right was an outstanding player. He had won the Best All-Around Player award at World Poker Finals a year or two before, and he made his living at the game. Let's call him Lance. Lance was aggressive, no surprise. In fact, I once saw him make a big raise against six limpers. When they all folded, he showed his hand and said, "How else do you play the ten–four of clubs?" Eventually, he and I were bound to have a confrontation. Sure enough, Lance raised on the button and I called from the big blind with a Doyle Brunson hand (sort of)—the eight–five of hearts. The flop came down king–king–queen with two hearts. Remembering Doyle's strategy of aggression, I bet right out at this flop. Lance asked how many chips I had left, a common practice in No Limit tournaments, I soon learned. I had bet T300 out of my T485 chips (meaning I was committed to calling if my opponent set me all-in). He thought for a long time. Finally he showed a queen . . . and mucked his hand.

Another time, Lance open-raised UTG for T500 total, with the blinds only T50 and T100. Brunson said the standard opening raise in No Limit should be about three times the big blind, so even I knew T500 to be a bit of an **overbet**. I looked down at my hand, expecting to fold . . . until I saw two aces. Remembering not to slowplay hands like this one, I immediately moved all-in for about T1,400 or so. Everyone folded to Lance, who instantly mucked his hand when the action got to him. Proud of my hand, I turned over the aces as I dragged the pot, without really thinking about it. Lance looked at me and said, "That's no surprise. I threw away kings." At the time I believed him. I believed him for three years. Now I'm not so sure. But as I told him then, I was happy to take 500 from a good player, given my inexperience—even when I was holding ace–ace.

My play on the above two hands was fine, but I made many bad plays as well. Specifically, I reraised an early position raiser, and then called all-in, holding just pocket fives. My thinking at the time was that any pair is a small favorite against two overcards, so if I could get the pot **heads-up**—down to just me and a single opponent—I would be making a profitable play. Can you see the problem with this logic? It's that I had no idea whether I was up against an **overpair** or overcards. While it's true that fives are about a 54 to 46 favorite over ace–king, they are an 82 to 18 *underdog* against any pair bigger than fives. So if the early raiser had turned over his hand and it was ace–king, I could have profitably called an all-in bet from him. But it's pretty rare that an opponent turns over his hand for you, so in practice we have to give our opponents a **range** of hands. By this I mean when we try to figure out what our opponents have, it's important to consider several possibilities and not to get locked into one choice (this is true in all forms of poker). When I had two fives, I could have called an all-in bet from my opponent if I gave him precisely AK. But what if I gave him the range of hands: AA, KK, QQ, JJ, TT, AK, AQ. Then I would've been about a 64 to 36 underdog and could not possibly have called.

Let me explain some of the math hidden in that last paragraph. I said that as a favorite, two fives can profitably call against AK. This is because the worst possible pot odds a player can get any time he's calling are 1 to 1. So in the most dire scenario, a player would need a 50 percent chance of winning to justify calling, assuming no further action (and when a call is all-in, there is by definition no further action). But how did I determine that two fives has a 36 percent chance of winning against the range of hands: AA, KK, QQ, JJ, TT, AK, AQ? Well, I used a computer program, but I can tell you how the program did it. Given the fifty-two cards in the deck, there are six ways a player can have AA (specifically, A♠A♥, A♠A♣, A♠A♦, A♥A♦, A♥A♣, A♦A♣), and similarly, six ways a player can have KK, QQ, JJ, or TT. There are sixteen ways a player can have AK or AQ. The program computes the chances of winning for each combination of possible opponent's hole cards against the two fives and averages them. It turns out that if our opponent is equally likely to have all those hands above, then we and our two fives are worth 36 percent of the pot against him.

It's not too important to understand the finer points of how this calculation works, but a serious No Limit player should understand that it's not the opponent's exact hole cards but the range of hands he could have that really matters. And it is important to think about your own equity against that range of hands. When I called all-in with five–five, my opponent could have had ace–king, as I believed that to be in his range of hands. But he happened to have two queens, which was also in his range of hands. It hardly matters that I **spiked** a five on the river to win—as it is very important not to let **results** influence our thinking.

I certainly didn't think in terms of ranges of hands in my first tournaments. I also committed the cardinal tournament sin of letting the blinds and antes (in No Limit tournaments, players are usually required to put an ante in the pot every hand during the later rounds) eat away at my stack.

It wasn't until after graduation that I had my first No Limit tournament success. To do well in any tournament usually requires both luck and skill. In a particular Foxwoods tournament on July 27, 1999, I had both. On a key hand, I called after many limpers with two eights on the button (I had learned my lesson about trying to get heads-up with mediocre pairs). The flop came down QJ8 **rainbow** (three different suits) and the small blind moved all-in, with a goofy smile on his face as he did so. Everyone folded to me, and I had to think. There were many ways I could've been beaten, but I remembered two things:

1. *Strong means weak and weak means strong.* This was the one piece of advice Ken Warren gave about tells. (I would learn much more about tells later on, which we'll get to in the next chapter.) Although he was referring more to a player's mannerisms, the same thinking can be applied to the amount of a bet. An all-in bet from the first player to act in a multi-way pot probably did not mean he had the nuts. It probably meant he was protecting a medium-strength hand.
2. *Do not fold sets.* That was Doyle's advice. Don't try to outthink yourself—if you flop a set, just be prepared to lose money with it. So I called.

The opponent in question showed his cards to his neighbor, giggling as another queen came off on the turn (this was back when all-in players were not required to turn their hands faceup for all to see). The river was a blank, and Mr. Small Blind showed his hand . . . queen–ten. "Eights full," I announced, turning my own cards up. The guy looked confused and kept looking at his hand, then at the board, then back at his hand again. The dealer also seemed unsure about where the pot should go. Eventually I had to help. "He has trip queens. I have eights full. I win." The dealer nodded along with me and shipped me the chips. My opponent, despite his disbelief, was out of the tournament. "Boy, that was a bad beat," another player at the table said. It's amazing how clueless some people are. A bad beat, as I explained in Chapter 1, is when someone puts money into the pot with slim prospects, and then gets lucky and wins anyway. In this particular hand, my opponent had about a 17 percent chance of winning after he went all-in and I called. If he had won, then it would have been a bad beat . . . for me!

Like KGB in the first scene of *Rounders*, I had flopped a set and turned a full house, and my opponent had given me all his money. This brings us back to our hero Mike McDermott and the way he goes broke to KGB. Knowing what we now know about No Limit strategy, can we make any comments about Mike's play? He open-raises before the flop on the button with A9s. So far, so good. He flops top two pair and makes an overbet of $2,000. I'm not crazy about risking a lot to win a little, but at least it's an aggressive play. Then, on the turn, Mike makes a full house and **checks behind** KGB; he checks after KGB has already checked. (Recall that KGB holds AA and has made a bigger full house, though of course Mike doesn't know this.) As I was first learning No Limit Hold'em, I didn't like this play. I wanted Mike to continue playing aggressive, because that was the only style I knew. Could Mike have folded if he had bet and Teddy had check-raised? Almost certainly not. But he might have suspected aces full by the river and **flat-called** instead of reraising. He might not have lost his entire stack. So I thought Mike could have played his hand better, but I still wasn't completely sure he could have avoided going broke.

I used my chips from the eights full hand to reach the final table of that post-graduation tournament. Once there, I had an early decision when the UTG player raised to 2000 with blinds of only 200 and 400, and I held two jacks, and not enough chips to cover the raise. I remembered that calling all-in with medium pairs could be a disaster. But luckily I also realized that I was running out of chips, needed to make a stand, and two jacks were considerably better than what the raiser was likely to be holding. When I called, my opponent looked ill. "Do you have a big hand?" I said. He shook his head, but when the flop came down with three low cards and two diamonds he said, "Well, now I have a big draw." Mortified that I was about to go down, I yelled, "Blank! Blank!" meaning I wanted worthless cards to come on the turn and river. I got my wish when no more flush cards came and the only thing of interest on the final board was a small pair. "Jacks up," I declared (this is poker-ese for "two pair, the higher of which is jacks"). My opponent mucked his hand. Soon we were down to the final four participants and played that way for an hour. At that point, someone offered a deal.

A deal is made at the end of a tournament when the players are not comfortable with the amount of money at risk, and they want to lock in some of their profits. For example, say a tournament gets down to two players and the prizes are $200,000 for first and $100,000 for second. The final two players, then, are playing heads-up for $100,000. That's a lot of money to gamble for, especially if the blinds are big enough to significantly reduce the skill factor. The players may very well agree to split up the money, maybe $50,000 each, or possibly less for the shorter stack. The point is to insure you get at least some of that $100,000 up for grabs, instead of going broke and giving it all to your opponent.

This particular deal was very favorable to the shorter stacks (and I was the shortest), and surprisingly all parties agreed. I netted $445, my biggest tournament score to that point, and the hand that made it possible was two pair, jacks and threes. Months later, when it came time to pick my rec.gambling.poker newsgroup handle, as well as my online poker screen name, the choice was obvious—"jacksup."

"He's got talent, he should go pro," Burke said about me after the Foxwoods result. I was flattered that he would make such a comment, but I pretty much shrugged it off. I was living at home in Westhampton, New York, at the time, during that awkward stage in between college and the real world. I was about to start a good job, and didn't want to throw it away for a career in poker. It was the right decision. I had far too little poker experience and not nearly enough bankroll to play full-time. Not to mention I hadn't faced anywhere near the number of stomach aches, bad runs of cards, and monetary swings every player should go through before deciding he's really cut out to support himself through poker. I strongly recommend that all players keep poker a secondary source of income for at least a few years before deciding to make poker their living. And no one should, in my opinion, play poker as his *only* means of earning money.

The last ferry back home to Long Island had left long before the tournament finished. So I played through the night, planning to catch the first boat in the morning. Since I had new money in my pocket, and a new job waiting for me in Virginia, I decided I could take a shot in a $10–$20 game—which was higher than any limit I'd played to that point. They say that $10–$20 is the first **middle limit**, and that play changes drastically at that point from the lower limits, even $5–$10. It seemed true during that first session. I could reraise before the flop with AK, get it heads-up, and win the pot with a bet on the flop. I could play a straight draw aggressively, with an actual chance of winning without a showdown. We'll get into middle limit strategy in Chapter 7, but it feels a lot more like real poker than low limit Hold'em—not to mention that, with the stakes doubled, the potential for a big payday is twice as great.

5

♠ ♣ ♦ ♥

Hosting a Home Game with Regular Opponents, and Spotting Tells

Poker night is up there with Monday Night Football, shopping the day after Thanksgiving, and sitting in rush hour traffic as a modern-day American tradition. People love to play poker, and they love to do it in their own homes.

Unfortunately, most people love to play those wacky games with wild cards and obscure rules that I mentioned earlier. If that's what you're into for your home games, have fun. I'm not going to stop you. But my ideal home game includes more serious poker than that. A weekly gathering of regular players is a way for me to work on my game and find new people to talk hands with. It's a great tool, and everyone should use it. Even those fortunate few who live close enough to play regularly in a casino should set up a home game. You'll want a chance to develop strategies against players you see repeatedly. The poker universe is small—if you encounter a tough player, you'll probably be playing against him, at least occasionally, until one of you is dead.

To get a home game started, my advice is to host it in your very own house, apartment, flat, dorm room, or whatever. The best way to do something right is to do it yourself.

As you know from Chapter 1, I had some experience in starting home games before I arrived at Yale. But there is a big difference between inviting friends over to your parents' house when no one has anything better to do, and getting a group of college students together at the same time. Groups didn't gather at Yale unless it was for some semi-official reason like a secret society, a study group, or free pizza. I had to work to recruit six buddies, and then get them to agree to a time and place. The only things in my favor were that risking money is inherently intriguing and that Yale students usually think they're smart enough to win at any game. When I finally got enough people together for a single-table tournament, the composition was something like this: me, a fellow math major, my history-major roommate, my psychology-major ex-roommate, my ethics-politics-and-economics major friend Burke, and Fabian.

The poker that took place in my dorm room, in the Saybrook College library (where we got the game underway after claiming to be convening a study group and kicking out another student), and a Linsly-Chittenden Hall classroom was odd in that we only played tournaments (sometimes two or three) and never ring games. I don't recommend this approach for bringing casual players into your home game, but the specific mix of personalities made it work for us. We had Burke and Fabian, who knew the adrenaline rush that came with tournaments and weren't interested in playing anything else. We had the psychology major—an ultracompetitive person who was more satisfied when there was a clear-cut winner surrounded by losers. And finally, we had the simple appeal of a fixed loss. No matter how badly someone played, the most he could lose was the initial tournament buy-in, usually $5 or $10.

As you might expect, I won more than my fair share of tournaments against my mostly inexperienced opponents. Not all of them were convinced skill played a factor in these results, but at least some were. One of the guys came up to me in our college courtyard while we were both out partying and said, "I just want to thank you for taking ten dollars from me over the past two days."

I was successful, in part, because I picked up on some of the habits, some of the specific tells, of my regular opponents. Doing this comes naturally to some people, and seems like a magic trick to others. It's odd, because in my life I have often erred on the side of being too trustworthy, believing people when they lied, thinking people would pay me back when they said they would. I once defended a fellow student after he denied having sent several malicious E-mails, only to have him confess the deed a few hours later. I got fooled because I thought people were inherently good. But I didn't get fooled at the poker table. There, I was a natural reader.

In case you're not one of the naturals, I'll let you in on some of the secrets of spotting tells. First, it's not magic. Reading tells is a science, just like every other aspect of the game. And like other sciences, there are basic principles from which the rest of the theory is derived. Mike Caro, America's Mad Genius of Poker, wrote an entire book on tells, called *Caro's Book of Poker Tells*, complete with photos of the hundreds of tells he describes. He also made a two-part video that supplements the book. I won't cover everything Caro does here, but I will explain the theory behind all his information.

First Principle of Reading Tells:
Most players are trying to fool you.

Don't believe people at a poker table. They might not be lying outright, but they'll usually be acting to conceal the truth about their hands. The underlying psychological reason for this (at least according to Caro) is that most people go through life putting on an act—pretending to like people they don't, trying to look fine when they feel ill, going to work at a job they don't really care about—so that unconsciously they think, because they fake everything else, they have to fake the strength of their hand to avoid being totally transparent.

The general concept *strong means weak and weak means strong* is typically valid, especially against inexperienced players. When you see or hear the following things that indicate weakness, be very afraid: a sigh, a meek bet, a lamenting speech, someone looking away from the table, someone starting to fold and then deciding to call, someone looking bored, a shrug, a hesitation raise, a head scratch, a hand gesture, a question from out of nowhere. These are all things a player might do, consciously or not, to try to convince an opponent his hand is weak. The vast majority of the time his feigned weakness will mean he has a strong hand. Play your own hand accordingly.

Similarly, your own hand becomes much more valuable when you see or hear anything that indicates strength: an emphatic bet, a stare right at you, an extremely interested expression, a player who continues to look at the flop long after the cards got there, a player with chips ready in hand, a player reaching for chips out of turn, a player eager to turn over his cards, a player who looks at his hand as you reach for chips. Don't let these antics convince you that your opponent has a strong hand. In fact, the opposite is usually true.

Not all tells are as clearly defined as in the examples I just gave, but some sure are. Let's take a look at a couple of the ones I spotted playing with my friends. Fabian, maybe because he spent so much time conserving funds for *The Herald*, was a gambler at heart and got involved in almost every pot. Usually he would call, hoping to catch some kind of hand. He would even sometimes say what card he needed (and he wasn't lying). But every once in a while things would change. He would say something like, "Hmmm, I'm not sure if you have anything," or "What should I do? Should I raise?" or something else entirely. The point is it didn't matter what he said. Whenever he said or did *anything* outside of his usual routine, he had a hand—probably a monster. He was one of the more obvious actors I've encountered, actually. He would sigh *and* act pained *and* give a speech. It was a classic case of *weak when strong*.

One time there was multi-way action before the flop, which then came down jack–jack–jack. Soon after, Fabian started talking. "It's the race to get a pair," he said. "Who will be the first to get a pair?" I wasn't in this particular hand, but I knew it would take much more than a pocket pair to win it. Fabian, of course, had the fourth jack. His thought process, I guess, was to convince everyone that the first full house would win the hand. But the observant player should have known that as soon as Fabian entered the conversation, everyone else was drawing dead.

I saw another, somewhat more subtle, tell when playing with my friends in Myrtle Beach, South Carolina. I guess I should first explain why we were there. The week after classes end, Yale graduates traditionally celebrate by taking a mass vacation in Myrtle Beach. Burke, Fabian, and I rented a condo with another male friend and two girlfriends. I did the usual stuff: clubbing, going to the beach, playing golf, sleeping late. But in addition, our condo held daily one-table poker tournaments, and we drew a crowd. Friends and girlfriends from nearby condos wanted to play, and we were happy to let them. All told, at least a dozen different people sat with us at some point. Fabian even answered our phone, "Myrtle Poker Room." The group made for an interesting mix of players. Some had been playing with us at Yale throughout the semester, and some had never played poker in their lives.

The hand with the tell involved Burke, a girl playing for her second time, and my girlfriend (let's call her Mylene), who had spent many an hour (bless her heart) listening to me blather about the game, had beaten me heads-up at least once, and who was the smartest person I'd ever met. Burke, despite his blustery personality, played a by-the-book brand of poker. When he bet he usually had the goods, but he would bluff once in a while just to keep us guessing. He was the most solid player of the people I went to school with. On the hand in question, Burke had an ace, and two more appeared on the flop. When another ace came on the turn, Burke let out a frustrated groan and shook his head in anger, pounding the table as he checked. The new player fell for this and bet, Mylene called, but when the action got back to Burke he raised. The new player called, but Mylene, confident Burke had **quad** aces, folded pocket kings! No one else at the table, including me, would have folded. So what happened? Burke's disgust definitely fell into the *weak when strong* class of tells, as he pretended to hate the ace on the turn when actually he loved it. But his angry check would seem to fall into the *strong when weak* class. Why would he make an emphatic check when trying to lure his opponents in? Think through his actions and it should be clear. Burke's check, despite being emphatic, was not a sign of strength. It was part of the rest of his act of hating the ace on the turn. It almost worked because he not only seemed frustrated, he actually checked after showing strength on a previous round. Many players' betting choices will belie their actions; Burke's didn't. But don't misinterpret force as a show of strength. Forcefulness can be part of a larger picture. If you can figure out why a specific player does the things he does, you will be able to correctly categorize his actions as strong or weak and reliably put him on a certain range of hands, just as Mylene did.

There are some tells that do not fall under the first principle, because there is another aspect of trying to portray a strong hand—it is difficult to do convincingly.

Second Principle of Reading Tells: *The more relaxed a player's body language is, the better his hand tends to be.*

Deep down, bluffing makes a person nervous. A bluffer might not change his facial expression, but he might unconsciously hold his breath. If you can succeed in getting him to talk, a bluffer will often mumble incoherently, incapable of speech. A player breathing and speaking easily is a player to be wary of. A player who seems frozen or who stammers, trying to get words out, is the one you want to call down. Bluffers don't want to give anything away, so they freeze without knowing they're doing it. Along these lines, here are some other indications a person may be bluffing: he was humming but suddenly stops, he was shaking but suddenly stops, he's holding his breath, his teeth are clenched, his fists are clenched, he's covering his mouth (he doesn't want to reveal his expression), he delays only slightly before betting (thinking an instant bet might be perceived as a bluff).

Have you ever noticed a player singing at the table? Well, if he makes a bet and keeps on singing, chances are pretty good he has a hand. He is in the opposite of bluffing mode. He feels no subconscious need to hide anything, so he doesn't. Don't call without a very strong hand if you notice that: a player was shaking before he bet and continues to shake afterwards; a player breathes easily with deep, satisfied breaths; a player bets instantly (hoping others think it's a bluff).

Third Principle of Reading Tells: *Reactions can't be faked.*

The last thing I'll teach you about tells (for now) is that it's important to watch someone's initial reaction. As I've already said, don't watch the flop, watch your opponents watch the flop.

One of the most reliable tells in poker is the glance at the chips as the flop comes down. I've seen world-class players do it. It almost always means the person flopped a big hand. Similarly, if a player immediately checks as the flop comes down, it's doubtful he's looking to check-raise. More likely, he just reacted to a flop that missed him. Pay attention to what a player does the instant he looks at a card. That's the best window into his true feelings about his hand. The way to practice observing reactions is to do it on every hand including the ones you're not in—especially the ones you're not in. You will be folding a lot, so you want to make use of your time between hands. Study your opponents during those intervals. This will keep you from getting bored, and it will make you better at reading your opponents.

If you're worried about giving away tells at the table, don't be. Most low limit players are not nearly sophisticated enough to pick up on tells. Bet the same way when you're strong as when you're weak and you should be fine. By the time you have to face strong opponents capable of benefiting from your tells, you should be experienced enough at the table to hide just about everything. Most top players have very few tells.

When the Myrtle trip was over, our rainy graduation day had come and gone, and the period of waiting around in my childhood home had ended, I finally moved into a two-bedroom apartment with Fabian (who coincidentally also got a job in Northern Virginia) in Fairfax. And the poker in my life suddenly stopped. I didn't play a single hand from July 28 until September 11, 1999—far too long for my liking. Atlantic City (AC) is a solid three-and-a-half-hour drive from the District of Columbia, and sadly AC had the nearest legal poker to my new place of residence. I tried to make the trip once a month, but I needed something more. So one day, while running a stress-test on my company's human resources database (my new job was to test software for a company called MicroStrategy), I ran a search to see who listed "poker" as an interest. I sent the result set—a bunch of names of random MicroStrategists—an E-mail, asking if anyone would like to play a regular low stakes game. Within minutes, I received a two-word response from Neal Bituin, a person I'd never met: "I'm in."

A few days later, Neal, his friend Rome, Fabian, and I got together for the first meeting of what became a regular game—a game that still goes today (even as I am living in New York and out of the picture). At least twenty-five different people have played in the Mohan Game (as it was dubbed, after a player named Shrimohan) over its lifetime. We've hosted tournaments, played in a half dozen different locations, and turned some ordinary Joes into some pretty good poker players.

As you can see, you don't need ten or twelve willing participants to get a home game off the ground, although it helps. But there are some things you do need. Home games everywhere are different but almost all of them will have the following:

1. *A host.* Again, I recommend this person be you, at least to start. A new game is not likely to get going if you have to rely on someone else to be hospitable and accommodating.
2. *A table.* This may be an obvious one, but I don't want you to get caught inviting your buddies over, only to make them sit around on your wooden floor, peering at their hole cards between ants and dustballs.
3. *Chairs.* Similar to a table, and also can't be overlooked. You may have a table that can fit nine people, but that doesn't do you much good if you only have four chairs. Ask for volunteers to provide chairs if you're going to be short. (On two separate occasions, Neal bought lawn chairs on his way to the Mohan Game and carried them in.)
4. *Poker chips.* If you or someone else in your game has sprung for the fancy clay kind, fantastic. But the cheaper plastic variety will suffice for home games, and they can be found at most drugstores and even some convenience stores. People like to have a lot of chips in front of them, so err on the side of buying too many. Also be sure to get more than one color, as you'll need to have different denominations of chips. (This is the only way to insure you'll always have enough chips for whatever stakes you want to play.) Most boxes of plastic chips have red, white, and blue in them, but do double-check.
5. *Two decks of cards.* Preferably brand new ones every game (or at least every other game). You need two decks so that one can be shuffled while the other is in play. Without a professional dealer, playing with one deck and shuffling between hands takes way too long. Even casual players will quickly see that using two decks

makes everything go faster, so the game can have more action, and people can have more fun. Oh, and make sure your decks are different colors (one red, one blue works well), or else they'll be very easy to mix up.

6. *Food and drinks.* I was delinquent in this area far too many times as a host. Especially if you have casual acquaintances in your game, it's important to make everyone feel as comfortable as possible. You want the losers to be losing their money happily. Try to have soda, beer, and some kind of snack food around for poker night. If your game starts going regularly and you find you're always providing refreshments, you can ask the players to start rotating turns to buy food and drinks, or just collect a couple of bucks from people once a month or so. If your players are enjoying the game, they almost certainly won't object.

Recruiting can be done in so many different ways. With more than 50 million poker players in this country, you're likely to find plenty of potential regulars if you just ask around. That should be all you need to do if you're only interested in a fun, gambooling home game playing all the wacky variations described in Chapter 1. But if you want your home game to make you a better poker player, you'll need people who have aspirations to be at least somewhat serious about the game, even if their goals are only to hold their own at the low limit tables in a casino. Finding these people is a little tougher. My database search was a neat trick, but I suspect most of you will find it hard to repeat. But you can sift through posts on the newsgroup rec.gambling.poker (RGP) to find players looking for a game in your area. Or you can post yourself, advertising your own game. If you're not sure what newsgroups are, or what RGP is, you'll find out in Chapter 8.

Some of you, however, might not be comfortable inviting total strangers to your home or, for that matter, telling the world and all law enforcement agencies that you're hosting a game. (By the way, laws on home games vary from state to state—the usual interpretation, at least from the players' point of view, is that as long as the house isn't taking a percentage of the pot, games are legal. But definitely look into your local laws if the legal ramifications worry you.)

So here are some other ideas on finding the real poker players lurking among your friends, family members, coworkers, and the rest of society.

1. *Talk up your game.* Mention that you're a poker player as often as you can without being obnoxious about it. You can usually tell by the conversation how serious another person is about it.
2. *Keep your eyes open.* One player got into the Mohan Game because a fellow player spotted him in Atlantic City playing Hold'em. He was a coworker of ours, and we had no idea he played until we saw him there.
3. *Have friends bring friends.* It's amazing how fast games can grow through friends of friends alone.
4. *Invite your coworkers.* Even if they have no idea what they're getting into, some of them might be intrigued at the idea of learning the game. Assure them the stakes are small, convince them they'd make good poker players, and you should be able to add two or three regulars to your game. A poker invite can also be a good way to kiss up to your boss, if that's something you need to do.

When Neal and Rome arrived in my Fairfax apartment for the first Mohan Game, they might have been a little intimidated by the poker books on display on the coffee table. In retrospect, that probably wasn't the best interior design decision on my part. If Neal and Rome hadn't been as desperate for a regular game as I was, the experiment might have ended right there. Luckily, my guests' only reaction was to say, "Uh oh!" and laugh. Besides, the stakes were small. That was one thing I did right—I started with extremely low limits. The first Mohan Games were 25–50 Hold'em; that's 25 and 50 *cents*. We bought in for ten bucks each, and twenty bucks would've been a mammoth loss for the night. (Although a guy who played every hand, and played them all badly, routinely took $40 and $50 losses on the few weeks he played.) We established a friendly atmosphere at the beginning so that a few months later, when I wanted to double the stakes, I got no objections.

I also started a tradition during that first game—a $5 buy-in No Limit Hold'em tournament to end the night. For me, and I think eventually for everyone else, this was the most anticipated, and most interesting part of the proceedings. In the ring game, people had fun, played a lot of garbage hands, and weren't too interested in whether they won or lost. But everyone wanted to win the tournament. It was a matter of pride. And since I had nowhere else to practice my No Limit, the Mohan Game was the only way I could stay reasonably sharp and keep my tournament skills honed.

It's hard to pick my favorite moment from the Mohan Game. There was the time Neal and I got heads-up in the tournament, and thirty straight hands were won with a preflop raise by the button. There was the tradition started by my friend Ben of moving all-in preflop with two–three offsuit and then showing the hand after everyone folded. There was the time Fabian flopped a flush . . . and I flopped a king-high straight flush. There were the many times Rome played his hand **blind** (without looking at it), and then turned over his cards to reveal he'd spiked a longshot on the river. In fact, Rome's blind play often created interesting scenarios. Once, he **straddled** (raised blind preflop from UTG) and then announced he would call every bet to the river without looking at his cards until the showdown. I was on the button with pocket fours and made it three bets. The blinds folded, and Rome (of course) called. The flop came eight–eight–ten rainbow. I bet, and Rome called again. Ditto for the turn card, which was a queen. A king fell on the river, and now I had a real decision. I was facing a random hand, but was I even a favorite against a random hand? Any eight, ten, queen, or king beat me, not to mention jack–nine and ace–jack. My instincts told me I was an underdog, so I checked and turned over my fours. Rome turned over jack–nine for the straight. A few days later I did some math, and it turned out my check was correct. There were 990 hands Rome could have had on the river (this is because there were 45 unseen cards, and there are 45C2 = 990 ways to make a two-card hand out of these unseen cards). It turns out my fours beat 492 of them, and lost to 497 of them. So I was *not* a favorite when called. (If you noticed that 492 + 497 = 989, you might be wondering what happened to the 990th hand. I'll give you a hint—if Rome had held that hand, we would've tied.) I've since done some more math, and it turns out my bet on the turn wasn't even correct! I only had slightly more than a 48 percent chance of winning at that point. If I knew my oppo-

nent would call (which I did), then I needed to be a favorite in order for a bet to be profitable.

Rome claims the reason he makes bizarre plays like this one is to create interesting and different situations like this one. I don't know if I believe him, but I do know that I learned a lot having Rome as an opponent for three years. I learned a lot from each of the Mohan Game regulars. Gary Carson, author of *The Complete Book of Hold'em Poker*, says you should be able to write a book on the people you play with every week. I think he might be exaggerating, but his point is valid. The more I watched Rome, the more I understood the rationale behind his seemingly illogical plays.

And I also picked up player-specific tells. For example, one of our regulars often talked during hands. But if he started thinking out loud, instead of just keeping up the usual conversation, he almost always had a strong hand. "Hmmm, do you have the flush? I raise." If he said something like this, I would consider folding a full house (and certainly wouldn't raise with it). It took me months of playing with him to pick up on this, but after I did I picked up on other things from other regulars. And as I learned to watch playing patterns in the home game, they became easier to pick up on in the casino games.

Improving my game and meeting new people were my two biggest goals for the Mohan Game, and I succeeded in both. Players from the game became my road-trip partners, my wingmen at bars, my sponsors in poker tournaments, and my helpers in moving to new apartments. They became some of my best friends. I understand, however, if making friends is not enough of a goal for some of you. Maybe you want to make some real money in your home game. In that case I suggest you try raising the stakes once every two or three months. Any faster than that, and your fellow players may start to feel things are moving too quickly (just like in a relationship). But as long as the game is fun for everybody—and you should have a pretty good sense of whether that is the case—the risk of pricing out a regular player is small, and you should be able to reach the betting limits you desire.

Our game never got bigger than $1–$2 (the limits it is still played at today) but we did experiment with alternating weeks of Limit and No Limit (25¢ and 50¢ blinds) ring games, a few nights of H.O.S.E. (where the games rotate between Hold'em, Omaha, Stud, and Stud

Eight-or-Better) and even tried a dealer's choice night once, with wacky games just to keep things fresh (again, like a relationship).

Decide what you want from your home game, and it should be easy to make it happen. Just make sure, whatever your goals, you remain a forceful competitor in your "real" poker games.

6

♠ ♣ ♦ ♥

Tournaments, the Next Level

Everyone knows the difference between playing a skins match with your golfing buddies on a Saturday morning, and playing in a PGA Tour event like the Pebble Beach National Pro-Am. Not everyone recognizes the enormous difference between playing poker with your buddies on a Friday night, and entering one of poker's **major tournaments**. These are annual events where you can be sure to find the tournament pros gathering to win some serious cash. Foxwoods, for example, has weekly tournaments with $35 buy-ins, but it also hosts two major tournaments a year: the New England Poker Classic (NEPC) in the spring and World Poker Finals (WPF) in the fall. The pros come all the way from Las Vegas for these—especially the latter, whose championship event is a $10,000 buy-in WPT No Limit Hold'em tournament—and they are advertised months in advance in *Card Player Magazine* and on poker websites.

As a kid, I never got excited by anything below the top tier. In junior high school, I wouldn't submit my truly awful thirteen-year-old writing to scholastic magazines but only to "real" publications. In high school, before I became a serious student of poker, chess was my game—and I had insisted on subscribing to *Chess Life*, the adult chess magazine, instead of the scholastic one. So as a twenty-one-year-old, the very phrase "major poker tournament" drew me in. Of course, so did the money. Why play a $20 tournament with the chance to win a few hundred bucks when I could play a $120 tournament with the chance to win a few thousand? Even better, satellites for the smallest NEPC events were dirt cheap, like thirty bucks or so. When the NEPC came around in April of 1999, I was ready (or at the very least, eager) to take the next step and enter the *major* tournament world.

Satellites, though, turned out not to be my thing. I knew little enough about general tournament strategy, and I had no idea how to adjust my play for satellites. A satellite is a one-table tournament where the winner advances to a bigger, multi-table tournament. Second place in a satellite is usually worth nothing, and it was worth nothing in the NEPC satellites I played.

Some say that proper strategy for winner-take-all tournaments like satellites should be the same as proper strategy for ring games. They reason that since the point is to get all the chips, and since they can't win any money by going broke (the way they could in a tournament that paid many people), then the best strategy is whatever will get the most chips in the long run, just as it would be in a ring game. I disagree with this as a blanket statement, but the point is valid. There is nothing to gain by finishing second or third, so you might as well get as many chips as you can with no thought of folding your strongest hands in the hopes of moving up a spot or two.

The problem is that satellites don't play anything like typical ring games. Players are much more aggressive and much more conscious of trying to accumulate chips than in a ring game—especially a low limit ring game, where most players just play passively and hope chips come to them. To win a satellite, you have to play more hands and play them more aggressively. This is not because satellite strategy is hugely different from ring game strategy, but because in a loose-hyperaggressive ring game, you would have to make these same adjustments. You'd have to adjust even more in a ring game where the blinds constantly doubled, as they do in satellites.

I didn't understand this when I sat in my first Limit Hold'em satellite. I played my usual tight-aggressive game, which left me playing far too few hands to have a reasonable chance of winning. People would raise my blind, and I would dutifully fold. If someone raised in front of me, I would fold all but my monsters. And I would rarely, if ever, try to steal the blinds by raising with a less than premium hand. Burke had told me to hum "Satellite" by Dave Matthews Band to myself as I tried to win my way into the bigger tournament. Although I did the humming, I couldn't do the winning. Maybe it should've been "Satellite of Love" by Lou Reed.

I became very successful at one-table tournaments later in my career, and looking back at those first few I played I came up with these Limit Hold'em Satellite Tips for New Players:

1. *Don't enter satellites until you're reasonably confident you're a winning ring game player.* Because the styles of play are so different, you run the risk of ruining your game if you jump into satellites before mastering the discipline required to beat a loose-passive Hold'em table. Get grounded as a grind-it-out, tight-aggressive winning poker player before you shoot for the big money in satellites (either that or become a tournament specialist and avoid ring games all together).

2. *Experiment and take chances.* You'll have to play more hands than you're used to playing, so think about different ways to do that. Steal-raise from different positions. Limp in once in a while with drawing hands. Play the small pairs **up front** (in early position). **Play back** at people (raise or reraise) who you suspect are bluffing, or at least call them down with medium-strength hands. Satellites are a good place to try out different ways to be a successful loose player.

3. *Don't make big folds.* Your opponents will be playing a lot of hands too. If you have a good hand, don't overthink your situation. It's Limit Hold'em, and your pot odds combined with the wide range of hands most opponents will have makes folding for one bet with a decent hand a bad play, especially on the river. Pay off, and hope your hand is best.

4. *Stay aggressive.* I can't emphasize this enough. You won't win a Limit Hold'em satellite by checking and calling.

Given my poor performance in the satellites, you might be wondering why I might have gone back to Foxwoods to enter an actual NEPC event. Well, that's simple. I was too young to lose my confidence, and I loved playing way too much.

The poker room was packed when Burke and I arrived for the first

Limit Hold'em event of the 1999 NEPC. For just $120, anybody could enter and have the chance to become a major tournament winner. This wasn't a good enough deal for Burke, however, as he planned to just play ring games and occasionally cheer me on from the rail. Many people did like their chances, though. We had about four hundred entrants in the tournament, and Foxwoods had to use tables in the poker room, in the craps area, and in what was usually a big empty space behind the blackjack games to accommodate them all.

I went to the registration area, forked over the cash, got my seat assignment, and went to the snack bar with Burke to grab a quick burger before everything got underway. Burke sat, staring at the big screens showing horse races he had no interest in, fidgeting even more than he usually did, watching me eat. Finally he told me he'd be right back, and I assumed he was going to the bathroom or something. I had finished my burger when Burke got back to the table. "I'm playing the tournament," he said, holding his receipt.

There were only two people in this enormous field who I would have recognized, with Burke being one of them. When I got to my table, I looked to my left and wanted to throw up. It was Lance, the man who claimed to have folded pocket kings against me preflop, the man I knew to have a fantastic record at Foxwoods tournaments, the man I feared most from the Tuesday night No Limit tournaments. My table assignment was definitely a bad beat, as the seating draw is often the biggest determining factor in who will accumulate chips. But I had already paid my money. I had no choice but to sit down and play my best.

On one of the very first hands, I got dealt ace–queen, limped in, and saw a flop of queen–jack–x (where x is an insignificant small card). I bet, and my lone opponent raised. This guy didn't seem to care about money, throwing chips into the pot as fast as he could. "Reraise," I said.

"Raise," he said immediately, quietly, as if it were a burden to him. At this point I figured him for queen–jack and decided to just call. I liked the ace on the turn very much, though, and I bet again. "Raise," he said, just as he'd said it before.

"Reraise," I said.

"Raise," the monotone came one more time. I just called. My major tournament career was getting off to a rollicking start. I had gone four bets on the flop and turn, and I had no idea what my opponent had. But after the ace on the river, I didn't really care. I knew I couldn't be beaten. I bet, and this time the raise-a-holic just called . . . and flipped over his king–ten for a straight.

"Aces full," I said. He didn't say anything, just took his cards and flung them in the muck. He had four-bet the flop with nothing but a straight draw, a strategy that worked beautifully when the turn card gave him the nuts and gave me top two pair. Unfortunately for him, the plan backfired when I made the nuts myself on the river. I think he played his hand very well, though. On the flop, he was aggressive with a draw in a heads-up pot and had me very confused (not confused enough to fold, but he had no idea I had top pair–top kicker). His turn and river plays were automatic.

From this first hand, you might think the rest of the tournament played completely different from a $3–$6 Hold'em table. It didn't. The raising war hand I started with was the exception, not the rule. Most hands were three- or four-way to the flop, with a ton of checking and calling and praying to hit a hand. As limits went up people got tighter, but it still felt as though little had changed. Even Lance was befuddled. "They're playing draws," he said. "In tournaments, they're playing draws." It is often correct to play a draw in Limit Hold'em, but I think Lance's comment applied to the general philosophy of most of our opponents, which seemed to be "Keep calling and hope to get lucky." Of course, the only reason Lance made the comment was that someone had played a draw, hit it, and taken a bunch of his chips. He busted long before I did, which I was happy to see.

There comes a time in every Limit Hold'em tournament when you have to get chips or die. It usually happens in the second and third hours. During the first hour, the blinds are low enough where the danger of going broke is small—the house wants to make sure everyone gets some bang for his buck. But the house also wants to make sure there is some **play** at the final table (that is, players have enough chips so they can be somewhat selective about what pots they enter). The typical solution is to lose half the field or more in the second and third hours of play by doubling the blinds at each new level. (Later in the tournaments, the blind increases are proportionally smaller.) There is some skill to getting through this insanity portion—for example, you can play aggressively and take advantage of players who fold too much. But the best way to survive the insanity is to find a hand and have it hold up.

I found a hand sometime in hour three of the NEPC event: good old **big slick** (ace–king). But I forgot to make it hold up, as I was beaten by an older lady holding ace–queen. It's fitting that I busted from my first major tournament with ace–king, as I can't count the number of times I've busted with it since. An old saying is "To win a Hold'em tournament you have to win with ace–king, and you have to beat ace–king." This, of course, is not universally true, but it does take luck to win a tournament. You'll need to have good hands, and you'll need to have some of them paid off in order to win.

My advice is to play your typical solid ring-game strategy for the first hour of bigger Limit Hold'em events. You'll be amazed at how many **fish** (weak players) you encounter, assuming you don't pick a WPT event as your first foray. Then, during the insanity portion, play more hands than usual or you run a serious risk of getting blinded out of the tournament. But be sure to play aggressively—you always want to have a chance to win the pot without a showdown.

When the insanity period ends, if you're lucky enough to be one of the survivors, you'll have entered a new stage in the tournament. Most of the remaining players will be strong and you'll have to either get creative or really lucky to accumulate chips. We'll discuss this stage much more in Chapter 14, when I enter the Tournament of Champions of Poker.

Foxwoods gave away a souvenir hat with the tournament buy-in. By lucky coincidence, Yale has a tradition where all the graduates wear some kind of funky hat (of the graduate's choosing) as they listen to the Class Day speaker in their caps and gowns during Commencement weekend. As I don't have a lot of funky in me, and wasn't about to wear a flamingo or Big Bird on my head (as some others did), my choice of hat was obvious. I was the guy in the Yale College class of 1999 wearing poker paraphernalia at his graduation.

The first few months after Yale were otherworldly. I was supposed to be this educated intellectual, but I didn't feel like one. I thought I had wasted four years without accomplishing anything, with my best days behind me. Although this sulking was foolishness, it wasn't foolish to me then. This period was the first of several since I took up the game that poker got me through an upheaval. It's ironic that a game of constant bankroll swings, changing fortunes, and uncertainty would be a stabilizing influence, but it has been. Why? Because I love the game. I love analyzing hands and determining the best way to play them. I love taking money from people who think they are better than everyone else. I love meeting brilliant game theorists and calling them friends. I love the rush of making the final table of a tournament. I love having $2,000 in chips in front of me. I love winning a hand. I love that the next hand is a minute or so away. I love figuring out exactly what a person is thinking. Love of the game finally helped me realize that my post-college life—new apartment, new job, new poker home to break in—wasn't so bad, even if my girlfriend was in England.

As I mentioned before, it took me a while to make my first Atlantic City (AC) trip. When I finally got there, the $5–$10 game at the Trump Taj Mahal was pretty similar to the ones I had played at Foxwoods and Mohegan. What caught my eye, though, was an advertisement for the upcoming U.S. Poker Championships—the 1999 version of the tournament where Phil Hellmuth had tilted away all his chips. I grabbed a copy of the schedule. Looking it over, I saw my opening odds of playing an event weren't good. I could only play weekend tournaments (it was far too early in my software testing career to be faking a sick day), and the smallest buy-in for a weekend event was $500. The only way I could afford to play in one of those was to win a satellite. Oh well, at least I could come up during the event and see a poker celebrity or two.

Three weeks after my first visit, I returned to the Taj Mahal, planning to take one shot in a satellite for the $500 events. I chose to play a Limit Hold'em satellite, as that was still the game I knew best by a wide margin. Again, I didn't play aggressively enough early. In fact, I limped with pocket queens after the first two players to act had limped in front of me. As you should know by now, raising is definitely the preferred play there. By the grace of the poker gods, my queens held up and won a huge pot. And as people began to bust out, I started raising more. Maybe it was instincts taking over. More likely it was all the shorthanded experience I had since the NEPC—with my buddies in the Yale dorms and in Myrtle Beach.

The next thing I knew the satellite was down to me and an old guy named Lucky. I had been afraid that when it got heads-up my opponent would want to make a deal. I really wanted to play for the full $500 **lammer** (a chip that can only be used to buy-in to a tournament) plus $65 cash that was at stake. I didn't want to get this far only to split everything up. It wasn't about the money. I wanted a chance to win this thing outright. Luckily, Lucky wanted to play it out as well. The only catch was that he wanted to **save** the $65 cash for whoever came in second. In other words, the prize pool would be readjusted so that second was worth $65, and first a $500 lammer. This sounded good to me, so we agreed to the save . . . and then the game was on.

Despite being fifty or so years younger than Lucky, I probably had more heads-up experience than he did, thanks again to all the one-table tournaments I played with my buddies. In heads-up Hold'em, the basic principles of starting hand selection change completely. Any two cards are playable, and folding is usually a bigger mistake than calling—the exact opposite of a normal full-table scenario. I could tell Lucky was folding way too many hands for a **heads-up match**. He complained to someone watching that he wasn't getting any cards. I have news for you, Lucky, no one gets any cards when it's heads-up.

I started the one-on-one contest with a decent chip lead, and when Lucky pulled even it only made me more determined to win. I kept raising, and he kept folding. Finally he decided to limp in on the button (in heads-up, the small blind is on the button and the other player has the big blind), and I checked from the big blind with six–four offsuit. The flop came with three low cards, one of which was a six. I bet and Lucky raised, putting himself all-in. I didn't have a great hand, but the pot was offering me 5 to 1, and a small pair is a legitimate heads-up hand. Besides, I didn't think Lucky had anything. I called. "Let's see if I can get lucky," he said, flipping over his ace–queen.

Suddenly aware that I was two rags away from winning the satellite, I watched another low card come off on the turn. "Blank! Blank!" I yelled (my signature line, I guess). I don't remember what the dealer turned up last, but I know it wasn't an ace or a queen. I jumped up from the table and probably pumped my fist a bit. Then I shook Lucky's hand.

"You're tough," he said.

When I called Mylene in England the next day I think she was more excited than I was. I told her I was thinking about selling the lammer. The only two $500 tournaments I had the option of playing were Stud Eight-or-Better (totally out of the question—I'd never even played the game) and No Limit Hold'em, a game I loved but really didn't know that well. I could probably get $500 or very close to it by selling my lammer the day of the tournament. Mylene, however, stopped all thoughts of that quickly. "It wouldn't be spiritually right if you didn't play," she said. Mylene was someone I listened to. I got off the phone, and started thinking about how to play a $500 No Limit Texas Hold'em event at the U.S. Poker Championships.

The first thing I did was read and reread the No Limit section of Doyle Brunson's *Super/System*. I also picked up T. J. Cloutier's No Limit Hold'em book *Championship No-Limit and Pot-Limit Hold'em* and absorbed his ideas. (He contrasts with Doyle in that he doesn't like to push draws. But he agrees with Doyle on a lot of things, like not slowplaying big pairs preflop.) After marking up the texts with underlines, I started working on an overall hand-by-hand strategy. I would play ace–queen suited a certain way from a certain position, seven–seven a certain way from a certain position, etc. This is not the best way to go about preparing for a No Limit tournament, as it is a rigid approach. But for a person still trying to nail down the fundamentals of the game, it isn't bad.

Next I had some conversations with Burke. He was the only person I'd ever talked poker strategy with, so he was the natural choice to bounce ideas off. Burke, as was his style, had done some thinking on my behalf to get me ready for the tournament. He thought middle-position decisions would be critical. Folding a lot in early position and stealing a lot in late position would be standard for everyone, but playing borderline hands when fourth or fifth to act would be what separated the winners from the rest. It was an interesting idea, and to this day I think it has some merit.

But it was more of a warning than strategic advice. What was I supposed to do in middle position? Play more aggressive? Play less aggressive? Play looser than everyone else? Play tighter than everyone else? As I sat in my hotel room the night before the tournament, looking over my No Limit notes, I decided I would take as few chances as possible with my chips. I would wait for the monster hands and hope someone doubled me up. I didn't trust myself to take chances with junk, and since anything other than ace–ace or king–king is potentially junk in No Limit, I was just going to stay out of the way in a lot of pots. With one exception. I would call the first raise with pocket pairs, planning to play them aggressively if no ace flopped, and maybe double up with them if I flopped a set.

In hindsight, the approach I came up with for my first big No Limit event was good and bad. It was good in that, by playing so tight, I was likely to stay in the tournament for a while and get the experience of playing with a lot of the big boys. But it was a bad strategy for trying to win money. You need to accumulate chips in order to win a tournament; surviving from hour to hour is not enough. You can survive by folding every hand; in fact, someone who does will last longer than most of his opponents. But you can never win any money that way. The prizes typically escalate sharply in the top three spots, which makes sense—the strategy for winning the tournament and the strategy for making the most money should be as close as possible. To make it to the top three, you need chips. And you usually won't get aces and kings enough times to wait for them.

My advice for new No Limit players is not to play $500 events. Get much more experience playing the game than I had before entering your first major. Don't even play a satellite for these events unless you're willing to write off the expense as tuition. I know this advice might be discouraging, but remember that I'm trying to help you learn from my mistakes. As excited and focused as I was going into the 1999 U.S. Poker Championships, the more sensible play in terms of short-term economics was to sell the lammer and pocket the cash, spiritually right or not.

But I didn't, and on the morning of the tournament there I was in the lobby outside of the Taj Mahal poker room, staring at Phil Hellmuth, Jr., in the flesh. He had a wad of $100 bills in his hand and was chatting it up with some other poker professional. That's one thing I noticed immediately—Hellmuth was always talking, even in real life. I didn't even consider approaching him. What would I say? I enjoyed watching you embarrass yourself on television?

Once in the poker room I quickly recognized Scotty Nguyen and T. J. Cloutier from their appearances in the 1998 World Series of Poker. This was the equivalent of a Little Leaguer walking to his baseball game and seeing Barry Bonds and Sammy Sosa milling around home plate. I didn't know whether to ask for their autographs or pretend to be one of them. I decided to just worry about my own tournament, and walked to the registration area where I handed over my lammer plus forty bucks cash (which went straight to Mr. Trump). I got my seat and settled in, putting my jacket over my chair, and placing my receipt on the table, **locking up** my spot. I was the first one there, the only person so new to this that he arrived at his seat ten minutes early. After not too long, people started filing in—an Asian guy on my right, an older guy a few seats to my left. There was nobody I recognized. That is, there was nobody I recognized until T. J. Cloutier sat down across the table from me. Great. Fantastic. My first big No Limit event, and I had the best No Limit player in the world at my table, a guy who had written several books on the game (including one I had read in preparation for this tournament), a guy who had reached the final table of the WSOP main event three times (four times, as of this writing). I got up from my seat and went outside to get cell phone reception and call Burke. I woke him up. "Cloutier's at my first table."

"Huh?"

"T. J. Cloutier is at my first table."

"Oh, shit," he said, coming to life.

"Yeah," I said. But once I had told him, I really didn't know what else to say. I couldn't do anything about it, and neither could Burke. "I'll talk to you later," I said, hanging up.

I returned to the table, ready to start folding. Before the tournament got underway, I noticed a few people giving T.J. their condolences about being at the same table with someone we'll call Pete. Pete was a chubby guy a few seats to my left (T.J. was a few seats to his left). I made a mental note to watch this Pete and see what was so sinister about him.

The event started, and the UTG player raised the very first hand at our table. Everyone folded. On the second hand, the UTG player (obviously a different player) raised again. "Is everyone in that spot gonna pop it?" Cloutier said. I was glad to hear him ask this because I was wondering the same thing. The first thing I learned about Hold'em was that you need a strong hand when first-to-act. The last thing I expected to see was an early position raise every hand. The next few UTG players folded, though, and things were closer to normal. One or two hands are not enough to judge the makeup of a poker table.

Ten hands, though, can be plenty, and I learned within that time frame why Pete would be a pain to play against. He was extremely aggressive and loved to make overbets. Even I knew that risking a lot of chips to win a few chips was not a good play. But many people fall into the trap of thinking it's a good play because an overbet will win some small amount most of the time. The problem, of course, is that when it loses, it usually costs your whole stack. Typical No Limit Hold'em bets are a little less than the size of the pot. This bet size is big enough to make calling a real decision for your opponent, but small enough so that you are not easy to **trap** (that is, you won't give a lot of chips to an opponent with a big hand). Pete didn't make typical No Limit bets. He was involved in a lot of hands, and made big bets with most of them.

A hand soon came up, in which Pete was second to act, where a pair appeared on the flop. I was watching Pete's opponent . . . and he immediately glanced down at his chips when the flop came. Well, we all know what that means. Pete's opponent checked, Pete bet, and then faced a check-raise. Pete reraised a very big amount. His opponent hesitated only a little, and then moved all-in. Now Pete went into a thinking mode. His problem was that so many of his chips were already in the pot. He had made it very difficult for himself to fold. Finally, Pete called. The guy who had glanced at his chips (Pete either didn't see it or didn't know what it meant, or both) had flopped a huge hand, and Pete had only a small pair. Pete's overbetting and failure to notice his opponent's tell got him knocked out of the tournament. Everyone at the table breathed a sigh of relief. Even though Pete's strategy was poor, it put all of us in serious jeopardy of getting knocked out at any time, which was stressful. That said, I found the situation stressful as it was, and might have preferred keeping Pete around, giving me a better chance to double my chips.

Meanwhile, T.J.'s stack was steadily rising, and he quickly became the chip leader at our table. And he was talking. He wasn't talking the way Hellmuth does, but he was talking. I don't know why I expected him to be the strong, silent type. Maybe it was because he spent three years playing football professionally in Canada, or maybe because he had learned poker as a road gambler out west, or maybe because he just looked like a strong, silent type, with his broad frame and big hands. But he was not silent. He constantly blurted stuff out. "Look at that flop, queen–queen–three, I had the gay waiter, a queen, and a tray." "Seventeen outs twice, he was the favorite." "Your first instinct is right 99 percent of the time." That last line was taken straight from his book—in fact it was one of its core philosophies. Go with your first instinct, don't talk yourself out of a read. If you think your opponent is weak, then call or raise. If you think he's strong, fold. This is solid No Limit advice, but it assumes you're good at reading people, a huge assumption. Cloutier certainly had been successful with it over the years.

I wasn't just lying down, though. In keeping with the plan I had devised the night before, I twice called a raise with a medium pair. Neither time did an ace flop, and on both flops the initial raiser bet and I raised. Both times I won on the flop, with my opponent actually showing me an ace on one of them. I couldn't believe that a play I had come up with in the middle of the night while fighting off insomnia had worked in exactly the way I'd envisioned it—twice.

About an hour into the tournament, Grandmaster T.J. made a fatal error. He made a pot-sized bet on an ace-high flop, and his opponent called. His opponent checked again on the turn card, and T.J. made another big bet. His opponent looked extremely pained, his face contorted as he stared at the board. But finally he called again. Cloutier put his opponent all-in for his last few chips on the river, and Cloutier rolled over ace–jack. His stunned opponent showed an ace–queen and raked in the pot. In one hand, Cloutier had gone from chip leader at the table to short stack. What had happened? T. J. Cloutier knew full well that a pair of aces with a jack kicker is not a real hand in No Limit Hold'em. Neither, for that matter, is a pair of aces with a queen kicker, which is why Cloutier's opponent nearly folded his hand. T.J., true to his word, had gone with his first instinct. "I put him on a weaker ace," he said. A few hands later, Cloutier busted. I had outlasted the four-time bracelet winner.

As the blinds went up, my chips were getting low, and I had to take a stand or be done. So when it was folded to me in the cutoff, I open-raised with ace–eight. Only the big blind called. I had just enough chips left to make a pot-sized all-in bet at the flop, which is what I did when it came jack-high (with no eight), and my opponent checked. This time, *my* opponent looked pained. He told me later that he hadn't seen me play a hand in an hour and was very scared I had an overpair. But finally he decided he couldn't fold his ace–jack for the first bet, and called. The turn card was an eight, giving me hope. Believe it or not, the river card was yet another eight. "Trip eights," I said, turning my hand over. His shoulders slumped and he stared, dumbfounded, at the board. "Sorry," I said, as I collected my chips and got up to go on break. This was the worst beat I have ever put on anyone, and will probably be the worst beat I ever do put on anyone. I had a 0.3 percent chance of winning the hand after the flop. I would've been about fifty times more likely to win with a gutshot straight draw, and *that*'s considered a longshot. Yikes.

After the break I continued to get no playable hands—at least, no playable hands by my definition. True, I never once saw ace–ace, king–king, queen–queen, or ace–king in this tournament, and that is an unquestionably god-awful preflop run. But I was just playing too tight. How tight? About three hours into the tournament, at a time I desperately needed chips, I looked down at two jacks in early position. I reached for my stack, ready to raise, but then thought, "No. Two jacks is a medium pair. We're in early position. We don't need to risk busting on this hand. Let it go." And I quickly fired them in the muck. The instant the cards left my hand I knew I'd made a mistake. Jacks are not a big pair, but they're much better than, say, sixes. And I was running out of time. It wasn't much longer before I busted (this is one of the few tournaments in my life where I don't remember the actual hand I busted on), with five or six tables remaining.

Christmas was just a few weeks later, and I got Ken Buntjer's tournament poker book as a present from my parents. As I read it, I remembered the Taj event and wished I'd read the book before I played it. There were three lessons to be learned from the experience that Buntjer hit home:

1. *You can't just survive, you have to survive with chips.* It's almost useless to preserve a tiny stack by folding every hand. Your goal should be to double your stack every hour. If you don't, it's not always a disaster because as long as you have chips you're alive. But on every hand you should be asking yourself, how can I get more chips?

2. *You have to take risks before you become a short stack.* You won't get anyone to fold if you don't have the chips to do it. So the time to take chances and be aggressive is *before* you get blinded down to where you only have three or four big blinds in front of you. Your raises and semibluffs must actually have a chance of winning with no showdown. If I'd had more chips on the ace–eight hand, my opponent may very well have folded.

3. *There are situations that require playing any two cards.* Especially in No Limit Hold'em, you need to give yourself the chance to get lucky, and you can only do that if you sometimes sneak into the pot by limping in late position (or even early position, if it's a passive table). Playing good starting hands is just not enough to make someone a strong No Limit player, or a strong tournament player in general.

If you are a beginning player, as I was, who can't resist the lure of a big-time No Limit tournament, then I hope at the very least you incorporate some of the ideas from this chapter. As for me, my next poker project was to strengthen my Limit Hold'em ring game. The next major poker tournament on the East Coast wasn't for another four months, and it was all the way in Foxwoods (now a seven-hour drive, or an hour flight, away). Luckily, I found the perfect opportunity to improve my ring game in my new hometown of the District of Columbia.

7

♠ ♣ ♦ ♥

Limit Hold'em, the Next Level

Some people wake up in the middle of the night wanting ice cream, or needing a shower, or overcome with the urge to call a friend across the country. As the 1990s were coming to an end and I was settled in my Virginia apartment, I woke up at night craving poker. The Mohan Game was fun but financially meaningless. I needed to play for real stakes; the occasional Atlantic City trips were not enough. There had to be something close by.

I responded to posts on rec.gambling.poker from people looking for a game in the D.C. area. Most of the respondents were hoping to find an existing game they could just jump into, but some guy who lived in Maryland seemed enthusiastic about hosting a game himself. The only problem was he wanted to build a poker table from scratch first. He sent a mass E-mail to potential players, informing us of this in the fall, and when he said things like "We're hoping to have our first game in February, after the holidays are over," I knew the game would never get off the ground.

Disturbed, I glanced over the recipient list and saw an E-mail address I recognized. It belonged to *CardPlayer Magazine* columnist Nolan Dalla, who included his contact information at the end of every column. I had no idea he lived in the poker hell of Washington, D.C., and guessed that he probably knew of a few games in the area. Feeling brazen and desperate to play cards, I sent an E-mail to Nolan, a man I had never met. I was very lucky that Nolan 1) is a class act who responds to E-mails from strangers, and 2) was looking to get some new blood into a local $10–$20 Hold'em—a game featuring a bunch of tough players. Nolan put me in touch with the self-described "Director of Player Relations" for this game—a man named Kim Eisler, who has written a book about Foxwoods called *Revenge of the Pequots*. Kim, in turn, sent me a detailed E-mail with a short bio of all the players, from both a poker and personal standpoint. The game in question was known as the Lawyers' Game.

It was too close to *Rounders* even for me. I couldn't believe I had found my way into a game like this one and had no idea whether I was good enough for it. I'd only played as high as $10–$20 once before. But I wanted a challenge, I could afford the stakes, and I needed to play. So I agreed to take a seat in this monthly game. Now all I had to do was figure out how to beat a bunch of the best poker players in D.C.

Hold'em Poker for Advanced Players (HPFAP) by David Sklansky and Mason Malmuth is considered the middle limit Hold'em bible. *The Theory of Poker* (TOP) by David Sklansky is a seminal work considered by many (including me) to be the best book on poker strategy available. I intended to master these two texts before my first $10–$20 home game session on January 21, 2000.

HPFAP is an interesting read, if nothing else. I don't consider it the sacred text that some others do, but it is still probably the best book on middle limit Hold'em available. It is really more a starting hand guide and a collection of plays than a strategic approach to Hold'em. Still, it does include some important concepts specific to middle limit games. For example, it discusses at length the use of the **semibluff**. A semi-bluff, as defined by Sklansky, is a bet with a hand that figures to be behind if called but has the possibility of improving to the best hand. Of course, you can only improve to the best hand if there are more cards to come.

As we discussed earlier, bets on the river are usually either value bets or bluffs. They are never semibluffs. The idea behind a semibluff is that there are two ways to win: your opponent can fold, or you can improve to the best hand if he calls. The semibluff is largely ineffective in low limit games because most players never fold. But it is enormously powerful against thinking opponents. Put yourself in the position of a player holding a small or medium pair. If a third flush card hits on the turn, do you really want to call a bet from your opponent? Probably not, and this is exactly why a player holding the lone ace of the flush suit can make a great play by betting there. He knows it will be tough for you to call, and even if you do he has at least nine outs to win the hand.

As for starting hand selection, HPFAP recommends playing more starting hands than Ken Warren does. This is not surprising because Warren's book is designed for rank beginners, while HPFAP is, as the title says, "for Advanced Players." (By the way, don't let this title scare you off. Anyone who has played Hold'em a few times should be able to understand and incorporate the ideas presented in the book.) As I said earlier, the more experience you get, the more hands you should be able to play for a profit. Specifically, HPFAP recommends playing more pairs (down to 88) and more suited hands (AKs, AQs, AJs, JTs, QJs, KJs, ATs, T9s, QTs, 98s, J9s, KTs) in early position than the low limit books do. It also advises open-raising in late position with hands as weak as 64s and suited kings, hands that I had thought were never worth playing. You only open-raise with these hands if there is a reasonable chance you will pick up the blinds immediately. Obviously these hands cannot be played based on their intrinsic value. But combine the possibility of winning the pot without a showdown and the possibility of making some kind of hand with these rags, and HPFAP says they sometimes warrant a play. Finally, HPFAP says you should sometimes mix things up by raising in early or middle position with suited connectors like 87s. The idea is to not be too predictable. If you only raise with big pairs and big aces, alert opponents will pick up on this.

Most of those alert opponents will have also read HPFAP, one of the most popular poker books around. Not all of them will have read TOP, a much more dense and labor-intensive read, but well worth the effort. Where HPFAP is a collection of hand-by-hand strategies and plays, TOP is an abstract study of poker in general. The tagline on the cover says it all: "a Professional Poker Player Teaches You How to Think Like One." The concepts in TOP apply to all forms of poker, and the book is a must-read for any serious player (Sklansky and Malmuth tend to say that about anything they write, but with TOP it's really true), if only to learn the vocabulary the rest of the poker community uses.

Two of the most important terms from the book are **implied odds** and **effective odds**. You already know that if there is $40 in the pot on the flop and you have to call $10 to see the next card, then you are getting 4 to 1 *pot* odds—not enough to draw at, say, a gutshot straight draw. But what if I told you another player would call on the flop, and if you hit the gutshot on the turn you could check-raise both opponents, they would both call, and one of them would call again on the river? Well, now you're not calling $10 to win $40, you're calling $10 to win $150. Suddenly this looks like a profitable play. Your implied odds—the amount you have to call compared to the amount you stand to win if you hit your hand—are 15 to 1, and it is only a 10.75 to 1 against hitting your gutshot on the turn (4 cards help you, 43 don't; 43 to 4 = 10.75 to 1).

Be very aware, though, of all the hidden factors we needed to make that call correct. We had to be sure the gutshot would give us the nuts if we hit it—not true on a paired board, or if our draw was not to the nut straight. We had to have four clean outs, which we would not have with a two-flush on board. We assumed our straight would still be the best hand after all the cards were dealt. You can never truly make this assumption, as the river can always pair the board or make someone a higher straight. For this reason, the implied odds must always be slightly higher than our odds of hitting (in the example I gave, we had a 10.75 to 1 shot and the implied odds were 15 to 1, probably enough to compensate for the times we would hit and still lose). Finally, we had to be sure our opponents would pay off all the way to the river. With **calling stations**, loose-passive players who often call, this assumption is reasonable. With players capable of folding, however, their unlikelihood of paying off is probably the biggest factor working against our implied odds calculation. If our opponents are good enough to read us for the straight when we check-raise the turn, it's almost certainly not worth calling the flop bet in the first place.

Poor players, or more specifically, players who have read the books but don't understand them and don't understand why they keep losing session after session, use implied odds as an excuse to call far too often. I hope it is clear from the last paragraph that the existence of the term "implied odds" doesn't make it correct to call whenever you have a draw. The decision of whether to call requires an accurate assessment of your opponents, the potential of your hand, and your opponents' perception of you. It's complicated, which is why this idea of implied odds is not usually presented to new players. It takes some experience to understand and apply it.

Can it ever be correct to *fold* when the immediate pot odds justify a call? Not if the odds are there to hit your hand on the very next card. But it can be correct to fold in some situations where calling would be the correct play . . . if it would set you all-in. This is because of effective odds.

Effective odds are the opposite of implied odds. You get them by comparing the amount you can win to the amount it will cost you to see a hand to the river. For example, let's say you and I are playing No Limit Hold'em. Before the flop, I've made it $100 **to go** (raised to $100), and you're on the $10 big blind holding AKo. You have a laser-like read on my play, and you're sure that I have two nines. You also know that I'm going to call any amount you may raise (I'm not playing very well). Finally, you know I'm going to bet my last $200 if and only if no ace or king appears on the flop, but I'm going to stop putting money in if an ace or king does come. Should you call? Well, your immediate pot odds are 115 to 90 = 1.28 to 1, and you're only a 1.24 to 1 dog to my nines, so it looks as though you should call. But you'll only outflop my nines about one time in three (30.6%, if we round to the nearest tenth), meaning you won't be able to call my bet on the flop two thirds of the time. So two thirds of the time you lose $90, and one third of the time you win $115. That's an average loss of over $20 a hand. A preflop call fails to take into account the effective odds. To **call down** this hand would cost not $90, but $290. You shouldn't look at your pot odds of 1.28 to 1 when making your decision but your effective odds of 315 to 290. This is a mere 1.09 to 1, and not enough to call even with two overcards against a pair.

That was a No Limit example, but effective odds come up in Limit Hold'em all the time. Say you've got a pair of kings on the turn, but your opponent bets $20, representing a flush. There is $120 in the pot after his bet. Should you call? You're getting 6 to 1 pot odds. So you need better than a 1 in 7 chance of having the best hand to call, right?

Well, no, because you have to assume your opponent will bet the river too. Your effective odds are 140 to 40, only 3.5 to 1. You need to have the best hand at the river over 22 percent of the time to make calling down profitable here. There are some passive opponents out there against whom you have much less than a 22 percent chance of winning (and there are some bluffers you would call down in a heartbeat).

TOP also teaches that poker begins as a struggle for the antes (or, in the case of Hold'em, blinds). If there were no money in the pot to start with, you could probably fold every hand except AA. Similarly, if Bill Gates walked up to a $3–$6 table and dropped a million dollars in the pot before a hand got dealt, any two cards would be worth playing. How does this concept apply in practice? Well, in a tight $3–$6 game (if such a thing existed) it would make attempting to steal the blinds less correct than in a tight $15–$30 game. This is because $3–$6 is played with a $1 small blind (one third of a small bet) and $15–$30 is played with a $10 small blind (two thirds of a small bet). A successful steal, then, is worth 25 percent more (relatively speaking) in a $15–$30 game. This blind stealing value is of little importance in loose games where steals hardly ever work, but it is definitely something to keep in mind at a tight table. The limit I was about to play in January 2000, $10–$20, has a $5 small blind (half a small bet), putting it smack in the middle of $3–$6 and $15–$30 in terms of blind-stealing equity.

If this seems like a lot of things to keep in mind, think how I felt sitting in my car in my company's parking garage after work, going over my notes from both books, trying to convince myself I could compete in a game where supposedly world-class players were regulars. Earlier in the day I had created a new user for my company's software and named him "icanplaytentwenty." The night before, I was playing for fun on Yahoo! and telling my opponents I was playing $10–$20 the next day. It was all I was thinking about.

I called my brother for a pep talk before pulling out of Vienna, Virginia. I drove over Chain Bridge and through residential streets to a large, plush contemporary home in Northwest D.C. When I got to the door, I didn't need a password or anything. I was Matt, the guy Nolan had brought into the game. That was good enough. Everyone even seemed pleased I was there, ready to donate my money (go figure). I felt at home, even if the funky, worm-shaped coffee tables and the modern art hanging on the wall weren't things you would've found in my house.

The felt top got placed over the kitchen table, and with two professional dealers at the ready, we were soon playing poker.

The players were all very familiar with each other. One guy gave a dollar to another guy whenever he lost a pot to him. When one of the "good" players lost a pot, people feigned astonishment. Everyone seemed to ignore an eccentric guy who was mumbling something about British troops burning Native American children. And another guy, a short guy named Russell Rosenblum, never shut up despite everyone's efforts to get him to.

As for me, I mostly watched everyone else for the first hour. I didn't say anything besides "raise" or "bet," and I didn't say those things very often. It's true, after everything I told you about semibluffing, mixing up your play, and blind-stealing, I resorted to standard tight-aggressive style at what turned out to be a very loose table. The lesson here is you can't change your game overnight.

On the first hand I actually played, I raised from UTG and got a cold call from one of the looser players. The flop came king-high. I bet, got raised, and I reraised. I bet the turn and river, and got called both times. My three kings were good.

The table had seen me play one hand, and it had been the stone-cold nuts. This might have had an effect on the next hand I played. In one of the blinds, I got to see a flop for free with an eight and some other rag in my hand. The flop came king–king–eight and I bet. My lone opponent called. The turn brought an ace making a flush possible, a card to kill my hand if there ever was one. I checked . . . and so did my opponent. The river brought another king. Well, now I could beat a flush, and it was almost impossible for my opponent to have a king or an ace. "All right," I said as I value bet my full house.

At least, I thought I was value betting. My opponent looked around the table for sympathy, sighed, and folded an ace faceup. I guess I had been bluffing. "Did you have it?" Russell said. I didn't say anything, just returned my cards to the dealer. As I did, Russell reached for them, as if to turn them over. I looked at him with what I thought was a startled expression. I don't think Russell saw it that way. "Whoa! I got the stare of death," he said.

Meanwhile, Nolan was playing far more hands than I had expected him to. The same was true for Russell. Both he and Nolan had been described as very good players by the Director of Player Relations. So why did they make so many calls pre- and post-flop? And why was Russell **stuck** (losing) $1,000 and happy about it, still talking nonstop, almost bragging about how much he had put into the game? It was something I'd have to think about while away from the table. For the time being, I would have to contend with them by playing the only poker I knew how. That is to say, I would get my chips in with good hands, hope people called me with bad hands, and hope they didn't get lucky.

I did, however, make some money from one final overly tight fold before the night was through. I had the ten–eight of spades and got the gorgeous flop of ace–queen–nine with two spades. Nolan bet, and the host of the game raised. I had twelve outs with my flush draw plus the gutshot (assuming both were good, which I was ready to do). These outs were plenty to call with, even without implied odds, and even to call a raise cold. I was a little less than a 3 to 1 dog to make my hand on the next card and I was getting 3.5 to 1 from the pot (assuming Nolan called). Reraising was even an option, as I was almost even money to make my hand by the river. But at that stage in my life, I didn't reraise with draws. I was content to call knowing the odds were there, and confident I would make some more money if I hit, given all the raising going on. The turn brought an offsuit ten. Nolan bet, and the original raiser folded. I didn't love this card. The board was now ace–queen–nine–ten with two spades. I still liked my flush draw, but it was now much less likely a jack would give me a winner, as Nolan would only need a king to make a higher straight. But another ten still might have been good for me. Even in my worst case, I had nine outs for the flush and was getting 5.5 to 1 from the pot. It was an easy call, and I made it.

As seems to happen so often in poker, the one card that made things interesting fell on the river . . . an offsuit jack. The board was now ace–queen–nine–ten–jack. I had the **ignorant end** of the straight.

I had to think through my options. I could check and fold. No way. Too easy for Nolan to bet two pair, or a set, or even his own busted flush draw. I hated folding for one bet on the river, and this was not the time to do it. I could check and call. A reasonable plan, but then again Nolan could easily shut down if he had two pair or a set, fearing the straight, and I would miss a bet. I could bet myself. It would be nearly impossible for Nolan to raise me without a king, and he would be forced to pay off with a lot of hands on this highly bluffable board. If Nolan raised me, I'd probably hate it and fold, but I would deal with that if and when it happened. I bet my straight.

"What an awful card for me," Nolan said, springing up from the table. "What an awful card for me! Good hand," he said, mucking jack–eight faceup. His fold cost him half the pot. There was $150 in the pot, and it would have cost Nolan $20 to call. Getting 7.5 to 1 on his money, and almost 4 to 1 for half the pot, he needed to be more than 75 percent sure I had a king to justify folding. It's tough to be that sure against a decent player. As I've said, it's unwise to make big folds on the river in Limit Hold'em.

At some point in that first appearance in the D.C. home game I was stuck almost $600. I didn't care. I was finally playing real poker. My nonconcern about the money, combined with some good cards in the early morning hours as the game got shorthanded, allowed me to come back.

I've said that my shorthanded experience in college helped me in many situations later down the line, but I haven't explicitly told you what strategy adjustments to make in those spots. Shorthanded play is very similar to a full game where the first few people have passed. For example, playing five-handed is like playing ten-handed after the first five players have folded. There is a slight difference in the two, however, because of what's called the **bunching** factor.

If the first five players fold in a full game, what does that say about their hands? We know for sure none of them had big pairs or AK, for example. This doesn't tell us much, but it does tell us there is a higher than normal concentration of aces and kings in the remaining hands. That's bunching. If there were no good hands in the first five, there is a better chance of seeing one in the last five. This means, then, that you should be *more* likely to open-raise in a five-handed game than you would be in a full game where five people have passed.

So what hands should you open with in a five-handed game? A lot of hands, for sure, but not as many as you might think. When I first started playing shorthanded I opened with any ace, any pair, any suited connectors, and any two big cards. This criteria can be successful in some games where opponents are playing way too tight, but in general it is too loose. I did okay in my first two tries at $10–$20 shorthanded. But that was mostly because I caught a lot of hands. In my third time out I got crushed. I was playing far too many hands. A better starting hand list for five-handed play is: AKs–A4s, AKo–A7o, AA–44, any two cards nine or higher, 98. Notice I dropped most of the suited connectors and the lower end of pairs and aces. In shorthanded games, high cards are where it's at. So many people are calling down with any pair (which isn't even a terrible play) that you need to get value from middle pairs and top pairs. Playing small suited connectors won't help you do this.

And, as usual, you want to be aggressive. I struggled for a long time to get the proper amount of aggression, as overaggression can be as much a problem as passive play. We'll discuss how far to take aggression in detail in Chapter 18. For now, let's just say that you shouldn't continue betting to the river with *all* of your opening hands. But if you only continue to bet top pair or better, you're going to get crushed. You have to be aggressive with unimproved AK and AQ and even some smaller aces. You should also play draws very strongly when you find yourself holding them. Again, you want two chances to win—hitting your draw, or getting your opponent to fold. The weaker your hand, the less inclined you should be to keep pushing it. This may sound obvious, but in practice the cutoff point is very tricky to find. It took me years to get it down, and for that reason I suggest only playing shorthanded for low stakes until you have the hang of it. Or at least finish reading this book first.

As I cashed out of my first Lawyers' Game, I noticed Russell had several racks of red chips (a rack of red is worth $500) in front of him. Somehow he had recouped his entire $1,000 deficit. Even I could tell Russell had a good, winning strategy that was different from any strategy I'd read about anywhere. His approach, combined with his hand-reading and player-reading skills, made him an exceptional player. Over the next few months of the game, I saw Russell:

1. Make an *overcall* on the river with an unimproved 33 . . . and win the hand.
2. Fold flopped trips on the turn, because he knew his opponent had *deuces* full.
3. Convince one opponent to call with a bad hand while at the same time convincing another opponent to fold a good hand.

I saw enough in the first few sessions of the Lawyers' Game to adopt Russell as my poker mentor. Luckily, he was willing to take me on. All the money I lost to him over the course of the home game easily came back to me (from other people in that home game alone). Sitting with him that night in January of 2000 completely changed the direction of my poker life.

8

♠ ♣ ♦ ♥

Pot Limit, Live

In the bowels of Cross Campus Library, in the heart of Yale University, I had my first newsreader experience. As most of you probably know, a newsreader allows access to newsgroups, collections of messages (posts) grouped by topic. Newsgroups, like E-mail addresses, have names with dots in them, and they cover just about everything you could think of. A few examples are alt.abraham-lincoln, sci.archaeology. mesoamerican, alt.robots.giant, rec.folk-dancing, and the ever-popular alt.amazon-women.admirers.

Browsing through this intriguing list, I found one I couldn't stop reading—rec.gambling.poker (RGP). People were sharing ideas about poker strategy, telling bad beat stories, and trading opinions over the Internet. Sometimes (often?) the opinions were personal attacks in disguise, but it was clear there was some valuable discussion going on, if you could just sift through the muck.

I didn't read the newsgroup from my room, though. I had the same computer all four years of college, and what was a state-of-the-art machine in 1995 was an obsolete and largely nonfunctional piece of junk in 1999. I had trouble accessing the Internet with my box and its dying eight megs of RAM, and I almost always just borrowed Burke's computer for checking E-mail or browsing the web. Burke was a great guy. I didn't want to take too much advantage of him by spending my entire life on his machine.

So it wasn't until after graduation, when I bought a new computer and started preparing for the $10–$20 home game, that I really started reading RGP. I made my first post to the newsgroup on December 16,

1999. I've since made more than three hundred (and that's lightweight compared to some of the other posters).

Russell, my new poker mentor, also read the newsgroup. Not only that, he attended real-life meetings for readers and contributors to RGP. There are annual get-togethers of these people in casinos all over the country— -ARGE events in Atlantic City, Foxwoods, Los Angeles, Mississippi, and, of course, Vegas. Russell insisted I join him at one of these and coincidentally, the Atlantic City version, ATLARGE (ATLAntic city Rec.Gambling Excursion), was the next one on the calendar. "What is it like?" I said.

"Oh, just go, you'll have a good time," was about the answer I got. I checked into it myself and it did sound fun. The scheduled events were a No Limit Hold'em tournament, a Seven-Card-Stud tournament, and an awards banquet. The unscheduled events included pink chip Hold'em, a dinner called the Smoker, and "baby" **Pot Limit** Hold'em games. Pot limit is similar to No Limit, the only difference being that you can only bet up to the size of the pot at any given time, not your entire stack.

I didn't know what pink chip Hold'em was, but a low-stakes Pot Limit Hold'em game sounded too good to be true, a perfect way for me to get some experience at big bet poker without losing my whole bankroll. And meeting these Internet people might have been fun too. ATLARGE, however, was scheduled for the same weekend as my mother's surprise fiftieth birthday party. Even I put family ahead of poker, but not without exhausting every possible means of getting some cards in. I decided to go to Atlantic City Friday night, play some baby Pot Limit, play the No Limit Hold'em tournament on Saturday morning, and drive to Long Island in time for Mom's party on Saturday night. The only potential snag was that if I did well in the No Limit, I'd never make it up to New York in time. Oh well, I would just have to bust out early. I put some cash in my wallet and left for AC.

If you're ever planning to drive from D.C. to AC on a Friday after work, don't. It adds two hours to what should be a three-and-a-half-hour trip. I was exhausted when I got there, but I knew I only had one night to try out baby Pot Limit. So I dragged myself to the Tropicana poker room and got on the Pot Limit list. I was relieved to see the blinds were $1 and $2 with a $100 buy-in, just about the stakes I wanted to play, a true baby game. I sat in the $10–$20 Hold'em game as I waited for a seat in the other game, and was fortunate to hold two kings when someone else had two queens. I was up $89 when they called my Pot Limit seat.

The instant I sat down, I knew there was a joke I hadn't been in on. This was not a table for beginners. The blinds were $1 and $2, but the first person to enter the pot was *required* to put in $5. He couldn't limp for $2, or raise to $7. He had to open for $5. The players after him could call or raise as usual. So despite the small blinds, even most unraised pots were $20 or more before the flop. And although the minimum buy-in was $100, no one at the table had less than $800 in front of him, all of which could be at risk on any given hand. The "baby" Pot Limit game could also be described as the biggest game I'd ever played in, against players who all seemed to know what they were doing.

Well, I'd come all the way to ATLARGE to play Pot Limit Hold'em. A table full of big stacks wasn't going to stop me. I didn't really care about the money. I just wanted to play big bet poker for meaningful stakes. With about $500 in front of me, I decided I would play until I lost what was there, or won a decent chunk of change. (This is called setting a **stop-loss** amount.) No matter what, I'd go home with a story.

I settled into my seat and stacked my chips.

"Do you want to post for two dollars, sir?" the dealer asked me. As you know, when you first sit down you have to post the big blind immediately, or wait for your natural big blind. Since posting is never a good play, I naturally decided to wait. As I told the dealer of my choice, the table erupted.

"For two dollars? You won't get a hand for two dollars?"

"This guy's the tightest player ever!"

I didn't know what to think, as waiting to post was customary in Limit Hold'em. How could Pot Limit have been so different? It turned out that in a game with $1,000 pots and people often betting $200 or more on a single card, the players didn't care about posting a measly $2 blind.

I laughed along with everyone else, trying to pretend I wasn't in over my head. On the next hand the dealer asked again if I wanted to post, trying, I guess, to spare me from all the crap I was taking from the other players. But by then there was no turning back. I'd chosen to wait, and wait for the big blind I would.

While waiting, I saw (or rather, heard) Russell, also in town for AT-LARGE, work his way around the poker room. I got up and asked him about my table. He looked over the faces and said, "Just play solid." He then gave me some more specific information about a player two seats to my left—Sippy. Sippy was a tough, experienced player, one to avoid.

By the time I posted my blind everyone already had me pegged as the tightest player in poker history. I thought I could use that to my advantage. I kept up appearances for the first orbit or so, folding just about everything and watching the other players to get a feel for their games. I threw in a raise once with a straight flush draw. My opponent had bet $20 into a $20 pot and I raised to $60, thinking I too was making a pot-sized bet.

"A mini-raise," mumbled a guy next to me who wasn't involved in the hand. "You don't want to be giving discounts on those raises." I stopped and thought about this. Why wasn't I betting the maximum? Luckily, I figured out the rules for pot limit betting right then and there.

If your opponent bets the pot, you can always raise up to four times his bet. This is because you're essentially matching his bet before you raise. In the above example, I could have matched his $20, and then raised $60 more (from the $20 in the original pot, my opponent's $20 bet, and my $20 call). It is a little confusing because you're raising, not calling. In fact if you say "call and raise" (as they often do in the movies) you'd be committed to just calling the $20 bet and wouldn't be allowed to raise. Conceptually, however, calling and raising is exactly what you're doing.

I think I won the straight flush draw hand without a showdown, but I really don't remember. Anyway, I know it wasn't my first big score. That came when I made a big-bet bluff against a middle-aged player across the table. There was $100 in the middle and a four-flush on board. I didn't think my opponent had the nut flush, and more important, I didn't think he'd call me with anything but the nut flush. I bet the pot—$100. This was more than I'd ever bet on a single card. My opponent showed his hand to the guy next to him . . . and quickly mucked it. He then moaned about how unlucky he was that he had the second nuts when I had the nuts. Well, I didn't have anything resembling the nuts. I didn't even have a flush.

At this point I understood that these guys, who all considered themselves good players, were scared to death to call me down. I could bluff and semibluff without fear, at least until I got caught by someone holding a monster.

A few hands later I played a pot I'll never forget. I picked up king of diamonds–queen of diamonds UTG and came in for the obligatory $5. Two others called and a late position player raised to $20. The guy to his left pulled out a big stack of chips . . . but he only dropped four of them into the pot, a call. I called, as did the other two players, and we all saw a flop of eight–five–three with two diamonds. I liked this flop—two overcards and a flush draw. I could have had as many as fifteen outs (nine for a flush, three kings, and three queens), and with my tight image I might not have needed to hit any of them. I bet the pot, $100. The first two players folded, but the preflop raiser called. The guy to his left started talking to me, scared. "Did you flop a set? You flopped a set?" But he called too. The turn brought an offsuit queen. At this point I was concerned about the preflop raiser. I really thought he had an overpair, and I was starting to get skeptical that he would fold it, even with my tight image. It's a rare player who can lay down a hand like pocket aces (which is why you often want opponents to have them). Rightly or wrongly, I decided to stop pushing the hand, and checked. The preflop raiser, though, surprised me by checking right along. The action went to the guy to his left, the one who had been babbling about my "set." All his body language was saying, "Please don't check-raise me." He finally bet $100, which might sound like a lot but even I knew was a weak bet into a $400 pot.

I wasn't about to fold to a player who I thought hated his hand, especially not when I had top pair plus a flush draw. My play was clear. It was a classic semibluffing situation. "Raise, all-in," I said, shoving my remaining $300 into the middle. The preflop raiser folded instantly, while the other guy said, "You must've flopped a set. You had to flop a set." He then proceeded to fold . . . his two black kings.

I gathered in the $800 pot and returned my cards to the dealer without revealing them. As I was stacking the last of the chips my opponent said, "You're not gonna tell us what set you had?"

I knew it was eating the guy up, and that he would keep bugging me about it all night if I didn't say something, so I decided to tell him the truth. "No set," I said.

"What did you have?"

"The king–queen of diamonds."

He didn't believe that for a second, and his disbelief started a roaring discussion at the table.

"I think he did, I think he had king–queen of diamonds," the preflop raiser said.

Another player who believed me was Sippy. He was one of the few who hadn't declared me the world's tightest player. He said he put me on the ace–eight of diamonds. "I thought you had a pair with the flush draw."

"I hit a queen on the turn," I said. This made sense to him.

The guy who folded kings, though, would never be convinced. "You're the most improved player at the table if you had king–queen of diamonds," he said. I guess that was one explanation. Another explanation was that I wasn't the passive tightass he decided to peg me as when I sat down.

As I said, Sippy knew better than to assume I had the nuts whenever I bet—he didn't just automatically fold like these other wusses—so I had to adopt a different strategy against him. I got the five of hearts–two of hearts on the button, and many players had limped for $5 when the action came to me. This was one of those hands Doyle Brunson liked to play in late position in an unraised pot—this exact scenario. I limped and the flop came down ace–five–two. It got checked to me, so I bet the pot. Only Sippy called. I didn't love this call. Sippy was the big blind and could've had anything, including ace–five, ace–two, and even three–four. I also couldn't imagine what hand he would be checking and calling with. The turn was a blank and Sippy checked again. Bottom two pair is not a monster hand in big bet poker, but I didn't want to let Sippy draw at whatever he might be drawing to, so I bet the pot again. Again, Sippy called. Thoroughly confused, I was ready to check behind on the river until another five fell. Sippy checked again, and now I was only concerned with maximizing the value of my hand. I bet $100 into the $200 pot, and Sippy called instantly, flipping over ace–queen. I turned up my hand and dragged the pot. "Would you have called two hundred?" I asked as I took the chips. Possibly this was bad form, but Sippy was a fellow ARGEr, and I really wanted to know.

"Yeah, because I don't put you on that," he said. So, because I was playing against a good opponent, one who knew he had to call me down with reasonable hands, I had missed a bet.

I could tell Sippy had a great feel for the game, and I didn't play any other pots against him. I also didn't see him again for quite some time after that night. In fact, the next time I heard anything about him was in May of 2002, when he won the Pot Limit Hold'em event at the World Series of Poker.

I won one more decent pot before I was through, and I did it with my favorite hand—pocket aces. Actually, aces are not my favorite hand in big bet poker when the stacks are deep, because they're so difficult to play. I knew what to do with them, though, on the big blind with six limpers. I raised the pot, making it $40 to go. Only one player, a guy I recognized from some of the Foxwoods No Limit tournaments, and who I knew to play loose and take chances, called. The flop came down queen-high, and I immediately bet the pot—$105. He called again. The turn was blank. Nothing on the board was too scary, no pair, no possible flush or straight, no likely two pair. About the only thing that could beat me was a set, and I knew my opponent played loose enough to be holding much worse. I bet the pot again, $315 this time, setting yet another record for most money I ever bet on one card. My opponent, a young guy who talked in a creaky high-pitched voice and always looked like he needed sleep, folded an ace–queen faceup.

The guy who folded the kings earlier said, "What did you have that time, three–four?" Since I was leaving soon, I figured there was no harm in showing my hand, and I turned up my aces. (In general, though, you still shouldn't do this, as you never know when you'll face your opponents again. Showing off aces is a beginner thing, and I was still a beginner.)

"I put you on bigger than that, the way you bet right away," creaky voice said.

When I finally cashed out, I had won $754 in the pot limit game, my biggest ever win at that point. It was a fantastic rush going to the cage with more than $1200 in chips, and it was a great confidence builder.

Let's look at the things I did right in this first pot limit session.

1. *I limped to see flops cheaply, especially in late position.* While tournament poker often comes down to picking the right spots to raise all-in preflop, in a ring game players typically have hundreds of big blinds in chips in front of them. There wouldn't be much value in moving in immediately, and of course, in Pot Limit Hold'em you can't shove your whole stack in preflop even if you want to. The pot starts out small and gets exponentially bigger. Implied odds, then, are enormous, and good players take advantage of them. I would not limp on the button in Limit Hold'em with a hand like 52s. In Pot Limit, I saw the flop for $5 and earned over $200 in profit with it, and I didn't even play it well. Of course, one result does not justify playing 52s, but the point is clear—get in cheap with a hand that has potential to win a big pot.

2. *I played the players.* It didn't matter what my opponent actually had when I raised all-in with my K♦Q♦. I knew whatever it was, he wouldn't call a $200 raise with it. It didn't matter what I had when there was a four-flush on board; it only mattered that my opponent wouldn't call without the nuts. There are many more situations in big bet poker than in limit poker where your own cards are just not a big factor. If you can recognize situations like the ones I was in, where making a move at the pot is a good play, you will be successful. Of course, the cards often do matter—I was semibluffing and had outs when I moved in against the guy with kings—but it is easier in Pot Limit for a good player to withstand a bad run of cards than it is in Limit Hold'em, where bad cards are death.

3. *The money didn't matter.* I've made this point before and I'll make it again. If I had been worried about what $300 could buy me, I might never have shoved it into the pot. The chips have to

be just chips, even when they represent all the money you have on the table. If they're money in your mind, and not chips, you'll get run over by any competent Pot Limit player. Luckily, money never mattered much to me, and I had a successful first session.

I went back to my room in the Ramada Inn and slept with my new winnings on the nightstand a few inches from my head. Throughout the session, I hadn't really felt part of any greater ATLARGE experience. Most of the people at the table were locals, not ATLARGErs making the trek from miles away to be with their fellow RGPers. I wondered if ATLARGE wasn't just a weekend where they spread a few new poker games at the Tropicana.

I got up the next morning to play the No Limit tournament, and found I was completely off base. As I stood in line to sign in, I noticed nobody could stop smiling. We had all already paid for the tournament, and everyone was giddy at the prospect of playing it. In most tournaments you'd be lucky to hear one chuckle from the registration area. I started chatting with another ATLARGEr. It turned out he was only in town for the one tournament, and had driven in from New York and was driving back the same day. "I just came to see everyone," he said. Huh? You came all the way to Atlantic City to see your friends from the Internet? I began to realize this -ARGE thing was bigger than poker.

During the tournament everyone wore badges with their wacky nicknames—Jaeger, Tiger, Iceman, Satan, jacksup (that was me). People applauded whenever someone got knocked out. Applause? It took me a minute to figure out it was a show of respect for the competitor who just busted. This applauding is done at all the -ARGE events. At a player's most painful moment, he or she gets to hear applause and sometimes even gets a bustout hug from an ARGEr named Beth. This ATLARGE was a convention of poker camaraderie. Granted, most of the people were geeks like me—poker geeks, math geeks, computer geeks, other kinds of geeks—but I enjoyed spending time with them more than I enjoyed almost anything else. And I realized the same was true for the ARGErs who'd been coming for years.

I got eliminated from the tournament when I moved in with a very weak hand and got called. The applause for this effort, strangely, seemed even louder than usual (maybe that was in my head). I walked over to the organizer, and he asked if I had a good time.

"Oh yeah," I said. "I had a great Pot Limit session last night."

"Well, the important thing is you had fun. If you won money, that's great. But that's not really what it's about."

I thought about what he said on the three-and-a-half-hour ride to Westhampton. When I had processed it, I wished I could've stayed the entire weekend: -ARGE events are the only poker played in any casino where people really don't care about the money. They're just there for the competition, and the fun. And that's the way it should always be. The money I got playing pot limit was nice, but it wasn't what has kept me coming back to -ARGE events every year since. The games there are not the most profitable, far from it. But they're the only casino games where people are laughing when a two-outer hits, where you might see an entire pot get **toked** to the dealer, and where everyone at the table is a friend to everyone else (even the people who haven't met yet). A few times a year, I get reminded why I love poker, and I'm eternally grateful.

Driving back to D.C. on March 26, 2000, I had won a lot of money, my MicroStrategy stock options were worth almost a million dollars on paper, and I was madly in love with Mylene, who was visiting from England the next weekend. Life couldn't have been better.

One week later, my company's stock had crashed, and Mylene had broken up with me. Thank God there was another poker tournament in my near future.

9

♠ ♣ ♦ ♥

Playing as a Maniac

The day before Mylene broke things off, I had made a spur-of-the-moment decision and booked a flight to Hartford and a room at Foxwoods for the next weekend's New England Poker Classic. When the day came to depart, my insides were still a mess. I had thought I would be spending the rest of my days with Mylene, and suddenly she was out of my life completely. Her reasons for the breakup were cerebral, like her. There was no one else, nothing in particular that happened, and no obvious change in the way things were between us. She simply felt it was best to end things because she couldn't see herself with me forever. It was nearly impossible to function after hearing this from her.

The options were to sit in my apartment and sulk, or spend the weekend in one of my favorite places doing one of my favorite things. Enough of my brain was working so that I made the right choice. Six days after a serious relationship ended, I was checking into the Two Trees Inn on the Mashantucket reservation, preparing for a No Limit Hold'em tournament.

I don't recommend doing something like this if you're interested in holding on to your money. Poker is a game of judgments, requiring constant subtle evaluations of your opponents. This is why almost none of the top players drink alcohol when playing—judgment is the first thing that goes. This is true when one's personal life is a mess too. Stay away from the poker table, at least if the stakes have meaning, when things aren't going well. Get your life together, then play cards.

By not following this advice, however, I created an interesting psychological experiment; far more interesting than the ones I did at Yale, where some grad student paid me five bucks to press a few buttons. Here at Foxwoods was a twenty-two-year-old male barely able to get himself out of bed, angry at everyone and everything, about to wage a war of nerves at the tables with a bunch of strangers. Get out your notebooks.

Despite my fragile mental state, I was a better informed player than I had been at my last major tournament. As I mentioned earlier, I had read Ken Buntjer's book, and I reviewed all its major concepts before sitting down at my first table. At the Taj, remember, I had folded two jacks in early position before anyone had even entered the pot. Contrast that to some of the hands you hear about in this event.

Foxwoods decided to make this first No Limit tournament at NEPC a rebuy tournament. All players were entitled to one $100 rebuy, regardless of their stack size, at any time during the first few levels. Rebuy strategy, choosing if and when to rebuy, depends on a bunch of factors, including how many chips a rebuy gets you, your current stack size, and your goal for the tournament. If your only goal is to maximize your chances of winning, then you should take any rebuys whenever they are available—the more chips you have, the better your chances of finishing first. But if you are trying to maximize your profit for the tournament, you clearly would not take a rebuy, for example, if it cost $1,000 for T1,000 additional chips when you only paid $100 for your first T1,000. That extreme almost never happens in practice. Much more common are what I like to call mandatory rebuys. These are rebuys that are technically optional, but you'd have to be a fool not to take. The Monday night tournament at Foxwoods has an "optional" $30 rebuy that gets you T1,000 in chips. But your initial $35 buy-in only gets you T500. The rebuy offers chips at more than a 50 percent discount!

At NEPC, though, the rebuy was not mandatory. The extra chips cost almost the same as the original ones. I spent a few minutes at the start of the tournament worrying whether I should rebuy. The worrying bothered me. I had enough trouble focusing on my hands, I didn't need any further distractions. "Rebuy!" I called out, immediately after which an employee came over and took my hundred bucks in exchange for more chips. I wanted my all-ins to be more meaningful, and I wanted to make more if I doubled up. But mostly I just wanted to focus, and to win. Nothing else mattered on that day. I wasn't thinking in terms of EV, I was thinking of taking revenge on the world.

This is not to say I played stupid poker. I just played a different style than I was used to. It didn't, however, start out that way. On one of the first hands, I went up against a big stack with ace–queen and bet out when the flop came queen–ten–six. The big stack paused briefly . . . and then made a large, all-in raise. I stopped and made myself think. That would become a common occurrence in this tournament. I knew I wasn't all there, so I forced myself to take a long time before making any decision. (This is a great habit to develop in general, by the way. Why wouldn't you want to consider all information before acting?) I had bet T400, and my opponent moved in for T1,300. I counted out T1,300 from my stack and looked at the remaining chips to see what I'd have if I lost. As I did this I studied my opponent. He was puffing away on a cigarette (smoking was still allowed at Foxwoods then) and seemed very relaxed. When I said I would need some time on this hand he said, "Go ahead, take your time." It just didn't feel right. All the tells were pointing at a strong hand, and T1,300 was a substantial portion of my stack. I finally folded. He took the pot without showing his hand.

On my way to the bathroom during the first break, I realized that despite my best efforts to consider everything, I had made a big mistake with the ace–queen. I was counting out T1,300 when it only would've cost me T900 *more* to call the raise. This difference might have changed my fold to a call. Furious that I could have made this relatively basic error, I questioned how in hell I was going to play this tournament when I couldn't even think straight.

When I returned to the table, something snapped. I had been getting run over in life and run over at the poker table. When I looked down at the guy who had just got me to fold top pair-top kicker, I decided I'd had enough. It would be betting and raising from here on in. Just try to get me to muck another hand. See what happens if you bet into one of my raises. I wouldn't be making any more "tough laydowns" on this day.

I found myself in a pot with two big stacks, one of whom was the guy I folded to earlier. Holding the ace of clubs and another small club, I flopped a flush draw and bet about the size of the pot. They both called me. On the turn I picked up a straight draw to go with the flush draw. No more timid play, no more big folds. It was time to semibluff. I shoved in all my chips, about T500 or so, hoping of course that both opponents would muck. Instead, they both called. As I had already taken my rebuy, all my hopes of remaining in this tournament rested on the last card being a club or making my straight. When the dealer turned over the king of clubs and both players checked, I jumped from my seat and screamed out, "Yes! Clubs!" I had no control. And I would have felt pretty stupid if one of them had turned over a full house, as the king had paired the board; but it was hard to imagine the river going check–check in that case. "Nice hand," the first caller said as I dragged the pot. I had tripled up, and now I was really ready to bully.

It's not usually a good play to semibluff into two people, especially with only one card to come. It's tough to get two people to fold, and your chances of improving aren't as good when you've only got the river to work with. My straight draw/flush draw all-in bet was a maniacal play (not to be confused with my pot limit semibluff at AT-LARGE, where I had very good reason to believe both opponents were weak). I didn't recognize the person moving my chips, but I liked him. I liked how he had no fear and just kept firing away at the pot.

He also had no qualms about playing weak hands. Ken Buntjer advises limping in with any two cards in late position when two or more players have limped in front of you and you have chips to gamble with. His advice is meant for Limit Hold'em, but it is even better suited to No Limit because the implied odds are so much greater. I took Buntjer's words quite literally when there were two limpers to me and I limped on the button with two–three offsuit. Four of us took a flop of eight–two–three rainbow, and the big blind led out for T800. The next two players folded, and I raised to T2,000. The big blind agonized for a few moments before deciding to call all-in.

"What do you have?" he said.

His head nearly fell off when I said, "Two pair."

"Two pair with the eight?" he said.

"Nope," I said, revealing my hand. He flipped over his king–eight, still staring at my cards trying to imagine how I made it into the pot with them. He was eliminated when he got no help from the turn or river. This hand had many of my opponents scratching their heads, but as far as I was concerned I was playing by the book.

This pot put me in comfortable chip position, but I was uncomfortable in my chair with one minute remaining before the break. I'd had to urinate for at least half an hour, and it was becoming painful. UTG, I looked down at my hand, praying it would be something I could muck. Unfortunately, I had two nines. I raised, hoping to win the pot right there and get it over with. I had the image of a lunatic, however, and the big blind had no problem calling. The flop came down eight–ten–jack with two diamonds, and my opponent checked. I almost always bet the flop after raising preflop, and I certainly was willing to bet with an open-ender plus a pocket pair that might still be good. I bet about the size of the pot, and my opponent called again. I figured him for a flush draw and was willing to test him on the next card . . . until the turn brought the six of diamonds. My opponent checked, and I checked right behind him. I wasn't about to fall into his check-raise trap. The river brought an offsuit four, changing nothing. My opponent immediately said, "I'm all-in."

"How much is it?" I said.

"I don't know," he said, getting up from the table and fidgeting with a cigarette.

I reached for my cards to throw them away. After all, I had put my opponent on a flush draw, the flush had come in, and he had just bet all his chips. But then I stopped. "No," I told myself. "Don't make any plays without thinking. Go to the bathroom later. Think this through first." The dealer counted down my opponent's stack, and I piled up my chips to see how much I'd have left if I called and lost, just as I had done earlier (this is a common practice in tournaments). The call would put a dent in my stack, but it wouldn't cripple me. I was getting a reasonable price—more than 2 to 1—so I had to be pretty sure I was beat to lay the hand down. And then I thought some more. I thought, "Yes he would play a flush this way, but he would also play this way with absolutely nothing: with overcards or a busted straight draw or possibly even a small pair." By this time the break had started and only a few people remained at the table to see how the hand went down. I finally decided there was just too good a chance he was bluffing. Given the pot odds, and the nervousness of my opponent who couldn't even sit at the table, I couldn't in good conscience lay my hand down. I gritted my teeth and said, "Call." One of the players who stayed to watch let out an "Mmmmph" from across the table.

There is a moment of nothingness just after you make a marginal call on the river. Everything happens in slow motion, and you are completely in the hands of fate. The poker is over, and all you can do is watch everything unfold around you. It's like being in a car accident (or so I'm told). I came out of the reverie by hearing two of the most beautiful words you'll ever hear in poker. "You win," my opponent said. I still wasn't convinced, however, as I only had a pair of nines, so I flipped up my cards. My opponent hesitated, looked at my hand, looked at the board . . . and threw his cards in the muck. I slammed the table and jumped up from my seat, pumping my fist. As I did, I heard the guy next to me say in astonishment, "He called him with a pair of nines!"

I spent the break basking in what I knew was the best call I'd ever made. Oh, I also used the facilities (finally). When the tournament started up again, some guy across the table said, "What happened to him?" meaning the guy I had just busted. I smiled over my now even bigger stack of chips.

"Oh, you missed it," someone else at the table said.

The original inquisitor looked at me. "You? Deuce–three again?" he said. I guess once you're marked as a maniac the label never leaves.

As we got back into the No Limit action, it became apparent the guy to my left, the one stunned by my call with the two nines, was a complete psychopath. Whenever anyone bet, including me, he raised all-in. If it sounds as though this strategy has some obvious problems, it does. But I promise it also caused me, an inexperienced opponent, some problems of my own. What was I supposed to call this guy with? Or what could I do to get his chips? I had tried bluffing him a few times before I figured out he raised any bet. So I decided I would only bet into him with a hand I could commit to. In our next heads-up pot I checked to him every street, and was surprised when he checked behind on the flop and turn. On the river he finally bet . . . and showed me a full house after I folded. Apparently this guy's strategy was to move-in with weak hands and check with his strong ones. It was only a matter of time before someone would trap this guy.

Sure enough, a few hands later the psycho raised preflop for the millionth time and got called by the big blind. The flop came jack-high, and the big blind checked. The Overbet King, who was an old, spastic guy who signaled his bets through odd gestures, began waving his hands towards the pot, indicating he was going all-in again. His bet was way more than the size of the pot.

"Nothing behind?" his opponent, a quiet guy who didn't miss anything, said. And then, in a cold, steady voice: "I call." They flipped up the hands, ace–king for the psycho, queen–jack for the big blind. The psycho got no help, and suddenly had very few chips.

At the time I thought this was the best call I'd ever seen, even better than my call with pocket nines. I would've had plenty of chips left if I'd lost—this guy was calling for all his chips with nothing but a pair of jacks with a queen kicker. I now recognize this as a standard trapping hand against a lunatic, but back then I was impressed.

The lunatic got knocked out not long after that, which left me free to return to my aggressive game plan if I so desired. As well as it had worked earlier, however, I decided to slow things down. I had enough chips to be an average stack at the final three tables (which should be your goal during the later stages of a tournament), and those last three tables were all in the money. I didn't need to take any ridiculous risks, and I recognized this even in my semidelirious state. I wouldn't get involved unless I picked up a hand.

The problem was that I did pick up a hand. It was ace–king, a mandatory opening hand, and I made a standard raise with it. One of the blinds, another big stack at the table, decided to call. Alarm bells should've been going off already. When a big stack calls another big stack, it almost always means he has a strong hand. I didn't consider this, though. We took a flop. I flopped nothing. But he checked, so I bet . . . and he called again. If there was ever a time to shut down and stop betting, this was it. The turn card came. I turned nothing. Now my opponent made a decent-sized bet at the pot. Hmmm, let's see. I had shown strength throughout the hand, my opponent was betting into me, knowing I was one of the few people who could bust him, and I had ace-high. It doesn't take a genius to figure out I should've folded. Instead, I raised. I really did. I have proof—in my notes written later that day it says, "Raised potential bluffer on turn." I guess everyone is a potential bluffer, but this player in this situation was one of the least likely bluffers you'll find. Of course he called my raise. On the river, I hit nothing. When he checked to me, I decided I had to bluff at this pot myself. I'll let my notes tell the rest of the story: "Bluffed river and had to fold to a raise." I wasted gobs of chips on this hand for no reason whatsoever. That was the bad news. The good news was I could officially revert to my maniacal style now that I needed chips again. It was, at least, more consistent with my mood.

I rebuilt my stack by playing aggressively. I raised with two biggish cards, and if I got called, I played it strong if I flopped something as weak as middle pair. I was in ultrafast mode. Just about any hand looked good to me. So much so in fact, that when I looked down at six–two suited in the cutoff I didn't fold. Instead, I made a standard raise. This raise was not as crazy as it might first appear, as the big blind was a very tight player. I had a reasonable chance of winning the pot right there. No one ever needed to know I didn't have anything. Except that the tight player reraised me when it got folded to him.

My first instinct, of course, was to fold. Folding was the clear play. I didn't have any other choice, right? But once again I stopped myself and decided to think it through. Maybe there were other options. Calling was obviously out, but what about moving in? My opponent was a tight player capable of folding, especially when a call would cost him all his chips. And I'd been raising a lot, so he might have reraised with a weak hand. And what a score that would be if I could pick up this pot uncontested. And why did I want to fold now—I hadn't been folding all tournament? "I'm all-in," I heard myself say. It was the first and only time I tried anything like that. I've raised with garbage since, but I've never reraised with anything nearly as weak as six–two suited. Unfortunately, the one time I did try this play, my opponent quickly said, "Call."

We didn't have to turn our hands up, a practice that is now required in most tournaments when one or more players is all-in, and neither of us did (I sure as hell didn't want to). When the flop brought a five and a four, I mostly just thought about how furious my opponent would be if I **spiked** a three and announced, "Straight." But, alas, no three came, and when all the cards were out I said, "I don't have anything."

"Queens," my opponent said, turning over his pocket ladies.

"That's good," I said, mucking my six-high. Just like that my chips had disappeared again. And I lost them on a hand I didn't have to get involved with. It's reasonable to think my opponent would've laid down all but his very best hands there. When a tight player reraises, however, he usually has a hand—even against a maniac. The best play, pretty clearly I think, was to throw my cards in the muck.

With five tables left, and the tournament paying three, I needed to recover a lot of chips if I wanted a shot at the real money. An orbit or so after the six–two suited disaster, I looked down at queen–jack off-suit on the button and opened for a standard raise. The small blind smooth-called and we took the flop heads-up. It came queen–six–four. My opponent, a huge stack, checked. Top pair–jack kicker, usually a mediocre holding, is a pretty solid hand at this stage of a tournament. I bet about the size of the pot, and my opponent called. The turn was a blank and my opponent checked again. This was another time when I should've smelled something unpleasant. One of Ken Buntjer's tips was, "Don't bet the turn unless you're semibluffing, or you have the nuts." The idea is more applicable to Limit Hold'em, but it has merit in No Limit as well. If you have a medium strength hand, you want to get to the showdown as soon as possible. You don't want to get check-raised and have to fold, when you could've spent the same amount of chips calling a river bet and seeing your opponent's hand. Well, I had a medium strength hand, but I didn't remember or didn't take (or both) Buntjer's advice. I made another sizeable bet, after which my opponent said, "Go all-in," and moved a bunch more chips into the pot. I thought. And thought. And I thought some more. For the first time in many hours, I was faced with a decision that could've meant my elimination from the tournament. I looked at the pot, a pot I had put so many chips into. I looked at my opponent's stack, and figured he could be bullying me without much of a hand. And finally I calculated my pot odds. I was getting something like 5 to 1, and I couldn't justify folding. So I called. The last card didn't help me, and I said, "Queens," as I turned up my hand.

"Kings," my opponent said, showing the two he had in the hole. A spectator (yes, there were some) groaned, suffering along with me. Whatever torment he felt, I'm sure mine was many thousands of times worse.

I said, "Nice hand," and immediately jumped from the table. I stood there long enough to count the remaining players—thirty-eight. I had finished thirty-ninth, twelve out of the money.

I walked around in a daze for a few minutes. I now do this a lot after tournaments, but this was my virgin experience of a true spirit-crushing bustout. While I was wandering in no particular direction, I ran into the guy who had made the call with the queen–jack on the jack-high flop against the psychopath. He stopped me and said, "Man, I really enjoyed playing with you. You got balls." It was about the last thing I expected to hear from anyone. Not knowing what else to do, I took the compliment and returned it by telling him how impressed I was by his call with the queen–jack. He introduced himself as Tom, and explained that play to me. "Well," he said. "What does it tell you when he moves in so many chips like that? It tells me he doesn't want me to call." This logic could easily get new players in a heap of trouble, calling huge bets with no prayer of winning. But for an experienced player like Tom, it helped him make a read that gave him a commanding chip position. All remaining tournament players were on a break, and Tom explained his strategy for the rest of the event. "Now the plan is to double up," he said. "Doesn't matter if it's against a big stack or a small stack. And you always have to have a plan."

I nodded, but talking about the tournament I had just been knocked out of was making me ill. I told Tom I enjoyed playing with him and walked the seven hundred yards back to my hotel room at the Two Trees Inn. After collapsing on the couch there, I cried for several minutes before I even realized I was doing it.

What did we learn from this psychology experiment disguised as a poker tournament? Well, we learned that you shouldn't enter a major event when your personal life is all screwed up, but I told you that from the start. Did we learn anything about poker strategy from the hands I played in this state of mental disarray?

I certainly think we did. To me, the biggest lesson is to use as much information as you can when making decisions. If this requires taking a long time, then go ahead and take it. Watch top pros like Phil Ivey, John Juanda, Andy Bloch, and Howard Lederer. They all play very deliberately, not giving anything away, thinking through all their options before deciding on a course of action. Juanda even takes several seconds on almost every hand he mucks before the flop, presumably because he is always considering a steal-raise.

Another lesson is to execute your game plan. Limping with the two–three was a calculated risk based on my stack size, my position, and the number of opponents. It wasn't based on ESP, or a lark, or a hope, or anything else. Whether it was a good play is debatable, but it was a play I had decided to make before the tournament even started. I failed to execute my game plan when I put money in on the turn, twice, when I wasn't semibluffing or betting a strong hand. My strategy going in was supposed to be to check the turn in those spots. Ignoring that strategy cost me dearly. The whole reason we think about poker outside of the table is to implement our ideas at the table. I'm not saying you never make plays based on on-the-spot analysis; I'm just saying you have to implement your away-from-table analysis in order for it to be relevant. I don't mind making a bad play, but I do mind when I don't play my best.

Finally, my tilt-a-whirl NEPC experience taught me that playing like a maniac has its benefits. I almost busted very early, but instead of busting I got a mountain of chips. If for every two tournaments that I busted early there was one where I got a ton of chips early, I'm confident I would make money as a tournament poker player. A big stack can be a powerful weapon, which is why so many of the top tournament players—John Bonetti, Daniel Negreanu, Phil Ivey (again), and the late Stuey Ungar—are considered maniacs by many people, and why my buddy Fabian was able to place third at Mohegan Sun eighteen months earlier. A player who takes a calculated risk during the first few levels, but knows how to use a big stack and a crazy image to reliably reach the final table, will do extremely well in tournaments.

My problem in this particular event was that I never turned the maniac off, and couldn't parlay my big stack into a nice score. Incidentally, this inability to back off is why most maniacs have little chance of winning a tournament. Eventually their crazy play costs them their chips. It's the maniac who can **change gears** who will really be a danger.

I have not adopted the maniac style for No Limit Hold'em tournaments, as I believe I have better ways to consistently build my stack. But the maniac style is a valid style, and possibly one to experiment with.

Although this tournament had an unhappy ending for me, I won more than $4,000 in the four months following my breakup with Mylene—in home games, in Atlantic City, in Foxwoods—by far the best run of my young career. This success turned out to be a mixed blessing, however, as I soon made the mistake of overestimating my skill based on results and sitting in games which were far too tough. Read the next chapter only if you have a strong stomach.

10

♠ ♣ ♦ ♥

Picking Your Game, in Vegas

BARGE (Big August Rec.Gambling Excursion) is the mecca of -ARGE events. It brings rec.gamblers from both coasts and everywhere in between to Las Vegas, Nevada, in the sweltering summer heat. Few tourists are savvy enough to visit Vegas at this time, so BARGErs pretty much have the town to themselves. BARGE is the longest and most mandatory of rec.poker gatherings. It is also, as the name implies, the biggest. BARGE spawned every other -ARGE event. It started in 1991 with barely a dozen people getting together to drink, play blackjack, play poker, and talk gambling. The 2002 version of BARGE featured more than two hundred attendees and a week's worth of poker and nonpoker tournaments. Although attendance has leveled off for a number of reasons, BARGE remains the one event rec.gamblers take "forced vacation time" for every year. In my 2001 BARGE trip report, I wrote: "The decision to come to Vegas in August wasn't a decision." I had to eat these words a year later when I missed BARGE for a family trip, but the point is clear: come to BARGE or face rec.humiliation.

BARGE 2000 fell at a seemingly perfect time. I was **running great** (catching a lot of good cards and winning money) and my last -ARGE experience had been a fun and profitable ATLARGE. When Russell insisted I go to Vegas for the *real* -ARGE event, I didn't put up much resistance. In the weeks leading up to BARGE, I would check the online registration list several times a day at work. Some intriguing names were on there: Chris Ferguson, reigning world champion and (not coincidentally) the highest ranked player in the history of IRC poker (a play-money Internet poker game); Melissa Hayden, a top tournament player who was reportedly also cute; and young poker stud Patri Friedman, who *Card Player Magazine* predicted would eventually be a world champion himself. I was dying to meet these people, to talk to these people, to play against these people.

The departure date finally came, and when my plane approached McCarron International Airport, Vegas appeared just as I'd remembered it—a neon orgy of lights breaking the hundreds of miles of desert blackness. I suffered through a tantalizing shuttle ride as we dropped people off along the Strip. They were staying at giant modern hotel/casinos like MGM Grand, New York New York, and the Luxor. When I finally got to Binion's Horseshoe (located downtown and a good five miles from the glitz and glimmer of the Strip), I didn't dare go to sleep after a long day of work, a drive through traffic to the airport, and a six-hour flight to Vegas. Of course not. I checked into my room and raced down to the poker area, where BARGErs were already running the place.

Binion's is nuts and bolts—no amusement park rides, few luxurious hotel suites, and tucked away from the usual tourist spots. It is, however, home to poker history. The World Series of Poker has been held there since its inception in 1970, and a photo of each champion hangs on the wall in the poker room. It has also been the host of almost every BARGE. In the summer of 2000, I sat in a $10–$20 Hold'em game at that very same Binion's, playing my usual style, losing a few pots to the local rocks. Really, though, I was just killing time until they called the Pot Limit Hold'em game. I hadn't played Pot Limit since ATLARGE, and I was salivating at the prospect of doing it again, experiencing another adrenaline rush. A bunch of BARGErs had requested the game and the Binion's floorpeople were scrambling to get it off. Finally, after I'd spent two hours and $313 in the $10–$20 game, a suit got on the microphone and said, "All right, you want it, you got it! New One–Two Pot Limit Hold'em game on—" I scooped up my chips and locked a seat at the new table. But I wasn't the first one there. A short guy with green hair had cried out in joy and raced to slam all his chips down at the Pot Limit table the instant it was called.

It was easy to recognize Patri Friedman from his photos in the magazine, and I happily chose the seat to his left.

Once we got the cards in the air, the BARGEr to my left, a polite and friendly guy named Oz, said exactly what I'd been thinking. "I'm so happy to be here. All day at work I was looking at the clock. Two. Two-fifteen. Two-thirty." Hallelujah, BARGE had arrived.

The table composition didn't take long to figure out (it usually doesn't). I was surrounded by eight good players and one fish. The good players ranged from the extremely loose (Patri would limp in position with literally any two cards) to the very tight (Oz never got involved without a premium hand). The fish played almost any two cards for any amount of money, and fell somewhere in the middle on the passive-aggressive scale.

I had an easy decision, then, when two players were in for $5 in front of me, and I looked down at two kings. I slid four $5 chips into the pot, only to watch Oz reraise the pot to $80 right behind me. Oz was playing tight, but I was still committed to my hand. If I wouldn't get my chips in with king–king, what would I get them in with? I was all set to reraise Oz, until the fish came in for a re-re-reraise. I would have to go all-in to call him. Normally, this fourth raise would make my decision extremely difficult. If it had come from a sane player, it would almost certainly mean ace–ace (or the other two kings), and I'd have to fold. But it didn't come from a sane player; it came from the only lunatic at the table. If anything, my decision was made easier. "I'm all-in," I said, and Oz's cards hit the muck before the final syllable had left my mouth.

"There's only one thing you can have," Oz said. He was wrong, however, as I showed him my two kings. My lone remaining opponent then turned up . . . his two jacks. They dealt out all the cards, and I did my usual routine of screaming at the board and getting way too excited when nothing of interest turned up. (It took me a long time to learn to win a lot of money without a spastic celebration, though I have always been a good loser. I hope you're a more natural winner than I am.) After the dust had settled, Oz revealed that he had folded two queens . . . and the player two seats to his left had folded the other two queens. I believed them both 100 percent, as they were BARGErs with no reason to lie, and anyone in his right mind would fold queen–queen to a reraise from Oz. Oz said his fold was automatic. He was even surprised at what I turned over. "Some people could get away from kings there," he said.

I nodded. "Not against him," I said, meaning the fish.

Soon afterwards, however, I picked up ace–ace and gave Patri more money than I should have. The board paired on the turn and Patri made **teaser** bets—less than the size of the pot—of $50 on both the turn and river. I never should've paid him off (although Patri correctly mentioned that if I folded aces every time in those situations, he could **exploit** me through bluffs; this is a **game theory** concept we'll get more into next chapter), but I did. I maintain that aces are the hardest hand to play in big bet poker. Luckily I mucked my ace–king a few hands later to the same teaser bet on a flop of nine–nine–x. Patri had flopped quad nines.

With most of my profits having disappeared, and with me almost falling asleep in my chair, I was looking for an ideal situation to get all my chips in before going to sleep for the first time in Vegas. (My previous Vegas experience consisted of one night during a post-college road trip with my buddies—and I didn't sleep.)

Before this trip, I had discussed several aspects of Pot Limit Hold'em on RGP with, among other people, Patri Friedman. A concept both of us seemed to embrace was the strength of straight flush draws with two cards to come. The idea is, with twelve or fifteen or possibly more outs, the hand is often a favorite against a legitimate hand such as top pair. But the hand is never such a big favorite that you want to invite callers with it. Therefore, it should be played aggressively. Making big bets with draws also adds deception to your game, and makes you more likely to be paid off when you play aggressively with the nuts.

These thoughts were swimming somewhere in my subconscious when I picked up ace–ten suited, limped, and flopped a gutshot straight flush draw, with my overcard ace possibly being an additional out. In early position, I checked, hoping to put someone to a decision by check-raising all-in (such was my stack size at that point). One of the good players bet, just as I'd hoped he would, but then the good player to his left raised the pot. It got folded to me, and now I had a decision.

Well, I really didn't have a decision. I couldn't fold, not when I was probably a favorite to win the hand and was getting 3 to 2 to shove my chips to the middle. "Raise all-in," I said. The initial bettor folded instantly, and the action went to the raiser. He looked ill, which was great news. I was in much better shape against something like top pair than I was against a set or two pair. My raise wasn't a real raise—let's say it was another $40 to my opponent, whose initial raise had been to $200. He couldn't fold, and as a good player he knew he couldn't fold. Even I was telling him to throw in the forty bucks (which might have been why he took so much time to do it).

Finally he did call, and he did have top pair with a mediocre kicker. I showed my hand to Patri and he said, "Oh, nice." My opponent then asked, rather urgently, to see it and I laid it on the table. He exhaled in relief—he must have been praying I didn't have a set and have him drawing almost dead. As it was, my fifteen outs made me only a slight favorite. The dealer burned and turned—no flush, no straight, no ace. With this new information, I was now about a 2 to 1 underdog with one card to come (which, incidentally, is why it's important to get the money in with two cards to come in these situations). I only had one more shot to win this thing, and it wasn't meant to be. Another blank came on the river, and all my chips were gone, good-bye. Rather than reach into the bankroll for more, I said goodnight to my new friends and took the elevator up to my room. I was confident I'd played well and learned something from this Pot Limit session against a tough field, and I slept like a baby despite starting the trip in a $596 hole.

I began the next day splitting a cab with Oz to the Orleans, another off-the-Strip casino known more for efficiency than glamour. I played in their noon Limit Hold'em tournament and managed to cash in it after a maniac gave me almost all of his chips. I would've won $150, but Oz had talked me into a 10 percent **trade** beforehand, meaning he would get 10 percent of whatever I won, and I would get 10 percent of whatever he won (which in this case was nothing, though of course I didn't know it would work out that way). So I only made $135.

We moved on to the Mirage, a beautiful casino on the Strip that smells like coconuts when you walk in. After booking a win in the $6–$12 game, I had recovered almost half of what I'd lost the night before and felt sure in my arrogance that I was on my way to a winning trip.

We had selected the Mirage in the first place because it had a $100 No Limit tournament that night, with an optional (but mandatory) $100 rebuy. Although two hundred bucks was more than I liked to spend on a tournament, I couldn't resist. Besides, it would be a really soft field—a bunch of BARGErs and the local Vegas pros. Okay, maybe it wouldn't be a soft field. Maybe entering this event was not a smart play from an EV standpoint. But it would at least be a learning experience, right?

My table had its share of BARGErs, including, through bizarre coincidence, Russell—the only BARGEr I knew well prior to the event—on my immediate right. I got some chips when I picked up ace–ace at the same time an unfortunate opponent (Bill Chen, a Ph.D. in mathematics who is now in the process of revolutionizing poker theory) picked up king–king. I also made a nice fold against Russell. An early position player had raised and Russell reraised. "I hope I have crap," I said to Russell. I then looked down at two jacks and said, "Shit."

As I was deciding what to do, Russell said, "Kings?" I had logged about fifty or sixty hours at the table with Russell, and I knew what this question meant. Yes, Russell was a great player, but sometimes he revealed information about his own hand in the course of probing his opponent for information about theirs. I would guess Russell was willing to take his chances that most opponents wouldn't catch on to this, and the few who did wouldn't be enough to turn his act into a bad play. But I knew the act. When Russell asked a player if he had a certain hand, it meant Russell had the hand exactly one notch below or above it. In this case, since he asked if I had kings, Russell had either queens or aces. I threw my jacks in the muck.

I also was subjected to an obnoxious young BARGEr across the table. Ninety-nine percent of the people I meet at -ARGE events are people I feel privileged to know. This player, however (we'll call him Joe), felt the need to comment on a hand I played by saying, "You played it to lose the maximum." Then, after I put in a steal-raise with jack–nine suited, Joe reraised me all-in. As I was debating whether to call based on pot odds, Joe looked right at me and said, "Call me. I want you to call me." I figured this was his way of luring a "weak" player to call, so I folded. He flashed two kings. "They wouldn't double me up with my kings!" he yelled out to Patri at another table. Well, I might have doubled him up if he hadn't put on that song and dance. I guess he was playing to win the minimum.

Eventually, Joe and Russell busted and I found myself in decent chip position at the final two tables. One of the players who had survived was a woman playing Hold'em for what had to be the first time (second or third at most). She had called a massive preflop reraise with pocket threes and spiked a three on the flop, and then caught big hands in other key pots to accumulate a mountain of chips. She even *left the tournament for an hour* to look for her husband, and came back with plenty of ammunition still at her disposal. (A player not at her seat will get her blinds and antes posted as usual until she runs out of chips.) Having outlasted many of the best Vegas pros, and almost all of the talented BARGE pool, I had a wrenching feeling that this clueless tourist would be the one to bust me.

We got down to the final ten people so we played **hand-for-hand**, meaning each table of five people would play the same number of hands until we lost a player, only starting a new hand if the other table had finished theirs. We were doing this because the final table of nine players were all in-the-money. Ninth place was several hundred dollars. The next person eliminated would finish **on the bubble** and get zero dollars. First place would earn several thousand dollars. I wasn't playing for ninth.

It got folded to me on the small blind and, with the clueless woman on the big blind, I resolved not to make a steal-raise because she would call with anything. But I looked down at a real hand, ace–queen offsuit, and put in a standard raise. The woman did call, and the flop came down queen–seven–two rainbow. I didn't want to talk myself into folding this hand, and I didn't want to give this woman any free cards to catch whatever the hell she needed to catch. I had more chips in front of me than were in the pot, but not by much. And I wanted to give her every reason to fold. "I'm all-in," I said.

"Me too," she said instantly.

The floor asked that we turn our cards over, and I obliged first. The woman then turned over a seven . . . and a queen. My heart sank and I shook my head. "She called my raise with a queen–seven," I mumbled, not that I was surprised. The turn brought a nine, meaning any ace or nine would give me the pot. But neither fell on the river, and I got up from the table, stunned.

The dealer insisted I might have her covered, and it seemed to take five minutes for them to count all of her mountainous chips and compare them to mine. In the end, she did have me covered . . . by one T100 chip.

I cursed myself for this play during the entire cab ride back to Binion's, but today I don't remember why. I'd made a fine play and gotten unlucky. It happens. This was one time I didn't need to beat myself up. Another important poker lesson is to learn from your mistakes, but don't destroy yourself over them, and don't find mistakes where there aren't any. As I said in Chapter 2, if you make the positive EV play, it doesn't matter what the result is. Poker players have control over their decisions, not the outcomes of hands. My decisions on the bubble against the clueless woman were solid ones.

I was on the wait list for the next day's BARGE Tournament of Champions (TOC)–style tournament, an event modeled after the real TOC, which included four different games and was considered by many the best test of a poker player's all-around ability. Some other wait-listed BARGErs sweated it out with me, including a fellow East Coaster named Len. When neither Len nor I made the cut, we split a cab to Bellagio, the reputed home of the nicest poker room, the highest stakes, and the best poker action anywhere in the world.

Comparing the Bellagio to Binion's is like comparing Wrigley Field to a Little League sandlot—the same kind of games happen at both places, but one is a posh baseball (or poker) cathedral in the middle of a city, while the other is just a place to play. The Bellagio has an enormous stained glass ceiling that greets visitors in the lobby, a giant lake whose fountains spout water choreographed to music, a labyrinth with swimming pools and jacuzzis hidden in every corner, hanging gardens that make you forget you're on arid land, and a poker room that serves strawberry juliuses and has cushioned chairs. Binion's has an alley filled with garbage some guests must pass through to get to their beds for the evening, and a smoke-filled poker room populated by locals and other malcontents.

I entered the Bellagio poker room, and after the awe wore off, scanned the lists of games. My options were $8–$16 or $15–$30 Hold'em. Most poker authorities say a player should have three hundred big bets *minimum* in his bankroll to sit in a given game. I didn't have $9,000 lying around in my bank account (I'd been employed less than a year and was spending plenty of money). But I did have four or five, and I figured if I lost all that money I could survive to my next paycheck. Besides, those bankroll requirements were for the long haul, not for a single session. I could survive on $800 bucks or so for the afternoon, couldn't I? In my brashness I decided that I would rather try than suffer the humiliation of playing lower than my now-usual limit of $10–$20. So when a seat opened in a $15–$30 game, I locked it up.

Now, I won't dispute that the $15–$30 game at Bellagio is often a *very* **good game**, meaning a profitable game for a good player. But if you've never played poker in Vegas before, I suggest you start with one limit lower than your usual. Every poker room has its own feel, its own style of play, and therefore its own best strategy. When you go to the Bellagio (and everyone reading this book should go to the Bellagio at some point), sip a strawberry julius and relax before jumping into a really big game. I eked out a small win playing tight in my first $15–$30 session, but the decision to play higher than I was really comfortable with would haunt me later.

Getting back to Binion's, I wandered into the poker room and spotted Patri, Melissa Hayden, and my non-friend Joe sitting in what looked like a Pot Limit Hold'em game . . . and there were plenty of empty seats. I knew I wasn't as good as these players. But when I asked what the game was and Patri said, "Pot Limit Hold'em, sit down!" I knew I would do just that.

Before I even played a hand I watched Patri and Melissa go at it. They raised each other until they were all-in and Melissa announced, "I have a set." Patri then said, almost laughing at himself, "I have a flush draw." No sooner had the words come from his mouth than the dealer burned and turned the third heart on board, giving Patri his flush. Even the dealer looked sick. Melissa now needed the river to pair the board, or it was Patri's pot. There was no justice when the river brought a blank, and Patri raked in the money. Rather than throw a fit, Melissa just said the dealer's name in a half-pleading half-scolding voice. "To-o-m," I believe it was.

I decided I'd have to mix it up with these guys (and girl). Playing tight/solid poker wouldn't cut it in this field. So when a pot developed and I held the ace–ten of diamonds (the same hand I'd gone broke with the night before), I vowed to get my money in when I flopped a flush draw with two overcards. It was bet and raised all-in for about $200 when it got to me . . . and I went with my game plan and shoved in my entire stack. The action was then on Joe, who looked at the mountain of chips in the middle and said, "I can't resist," calling my reraise.

With about $1,200 on the line, the dealer burned and turned the next card. Nothing. But then the river came. And it was a low, but perfectly valid and perfectly acceptable, diamond—a diamond that didn't even pair the board. Joe said, "I have a straight," but he was drowned out in my cry of "Yes!" as I turned over the stone cold nuts. The poor guy who had raised all-in on the flop had two queens, now the third best hand.

As I raked in the pot, Melissa said, "Nice hand, Matt." I thanked her and apologized for all my blubbering over the money. "I know this isn't a lot of money to you guys, but it's a lot of money to me," I said. Admitting you're playing poker for what you consider "a lot of money" is a solid sign that something is wrong. Playing for "a lot of money" against three of the best poker players in Vegas (yes Joe, despite being a jerk, was a very good player)—well, that's just stupid.

Many players say **game selection** is the most important skill for a player to have. I don't agree, as I think learning proper strategy is more important than picking a good game, but I promise that poor game selection is a recipe for disaster. There's an old adage that says you could be the tenth best poker player in the world, but if you sit in a game with the best nine you're a fish. We make money in this game from bad players. We don't make money getting into pissing contests with professionals. You should play against good players every once in a while to improve your game, but you shouldn't play for high stakes, and you certainly shouldn't play a game you don't know well. I had played Pot Limit Hold'em a grand total of twice prior to this experience.

My fate was sealed long before I picked up ace–queen and made it $20 to go. Four people called, including Joe and Melissa, and we all saw a flop of jack–ten–nine rainbow. Melissa led out and went all-in for $100. "Stay aggressive," I told myself. "Don't let these people run over you." I made it $300 to go, which I thought was a decent bet given my open-ended straight draw and two overcards. But then Joe looked me over and declared he was raising the pot. The action came back to me, eight hundred smackers to call. Whoops. What had I done? My first thought was, "Damn, now I have to fold." That should've been my final thought. Except I realized I was almost all-in if I called (I'd have $100 or so left), so I didn't have to worry much about the turn or river action. The only thing that mattered was whether I was getting the right odds with two cards to come. And I actually said aloud, "There's sixteen hundred dollars in there, right? So I'm getting two to one." While I was getting 2 to 1, which is about the right price for a straight draw, I still had no business calling. As Patri said later, when we discussed the hand, "In your best case, with all your straight outs being good, you're getting two to one on a two-to-one shot. That's zero EV. And that's the best you can hope for!" He was right, but I didn't see it that way as I played the hand, and I watched myself fire eight $100 bills into the pot.

The turn brought a blank and Joe set me in for my last few dollars.

"I put you on queens," he said after I'd called his bet.

"Do you have kings?" I said.

"I've got queens beat," he said. "Good luck on the river."

"Thanks," I said, sure he didn't mean it.

The river, for better or for worse (I think I was destined to lose my stack in this game at some point anyway), did not bring an eight or a king. "I missed," I said, flipping over my cards. Joe scooped the main pot and the side pot with jack–nine—top and bottom pair on the flop— beating Melissa's queen–jack. "Nice hand," I said, getting up from the table. The game had drawn the attention of several railbirds, and one of them looked at me with pain as I walked away. "If I win, I make a lot of money," I said to him. He nodded wistfully. The man had obviously been living vicariously through me for the last several hands.

After wandering around for a few minutes, now stuck more than $1,000 for the trip, I returned to the table to talk about my call with Joe and Patri. I already described Patri's excellent analysis. Joe's was less useful. "If you call me with draws all day, eventually I'll have the money." Wow, that's really helpful. I thanked him (Lord knows why), and then he left me with this beauty: "Yeah, and I hope we can play again . . . if you win the Lotto or something." Over the past few years, Joe has been much more respectful of me and my game (I'm a much, much better player now than I was then), and has grown up a little himself, in my opinion. But I don't think we'll ever be friends. I could be wrong.

I must've still been in a daze the next morning, as I was the only BARGEr eating the breakfast buffet at 10 A.M. It turned out the BARGE No Limit Hold'em tournament started at ten, not at noon like all the others. I missed the first twenty-five minutes while enjoying some stale pancakes and bland orange juice.

When I finally got to the tournament, I played the best No Limit Hold'em I knew how. Either it wasn't enough, or I didn't get any cards, or both. I made it through more than half the field before busting out.

With nothing else to do, I soon found myself in another Pot Limit game, where once again I went through a $500 buy-in. This time it took six and a half hours, and I didn't lose all my chips on a bad call. Instead, I lost them by betting. My opponent had bet the pot on the flop and I had called with just two sevens, despite the overcard that was on board. I felt strongly my sevens were in the lead, and that my opponent had some kind of big ace. When he checked the ace on the turn, I didn't know what to think. If he had the ace I originally put him on, why did he check? I still thought he was weak, and that he might fold an ace even if he had one. So I made an all-in pot-sized bet . . . and he called with ace–ten. If I'd had another $500 behind ready to bet on the river, maybe my opponent would've mucked. As it was, I was busted from another Pot Limit game and now stuck more than $1,600 for the trip.

This was more than three times as much as I'd ever lost in a weekend, and I walked around the casino not sure of my name.

My spirits brightened during Chris Ferguson's fantastic speech at the BARGE banquet (I'll tell you about its content next chapter). When it ended, I was ready to win back some money. Russell and I ventured over to the Bellagio. The natural choice was to play $15–$30 again, as I had already done it once and I needed to play big to get myself unstuck (can you spot the flaw in this logic?). I proceeded to dump yet another $900. A loss like this is a fairly typical occurrence at that limit, a limit 50 percent bigger than my usual stakes. But it shocked me nonetheless. Losing $900, let alone $2,500, was just something that didn't happen to me.

There is more to game selection than finding a table full of bad players. There is finding appropriate stakes for your bankroll. I had failed to answer two important questions before sitting in that $15–$30 game: (1) Do I really have the bankroll for it? (I didn't, because I wasn't really prepared to lose all my money and live paycheck-to-paycheck); and (2) Can I stomach a big loss in it? (I couldn't, especially not in the middle of a money-hemorrhaging Vegas experience.) I had committed the rookie mistakes of chasing a loss by playing too big and feeling invulnerable at the poker table. I couldn't admit to myself that I just might lose a lot of money at these limits, and that made everything all the more agonizing.

Russell paid for the cab ride back to Binion's and listened to me moan. "What are you stuck for the trip?" he said.

"Twenty-five hundred."

"That's a bad trip," Russell, a multimillionaire, said. Indeed it was.

Back in my hotel room, I resolved to have fun during my last day in Vegas. I resolved not to care about money anymore, to laugh when I got good cards cracked, to enjoy my time playing poker with BARGErs, and to remember why I played poker in the first place.

I only had time for a two-hour $10–$20 session before my flight on Sunday, but I made several new friends in that time, laughed when my ace–king went down in flames, and told everyone I'd see them next year before catching my cab to McCarron. And, oh yeah, I won $192.

On the flight home, I wondered what a $2,365 loss would look like in my records, and then decided not to think about it. I pulled out my notebook and wrote: "Always have bankroll for the game," and "Have fun, it's supposed to be fun."

It took me more than seven months to win back all that cash (but, to my credit I think, I did). Now I don't sit in bad games for high stakes. I play against fish to win money. I play against tough players for small dollar amounts. I don't let my ego get in the way of choosing stakes. I'm a graduate student now, and for a long time I stayed away from the juicy $15–$30 game at Bellagio. I didn't play it again until I'd built up my bankroll through two years at the proper, lower, limits.

11

♠ ♣ ♦ ♥

Game Theory

You and I are playing No Limit Hold'em. The blinds are $1 and $2, and we each have $50,000 in front of us. It's folded to me on the small blind, and I make it $5 to go. Before you look at your cards, I accidentally expose my hand, revealing two black aces. You now know my cards, and I know that you know my cards. What hands should you call with? What hands should you raise? What hands should you fold?

This was the problem posed to BARGErs by then–world-champion Chris "Jesus" Ferguson (the nickname comes from his long, flowing locks) at his speech during the BARGE2K banquet. Immediately after Ferguson did so, Bill Chen blurted out, "I would think you have to fold all hands." And Bill Chen is one of the smartest people in the world.

The answer is not, of course, that you should fold all hands (as Bill realized about two seconds after he opened his mouth)—that wouldn't have made for a very interesting problem. It should also be obvious, however, that you can't raise, because that reopens the action for me, and I'm just going to move all-in and be done with it. It is far from obvious, however, which hands should be mucked and which should be played. Take some time to think about this problem on your own. I'll reveal the answer toward the middle of the chapter.

Problems like this one are problems of game theory, a branch of mathematics developed to study decision-making in situations where two or more parties have competing interests. The field began with the mathematicians John von Neumann and Oskar Morgenstern, who observed games of poker and tic-tac-toe in the 1940s and wrote the landmark work *Theory of Games and Economic Behavior*. In 1950, John

Nash (the mathematician made famous in the Oscar-winning film *A Beautiful Mind*) wrote his doctoral dissertation, entitled *Noncooperative Games*. Forty-four years later he was awarded the Nobel Prize. Nash's work proved to be a foundation for modern economic analysis, an implication he supposedly never saw coming as a twenty-two-year-old graduate student.

The most common example of a game theory problem is the prisoners' dilemma. Here's how it works: Two suspects in a crime are put into separate cells. If they both confess, each will be sentenced to three years in prison. If only one of them confesses, he will be set free after testifying against the other, who will receive a sentence of ten years. If neither confesses, they will both be convicted of minor offenses and spend just a year in prison. Naturally, if the prisoners could somehow be forced to cooperate, neither would confess and both would be out of jail in a year. This, however, is a noncooperative situation, of the type Nash studied, where the prisoners have no reason to trust each other. It turns out that the Nash equilibrium for the prisoners' dilemma is for both prisoners to confess. This is because, at that point, there is no way for either prisoner to gain by making a unilateral change in his strategy (that is, once one prisoner has confessed, it does the other prisoner no good to remain silent). Nash showed that this is actually the best solution, for both prisoners to confess, even though there are scenarios where each individual could do better. It is these kinds of counterintuitive insights that make game theory fun.

The math geeks of poker are game theorists, taking on game theory problems—they are not computing pot odds to more decimal points. During his speech, Chris Ferguson said, "People who think math isn't important in poker don't know the right math." He also said, "If you're going to deviate from the correct play, you better first know what the correct play is." Ferguson has a doctorate in computer science, with a focus on artificial intelligence. In the course of his education, he has probably forgotten more game theory than 99 percent of the poker tournament world knows. Chris, as he told us we should call him (I don't know why I expected him to prefer Dr. Ferguson, or His Majesty the World Champion, or something like that) got his start playing poker on IRC, an old version of Internet poker played for no money. He held the highest tournament ranking of the hundreds of players there, most of whom took the game seriously. When Chris won his world championship, his heads-up opponent was T. J. Cloutier, a man who got his poker education as a road gambler in games run by crooks. The difference between the two players' approaches couldn't have been exaggerated—Chris, the (over)educated theorist, against T.J., dean of the school of hard knocks. Education had to get lucky and spike a nine on the river to win the match, but it was certainly more than luck that got Chris heads-up with the chip lead in the first place.

Chris's words at BARGE paint a picture of a poker universe where every hand has a correct play, known to game theorists and possibly a few select others, and where everyone else is doomed to lose their money. Well, his picture isn't exactly that straightforward. Chris would be the first to admit that it is rarely possible to determine the correct play for multi-way poker hands. This is because the solutions in those cases often require players to work together, and it's not clear which alliances could or should be formed. Furthermore, every situation at a poker table is unique. There is no way to judge in advance what will be the best play against a randomly assembled group of players, each with their own idiosyncratic playing styles.

When Chris talks about the "correct" play, he is really talking about the **optimal** play. In game theory, the optimal play is one where even if your opponent knew exactly what your strategy was, he couldn't do anything to counter it. For example, suppose there is $100 in the pot, and you have a pair of aces on the river. You're sure that I either have a monster hand or absolutely nothing. I then bet $20 and tell you exactly what I'm doing. "Reader," I say. "There is a one in seven chance I am bluffing, and a six in seven chance I have the nuts. Go ahead and call if you like." It turns out it doesn't matter if you call or fold. If you call, you'll win $120 one seventh of the time and lose $20 six sevenths of the time. Your EV is $0 (and mine is $100). And of course if you fold, your EV is also $0 (and mine is $100). It's the same either way. This is because I am bluffing with *optimal* frequency. If I were bluffing any less often, your best play would be to fold. If I were bluffing any more often, your best play would be to call. If I'm playing optimally *it doesn't matter what you do*.

But what about you holding your aces? Do you have your own optimal strategy? Well, obviously you can't call with them every time.

That strategy would be **exploited** by a savvy opponent. If you decide that you never want to throw away the best hand, and you're going to call every one of my river bets with your aces, then I'm going to deviate from the optimal strategy. Now I'm going to only bet when I have the nuts, and check and fold the one-seventh of the time I have nothing. Your EV just dropped from $0 to negative $2.86, and mine increased from $100 to $102.86. I have employed an **exploitative** strategy to take advantage of my dumb opponent and increase my profit.

Note that I would still make money using optimal strategy against an opponent who calls every time—I would make the same $100 I made before. Why? Because if you play optimally, it doesn't matter what your opponent does. Some people therefore view optimal play as a guaranteed way to break even, but a lousy way to make money. Chris Ferguson surely deviates from "correct" play all the time, because optimal play is only correct against an opponent playing optimally. Since real world opponents play suboptimally all the time (thank God), the optimal play is rarely the right one. But as Chris says, it would be nice to always know what the optimal play is, and you rarely lose *that much* in expected value by playing optimally.

We discussed how to bluff with optimal frequency in theory, but how do we do it in practice? In real life, you're either bluffing or value betting (usually), so it can be difficult to say, "Well, I was bluffing so that my ration of bluffs to value bets is $1/P + 1$, where P is the size of the pot in big bets." (In the example above, the pot size after I bet was six big bets, and optimal strategy was to bluff one seventh of the time.) How could you possibly know you're bluffing exactly that often? David Sklansky offers one suggestion in *The Theory of Poker*. His idea is essentially to pick certain cards out of the deck to bluff with. Let's say your optimal bluffing frequency on the river will be one in ten, and unbeknownst to your opponent you have a flush draw. (Assume for the sake of the exercise that your opponent thinks you have either the nuts or nothing, and is pondering whether to call on the end with one pair.) You know you're going to bet the river when any of the nine flush cards come—so in order to be bluffing with optimal frequency you need to also bet on one other river card. So just pick one at random, like the nine of clubs, and bet whenever you hit the flush, or whenever that nine of clubs appears on the river. You will now be bluffing with optimal frequency. If optimal bluffing frequency had been one in four, you would've needed to bet three non–flush cards on the river. Do you see why?

Okay, I admit I never pick random river cards to bluff with. I bluff when I think it's a profitable play, based on the logic I outlined in Chapter 2. I think that's a better exploitative approach. Players tend to fold the river more than they should, and a player bluffing optimally is not bluffing enough, in my opinion. I do, however, think it's important to understand what bluffing optimally means.

Chris seemed only to think about poker in terms of game theory, not in terms of staying disciplined, learning from experience, or finding your own winning style like the rest of us mortals. He told us that he learned poker with a pencil and paper, working out problems like the one he had given us. There was more. He played no more than ten hours of ring game poker per year—he was strictly a tournament specialist. I guess if you're going to study a game so thoroughly, the slightest change in parameters (like switching from ring game strategy to tournament strategy) could potentially lead to a whole lot more work. I still find his tournament preference curious, though, since early tournament strategy is basically the same as ring game strategy.

But most astounding of all, Chris Ferguson, winner of $1.5 million in the world's biggest tournament, said he did not use physical tells when studying his opponents. Didn't use them. Most of us had entered the banquet thinking world-class players were separated into different skill levels by their abilities to read body language. Now one of the best players in the world was telling us he didn't even look at body language. The idea, of course, was that if Chris was making a near-optimal play, it didn't matter what his opponents had—no one could exploit him. Chris therefore devoted his energy to studying poker from a game theory standpoint, not to studying the way someone breathed or smoked a cigarette at the table. Needless to say, he has had some success with this tactic.

Chris would only give us two strategic tips. They were: (1) Leave calling to the experts, and know that the experts don't call very much; and (2) Make very small bets and raises in No Limit Hold'em.

Point One seemed natural to me at the time, as I pretty much followed an aggressive raise-or-fold philosophy. Today, however, it surprises me that Chris gave us this advice. Many of the game theory players I know often check and call as a way to maximize value for their hands. Point Two seemed counterintuitive to everyone. Just about every No Limit book in print said preflop raises should be about three or four times the size of the blinds, and postflop bets should be about the size of the pot. Ferguson was saying to make minimum raises preflop, and half-pot-sized bets after the flop. I've since learned that Chris's advice comes largely from a game theory result called "geometric growth of pot." It says that in a heads-up, multi-street game where one player has the nuts or nothing and his opponent has a hand, EV is maximized by betting one third to two thirds of the pot when a bet is called for.

The intuitive explanation for me is that by betting or raising, you always stand to win the same amount if opponents fold—the amount of the pot. So why not risk as little as you can? I'm sure Chris's analysis goes deeper, and that he considered other effects of the small raise (for example, the potential for losing value on big hands and the reduced chances of winning the pot) and other results from game theory land before coming to the conclusion that the small raise is the best play. Indeed, without being a game theorist, it is very hard—no, impossible—to prove him wrong.

Game theory sounded too good to be true to an aspiring world-class player like me, and in some ways it was. Problems in multi-way pots are almost impossible to solve. Even the solvable problems take a tremendous amount of work and don't always provide helpful insight into the game even after they're solved.

One of the biggest issues I've always had with the game theoretical approach to poker is that it completely ignores execution of the optimal plays. Let me explain. If you tell me you're bluffing optimally on the river, it's true that it doesn't matter if I call or fold. But that's only if there's *no difference in your bets* when you're bluffing or when you're calling. You could be the most optimal player in world history, but if you have a tell every time you bluff, I'm going to slaughter you. Sklansky makes statements like: "It is against such expert players, whose calling and folding are right on target, or whose judgment is as good or better than yours, that game theory becomes the perfect tool. When you use it, there is no way they can outplay you." (*The Theory of Poker*, page 187.) No way? What if these expert players know when you're bluffing and when you're value betting? I think they would probably outplay you in that case. This oversight in the game theory approach is rarely mentioned. I guess it is assumed that all good players will get to the point where they don't give off too many tells at the tables. I think this is a terrible assumption, as I know one of the top game theorists in the world gave off a major tell at the final table of a big tournament, and that his opponent was aware of it. Game theory is without question an outstanding tool, but you better put your hours in at the table to make sure your bluffs look the same as your value bets.

The conversations after Chris's speech were all over the place, but most were one way or another related to the exposed aces problem. One confused -ARGEr claimed there were some hands the big blind could reraise with before the flop.

"You can't possibly raise before the flop," I said.

"Game theory says you can," was his ill-informed response. As Russell rhetorically asked later, "What does 'game theory' say to do when the aces reraise you all-in?"

After BARGE ended, Chris posted his problem to RGP. It got more than one hundred responses, among the longest threads in the history of the newsgroup. I had no idea how to go about finding a solution, but in reading the responses I started to develop an intuition about the answer. First, I noticed it would be silly for the aces to make big bets or raises after the flop (except, of course, if the aces flopped the current nuts, in which case they should move all-in and the hand would be over). This is because his opponent has perfect information. Let's say the aces decided to just move-in on any flop. Well, then the big blind simply calls when he's ahead and folds when he's behind. The aces would be risking $49,995 to win $10. He'll be behind on far too many flops to make this play profitable.

But it turns out even much smaller bets would not make sense for the aces, and the rationale behind that is the crux of understanding the entire problem. Let's approach it backwards, starting from the showdown and working our way to the preflop strategy. First, we should note that a random hand has about a 15 percent chance of beating aces. It is clear, therefore, that the big blind will be able to make a large overbet on the river about 15 percent of the time. But the big blind can also bluff optimally on the river, and since his bet will be very large, he will only be offering the aces around 1 to 1 to call. The big blind, then, can bluff with almost as many hands as he value bets on the river. In all, the big blind will be betting on the river about 30 percent of the time, and the aces might as well fold (since the big blind will be playing optimally, and it won't matter if the aces call or not). Now let's back up to the turn. The big blind can bet the turn as often as he can bet the river. If he bets the same 30 percent of his hands, the aces can't call because they'll always be facing another bet on the river they can't call. Calling on the turn would just be throwing away money. It gets better. The big blind can add *another* 29 percent of his hands or so to bet on the turn with—and the aces still can't call. If they did, they would only be getting about 1 to 1 on their money, so they'd need to win more than half the time to make the call profitable. But they'll be *folding* more than half the time on the river, ergo, they *won't* be winning more than half the time. Take this logic one more step, and you see the random hand can overbet *every* flop, because the aces will have to fold on the turn more than half the time. Therefore, before the flop, the big blind should call with any two cards.

This argument was put forth on RGP by David Sklansky. It is not a rigorous proof, but it is the idea. One hole in the argument is that there are flops where a random hand has worse than a 15 percent chance of beating aces. For example, on a flop of KKK, a random hand has only a 4.6 percent chance of beating the aces. (Conversely, on a flop of 5♦6♦7♦, a random hand has about 40 percent equity against black aces!) Not to mention that when the aces flop the nuts, the random hand has to fold to the aces' all-in wager.

In the cases where the random hand is bigger than a 15 percent underdog (true on flops like KK2 and Q83 rainbow), his strategy is not as clearcut. It turns out he should sometimes check and sometimes make an overbet on the flop (the exact frequencies decided by some complicated math). The big blind's EV in this scenario still ends up being positive. If, on the flop, a random hand has better than a 15 percent chance of beating aces, the big blind bets and the aces have to fold. The big blind's EV in this scenario is $10 (the whole pot). Notice that it doesn't matter if the big blind's particular hand has a 15 percent chance of winning, only that a random hand does. As far as the aces are concerned, the big blind is a random hand. In other words, what matters is the big blind's range of hands (in this case, all hands), not his specific hand, because his opponent doesn't know his specific hand. From a game theory standpoint, the big blind can announce that he'll play his random hand by betting any flop on which his range of hands has a better than one in seven chance of winning . . . and the aces have to fold.

This sketch of a proof was provided for RGP by its resident game theorist, Tom Weideman. Tom told us that in order for the big blind to have positive EV, his range of hands has to have better than a 3/70 chance of winning. Since every hand is at least that likely to beat aces, every hand is playable. The only catch is that Tom did not account for the times the aces flop the nuts and the big blind has to fold. Tom, however, was confident this happens infrequently enough so that the correct strategy is still as described above. It certainly seems intuitively correct.

What did we learn from Chris's question? First, the additional rounds of betting help the random hand. If the betting ended preflop, there would be no way a random hand could make money against aces. If the betting ended on the flop, there would be no way a random hand could overbet the pot every time—as the aces would always be a favorite. But because there are three rounds of betting, the random hand will win often enough, and have enough chances to bluff, so that the aces cannot continue. The perfect information the big blind has becomes more useful with more rounds of betting.

But the most interesting part of the problem, I think, is the result itself. By revealing his hole cards preflop, the player with the aces must fold even the best possible starting hand in the game whenever he doesn't flop the nuts. I'm pretty sure this realization is why Chris posed the problem in the first place. In poker, information is everything. You're only as good as what you know about your opponent, and what your opponent knows about you. The cards are insignificant in comparison.

The more I thought about the Ferguson Problem (as it came to be known), the more interested I became in game theory. Despite having a degree in mathematics, I never took a formal course in game theory, and I came to the conclusion that I better learn some if I wanted to be a serious poker player. I didn't think I knew, in Ferguson's language, "the right math."

I looked into buying a game theory textbook, but all the titles I found were outdated, unwieldy (filled with jargon and not really usable by a layperson), or both. Luckily, just as I started to get frustrated, Tom Weideman posted his own game theory problem to the newsgroup. I E-mailed him back with a perfect solution (it was really just a relatively simple pure math question), and we ended up exchanging some E-mails. Tom, a Ph.D. in physics, is one of the most knowledgeable and most intelligent members of the newsgroup (a scary combination at the poker table, by the way). He is one of a handful of people contributing to the science of poker through game theory research. Poker, as a game, is very, very poorly understood, even compared to complicated games like chess. This is because chess is a game of complete information. While chess is far from solved, the correct chess move is almost always much easier to determine than the correct play at a full poker table. In poker, we never know what the other player is holding, or even what range of hands he could have. It is therefore usually impossible to say what the correct play is with certainty.

Over the next few years I worked on problems presented by many RGPers including Tom, David Sklansky, Bill Chen, and Jerrod Ankenman. I solved most of them on my own, and the rest with help. They were problems with phrases like, "With what frequency should you call on the end to prevent your opponent from exploiting you?" and "With what percentage of your hands should you value bet in this spot?"

Bill and Jerrod are now doing some of the most interesting work in poker theory. They have fully analyzed what they call the [0,1] game—an invented game where each player is "dealt" a real number between 0 and 1, there are one or more betting rounds with fixed or unfixed bet sizes (depending on the variation), and a showdown comes at the end if necessary, with the lowest number winning. Their results, which they have started posting on RGP, have definite applications to poker situations. Without getting into specifics, it's safe to say they have contributed to my understanding of the game. Jerrod and Bill are now working on actual poker problems instead of [0,1] problems. Their work to this point, along with the work of another RGPer named Andy

Latto, will be published in the book *The Mathematics of Poker*. I predict it will have far-reaching effects on the educated poker populace.

If I ever go back to school (again), it would probably be to get a degree in game theory, specializing in poker (might as well go to school for something useful, eh?). One person already doing something similar is RGPer Darse Billings. A doctoral student in computer science at the University of Alberta, Darse is working on writing *bots*, computer poker players that can outplay even the toughest of humans. Darse's work was featured in a 2003 *New York Times* article. In it he is quoted as saying: "The program is the first decent approximation of a really balanced strategy. It does a really good job of bluffing with an appropriate frequency, as well as check raising and slow playing." Many knowledgeable people believe that bots will one day dominate online poker, and that the day might be soon. It's easy to understand their reasoning—just think of all the advantages a bot has over a human: (1) A bot will never get tired; (2) a bot will never tilt; (3) a bot will have perfect recollection of every hand its opponents have ever played against it; (4) a bot will never be afraid of losing money; (5) a bot will always make what it thinks is the correct play; (6) a bot will never misclick.

What advantages would a human have over a bot? Aside from possibly getting a read on a person based on a screen name or chat box text, I can think of none. Count me among those who believe bots are the future of poker. In twenty years, any serious player will have to study their algorithms and the game theory behind them.

In my own search for game theory problems back in the fall of 2000, I inadvertently discovered another Internet poker forum—twoplustwo. com. This is Sklansky and Malmuth's forum, moderated, and more focused on strategic and theoretical questions than its unmoderated rival, RGP. There are downsides and upsides to each forum. At twoplustwo, you get interesting theoretical questions from one of the game's greatest minds (David Sklansky) and a lot of focused, thought-out responses from dedicated twoplustwoers. The problem is that Sklansky and Malmuth are treated as gods, and there is often little difference of opinion when analyzing hands. Everyone there seems to think and play the way Sklansky and Malmuth tell them to play; or at least, they think they're thinking and playing the way Sklansky and Malmuth tell them to. In my opinion, most twoplustwo posters are overly cautious in their approach to poker, more concerned with saving bets and getting away from hands than getting value out of their good hands. I consider value betting one of my biggest strengths, and I am often stunned by the situations where twoplustwo posters recommend checking a hand down, or even folding.

By far the biggest problem with RGP is the large number of lunatics posting there. You have to sift through far too much spam, personal attacks, and off-topic posts to find the good poker content. There is still some, but sadly many of the best posters have given up on RGP as a place to discuss poker. Still, RGP's openness is both its biggest weakness and its biggest strength. You're liable to get five different ideas about how to play a particular hand when you ask for comments, and they won't all be from the school of Sklansky and Malmuth. Also, personalities come out in the newsgroup, as there is no one to censor them. Often this lack of censorship is a bad thing, but sometimes it is a great thing. On many days, RGP is the best comedy I can find.

And of course, RGP is where I got the solution to the Ferguson Problem. As RGPer Steve Brecher said during the discussion, "This is a problem in game theory, the kind of problem that so-called 'math weenies' like to think about. If you think that this kind of stuff is too theoretical and abstract to have practical value, consider this: The guy who posted the problem is probably the world's top game theoretician with respect to No-Limit Hold'em poker. In coming up with his strategies for playing poker tournaments, he did original work in this highly theoretical and abstract field, and that work is the primary source of his development as a player."

Game theory is not easy. Far from it. I'd say the biggest reason most players don't use game theory in their thinking processes is that it's way too much work. And because most people don't use game theory, game theorists get infuriated when a so-called "intuitive" player makes unfounded claims about the correctness of a poker play. As Bill Chen once posted on RGP: "We are in a scary place when we rely on experts to feed us facts like what group of hands we should play in a loose-passive game in early position or what this DNA evidence means or whether we should go to war." For Bill, a solution to a question derived from analysis is much better than an "expert" declaration. Even "experts" basing their opinions on years of trial and error do not carry as much weight with game theorists as a proof, or a computer simulation, or any opinion founded in logic.

An irony to all this is that I've found many (not all, of course) game theory-savvy players to be more exploitable than average players. This is because most game theorists call a lot more than other good players do. Maybe they've done the math and know that they are often getting the right odds against many ranges of hands. But it seems many of them do a poor job of estimating an opponent's range of hands to begin with, possibly assuming their opponents are playing closer to optimally than they actually are. I've seen a mathematically inclined player call a huge raise with pocket sixes when it seemed clear his opponent's range of hands was something like 88–AA, AK, AQ (making the sixes almost a 2 to 1 dog). My advice to you if you find yourself playing a game theory expert is to bluff much less and value bet much more. Then, if you feel your opponent start adjusting, you're on your own.

Is it essential to understand game theory in order to be a world-class poker player? No, but it's getting more and more helpful all the time. Think turn-of-the-century (the previous century) America. Everyone riding around in a horse and buggy must have been satisfied with their method of transportation; while in the background Henry Ford was toiling away at some theoretical abstraction called the automobile. That's analogous to what's going on in the poker world today. When the game theorists make serious advances with their research, those who can successfully implement their strategy at the table will be light years ahead of everyone else. Anyone who ignores game theory does so at his own peril.

This is not a book about game theory, this is a book about learning poker the way I learned it. These days, however, I'm learning about poker through game theory—and I plan on learning a lot more.

12

♠ ♣ ♦ ♥

Learning Omaha and Stud
(at FARGO)

"Worlds are colliding!"

George Costanza of the world-changing sitcom *Seinfeld* utters these words when his girlfriend Susan and his longtime friend Elaine meet up for coffee. Paranoid individual that he is, George worries about this rendezvous and spells out his concerns in his best friend Jerry's apartment.

"I have relationship George, but there is also independent George—that's the George you know . . . movie George, coffee-shop George, liar George."

"I love that George," Jerry says.

"Me too," George says. "And he's dying, Jerry. If relationship George walks through this door, he will kill independent George."

I sort of felt like George when I brought my father to the 2000 version of FARGO (Foxwoods Annual Rec.Gambling Outing). If family Matt walked into the poker room with father in tow, would he kill -ARGEr Matt, straddler Matt, poker Matt? I liked that Matt, and I know some FARGOers did too.

Bringing Dad to FARGO could kill this Matt because ARGers were not just poker players—they were a different breed entirely. Even though Dad was the one who taught me to play poker in the first place, he wouldn't necessarily fit in.

My fears seemed well founded in the weeks leading up to the event. "These guys are crazy," Dad said to me while reading the FARGO E-mail list. I guess he was surprised to see messages with subjects like, "Nolan Dalla is a heterosexual!!"—an inside joke responding to some nut on RGP who had posted a flame of Nolan—and "Ha! Ha! Ha! I'm at Foxwoods and you're not!"

ARGErs say whatever they want, conventions be damned. Maybe this comes from the ability to hide beyond a keyboard. Maybe this comes from playing so much poker, where you're free to play your chips however you please at any time. Probably it is a combination of both.

For whatever reason, Dad was skeptical about even attending. "The tournaments are for money, right?" he asked. Yes, Dad.

Skeptical or not, Dad picked me up from the airport in Providence on the night of October 12, 2000, and we listened to my beloved New York Mets triumph in Game Two of the National League Championship Series on our way to the casino. Despite it being midnight when we arrived, and both of us having worked a full day before traveling, we made the journey from the Two Trees Inn to the poker room just to get it out of our systems.

Dad thought he was hearing things when everyone greeted me as I walked around with a, "Hi, Matt!"

"How does everyone know you?" Dad said.

I explained a little of the group dynamics, how we were one big East Coast poker family, why it was fun to play at these events; but I didn't say much. The best way for him to understand -ARG was to experience it himself. I began to realize that I had been worried about nothing—that Dad, a goofy, geeky math teacher who plays loose and loves to have fun, would fit in perfectly.

We sat in the same $4–$8 Hold'em game, which featured fellow FARGOer Nolan Dalla (the guy was everywhere). I didn't concentrate much on the poker, as I was playing the low limits to socialize, unwind, and mark the beginning of my first FARGO, but there were two interesting hands.

I had gotten a free play on the big blind and flopped top pair on a jack-high board with a two-flush. I bet out, Dad raised, another player cold-called, and I called. I figured Dad was doing the old "take a free card with a flush draw play," as he had read the same book I did. So when an offsuit ace came on the turn, I bet out again, saying, "Just in case you were on a flush draw." Dad shrugged and called, which (I thought) confirmed my read, and the other player called behind. The river was a blank and I bet one last time. Dad folded and the woman called. I announced my jacks, and she mucked her hand. "Oh God," Dad said. "I threw away pocket kings."

This was a rare case of father giving son too much respect. To begin with, Dad should have raised preflop, but once he called on the turn, he should have forced himself to call on the river. He was not calling on the turn to try to spike a third king (a 22 to 1 shot); he was calling because he thought there was enough chance he had the best hand. The same logic should have applied on the river. If you learn one thing from this book about river play in Limit Hold'em, learn not to fold a hand like king–king for one bet.

The other interesting hand came when I limped in with five–five—a sacred RGP hand known as **presto,** which is said to bring good fortune to all who play it—in middle position, and we took the flop seven ways. The flop came down ace–six–six with two hearts. It was checked to me, and for some reason I bet (not a good play). When it came back to me, there had been two callers, a raiser, and then two cold-callers. I felt strongly that the first cold-caller—the button—was slowplaying a six, so I called one more bet getting about 18 to 1 on my money, figuring to win a big pot if a five hit. Sure enough, the five of hearts came on the turn, bringing a flush but giving me a full house. It got checked to me, I checked, and then Nolan bet. The next player called, and the button raised. It got to me, and I reraised. Nolan showed the guy next to him what I later learned was a queen-high flush and folded. The original bettor called, but the button capped it. Now I feared he'd been slowplaying not a six, but sixes full or even aces full. But there was no way I could fold at this point, so I called, and then checked and called on the river. (The other player still in the hand overcalled behind me.) The button reached for his cards . . . and turned over two sixes. He had flopped quads, and all of us fine contestants had been drawing dead (the overcaller had the "nut" flush)—thanks for playing! Notice that folding the river here would have saved me eight dollars, but it would have cost me several hundred if I'd been wrong.

Despite this massacre, I still managed a two-dollar win for the one-and-a-half-hour session when Dad (who had also eked out a profit) and I went back to the Two Trees. We needed to get some rest for the Pairs tourney the next morning, which was not FARGO's main event but was the main recruiting weapon I'd used to get Dad to FARGO.

A uniquely FARGO event, the Pairs is a competition between teams of two, where one person plays Limit Hold'em and, after twenty minutes, the other comes in and plays Omaha Eight-or-Better using the same stack of chips. Since Dad's favorite game was (and is) Omaha, and my best game was (and is) Limit Hold'em, the Pairs was a natural event for us to conquer.

You might be wondering what exactly this Omaha game is. Omaha Eight-or-Better (to be referred to as Omaha, for short) has a flop, turn, and river, a small blind and a big blind, and the exact same betting structure as Limit Hold'em. And that is where the similarities end. In Omaha, there are two ways to show down a winning hand. You can have the best hand, as usual, or you can have the worst hand. Games like Omaha are known in kitchen table poker as hi-lo games, where the high hand and the low hand each get half the pot. But it's not that simple. Having the worst hand at the showdown does not guarantee you half the pot. Your low hand has to be so bad that it **qualifies** in order to be worth any money. Eight-high is the first qualifying low hand (hence the name, "Eight-or-Better"), so hands like 8–6–4–3–2 could potentially earn you half the pot. But straights and flushes do *not* count against you, and an ace can be used as a one if it helps you make a low hand. The best possible low hand, therefore, is 5–4–3–2–A—the wheel. The worst low hand that still qualifies is an eight-high straight—8–7–6–5–4.

There's more. You're required to use exactly two cards from your hand and three from the board to make your five-card hand (unlike Hold'em, where you can play all five cards from the board, or four from the board and one from your hand). Some examples where this rule comes into play:

Board—9♠9♣9♥4♦K♣
Your hand—Q♦K♠3♥3♦
You do NOT have nines full of kings, as that would require using
   four board cards. You DO, however, have nines full of threes, and
   would beat anyone holding an ace or king without a pocket pair
   to go with it.

Board—4♠5♠6♠7♠8♠
Your hand—9♠6♣6♥6♦

You do NOT have a straight flush. You do NOT have four of a kind. You do NOT have a flush. You can't make any of those hands by using two of your hole cards and three cards from the board. What you have is a nine-high straight (playing a 96 from your hand and the 5♠7♠8♠ from the board).

Board—8♥9♦3♣J♠K♥
Your hand—J♣J♦9♥2♦

You do NOT have a full house, as you'd need to use three of your hole cards to make one. As in Hold'em, a full house is only possible when there is a pair on the board. In this hand, you have a set of jacks.

In none of the above hands did your hole cards even give you a chance to have a qualifying low. Let's look at some examples where you do have that chance:

Board—4♥5♥6♠K♣J♦
Your hand—A♠2♣7♥8♦

You have what's known as **nut-nut**, the best possible high hand (an eight-high straight) *and* the best possible low hand (6542A) on board.

Board—A♥2♥3♠K♠Q♥
Your hand—A♠2♠3♣4♥

You had a fantastic starting hand, but with this board you do NOT have a low. To make a low, you need to have five unpaired cards. You don't have that using only two cards from your hand. All you have is aces and threes for high, and no low. This is not a good hand in Omaha. You'd often have to fold this hand (unlike in Limit Hold'em, where you'd almost never fold aces-up on this board).

Board—A♣2♣3♥4♠9♦
Your hand—2♥3♠6♦T♥

Here you do have a low, even though two of your low cards match cards on the board. You can use the six and the deuce from your hand with the A34 on board to make 6432A. When there are four low cards on board, you only need one unmatched low card in your hand and one that matches the board to have a low. In this case, you have a **live six**, meaning your low hand is the four low board cards (even though you're not using all four board cards), plus a six. Although this looks like a decent low, anyone holding a five and any other card below five has a wheel, the best possible low. Since you have a measly threes-up for high, you would again usually fold this hand on the river, if not long before then.

Omaha is not only complicated but tedious. Between the extra hole cards, the many, many people who usually stick around to see the flop, and the time it takes to read the board and split the pot, Omaha gets in about half as many hands per hour as Hold'em does. Not only that, but a very tight strategy is needed to play Omaha well. In low limit Omaha games, there is even less opportunity to bluff than there is in Hold'em. The only good low hand is the nut low, and good high hands tend to be pretty close to the nuts as well. Don't even think about drawing to non-nut flushes or straights in Omaha. And if you draw to a flush with a pair on board, you might as well just write out a check and leave it on the table.

Because it takes such a premium hand to play, good Omaha players often go hours without getting past the flop. It's excruciating. I only play Omaha online (where play is significantly faster), and even then almost always two or three tables at a time.

Here is a basic starting hand guide for a full table of Omaha Eight-or-Better (little "s" indicates a suited ace).

Early Position
Raise—A23x, A34x, AA2x, A24x, As25x, As26x, AA3x, AAs4x, KQJT, AAKQ, AsAsxx
Call—A45x, A35x, A2xx, As3xx, A567, 2345, 2346, AA5x, AA6x, four cards 10 or higher without trips
Fold—everything else

Middle and Late Positions
Raise—early raising hands

Call—early calling hands plus 235x, As4xx, As5Kx, As5Qx, As5Jx, AsKQx, AsKJx, 236x

I am not an Omaha expert, but I play the game well enough to hold my own. The rankings I just provided would be approved by most experts as a decent approach for beginners. Notice a few things about these rankings.

1. *Position is not as crucial as it is in Hold'em.* Don't misunderstand—position is still important. But in Omaha, you'll almost never want to draw to non-nut hands, and you need a very strong hand to bet with confidence. This holds true no matter where you're sitting. The other factor is that, for some reason, there is very little preflop raising in Omaha. You can take advantage of this oddity by limping more often without fear of a raise. You can't loosen up very much in late position, but you can play more hands than you might expect from up front.

   Incidentally, it is a myth that raising preflop is a bad play in Omaha. The reasons to do it are slightly different than they are in Hold'em, where raising increases your chances of winning without a showdown. It's hard to win a pot in Omaha without a showdown, but a raise gives you a ton of equity if everyone is going to call you with junk. It's like putting dead money in the pot for when you flop your nut hands.

2. *Most pocket pairs are junk.* This is because the point of Omaha is to **scoop** the pot, meaning win the entire thing. There are two ways to scoop—have the best high hand with no low on board, or have the best high AND low hands. (Yes, you can use different hole cards when making your five-card high and low hands.) Pairs have little potential to do either. With low pairs, when you hit your set there is at least one low card on board, and you're likely fighting for half the pot. With bigger pairs, you're hoping to hit a set, but sets aren't nearly the monsters they are in Hold'em. It takes close to the nuts to win an Omaha pot, and sets are almost never the nuts. The only sets even capable of making the nuts are queens, kings, and aces, and it takes a rare board for those. Usually when you hit a set in Omaha, you need to fill up

(make a full house) and hope nobody has quads. That's a lot to ask, and these prospects certainly don't justify playing garbage like QQ74.

3. *Scooping hands are the most powerful.* I can't stress this enough. Playing for half the pot will not win you money in this game. A great Omaha hand is the wheel, because it is the nut low and a strong high. The idea, then, is to play wheel cards.

   When you have a hand like A347 on a board of 258, you have a monster indeed. Not only do you have a guaranteed nut low, you have a **wheel wrap**, meaning any A, 3, or 4 will give you a wheel. Furthermore, any 6 or 7 will give you a straight. This two-way hand is the kind of hand Omaha players dream about—you have about 70 percent equity against top set!

   Another great situation is when you hold something like A♥Q♥J♠T♦ on a board of A♠K♥J♥T♣. You have the current nut high, but you also have six outs for a full house and eight outs for the nut flush. You could very well be freerolling a player who gets into a raising war with you, thinking he is correct to do so because he has the nuts.

   Now, I'm not saying you need situations this good to warrant playing in Omaha; but I am saying you should recognize and get value from them when they arise. I'm also saying that if you don't have a reasonable chance to scoop the pot, you should muck your hand. The good thing about nut low draws is they often have scooping potential with a low straight.

4. *Pocket aces ain't what they are in Hold'em.* The best part about holding AA in Omaha is that it's unlikely for your opponents to have a nut low draw or a nut flush draw. The pair of aces itself isn't much more valuable than any other pair (and actually has the same problem as other low pairs in that it puts a low card on board when it flops a set). There is no concept of aces "holding up" in Omaha. If you don't flop a set or a nut draw with them, *throw them away on the flop.* Hands like AA98 can even be mucked preflop.

Dad knew all this stuff when he came to FARGO. He's the one who explained it to me. You can imagine my horror, then, when I sweated him during the first few minutes of the Pairs tournament and saw him limp UTG with three–three–king–queen. He was haphazardly tossing chips into the pot, chips I was supposed to have when I sat down to play the Hold'em round. And then Dad made a comment to me about how tight he was playing!

"What about that three–three–king–queen under the gun, Dad?"

"Oh yeah, that was a little crazy—ha ha!" he said.

This pattern repeated itself for years. Dad would go through great pains to devise a playing system, and then do nothing remotely like it at the table. Dad loves to gamble, he is just incapable of playing tight. He has learned to play loose better than most people, and he does what he likes to do. There's something to be said for that.

And it was actually I who lost the last of our chips in the Pairs tournament, reraising an aggressive player with ace–jack and getting it all-in on a jack-high flop, only to be shown two queens.

The main event of the weekend, however, was not the Pairs tournament. It was the No Limit Hold'em tournament. I entered it with confidence, something I was gaining more and more of as I developed as a player and continued to absorb information from my mentor Russell. Early in the event, I raised the minimum with two jacks and faced an enormous overbet reraise all-in from my opponent. The thing was, it was the same opponent I had called with two jacks in that Tuesday night tournament a year and a half earlier. My memory of his play from all that time ago greatly contributed to my read. Against an unknown opponent, I probably would've mucked. But this player, I just felt sure he was overplaying some mediocre hand. I gritted my teeth and called. Sure enough, he had two sevens, and I doubled up to a very nice stack.

I busted myself a few hours later, however, by trying to bluff an unbluffable opponent. This is one of the most common mistakes I see good players make. Even in No Limit Hold'em, bad players call. You cannot bluff a calling station. There is no way around it. Players who can't fold are sure to go broke, but they will take all your chips on their way down if you try to bluff them. It took me a long time to stop myself from doing this. I would correctly put my opponent on a weak hand and think, "He can't possibly call a big bet." But I would be wrong. Time and again these players throw their chips into the pot with garbage hands. The only consolation is that the few times they win by snapping off bluffs virtually insures they'll continue to call in the future.

With the No Limit tournament having been a failure, I had only the Seven-Card Stud event left. I, of course, had signed up for every FARGO tournament, so even though I almost never played Stud, I needed to come up with a winning strategy.

I had read *Seven-Card Stud for Advanced Players* by Sklansky and Malmuth, and did know a little something about the game. I had reached the final table of the only other stud tournament I'd ever entered, on a Wednesday at Foxwoods in the summer of 1999. Burke used to say that I "loved my Stud," even though I always declared myself a Hold'em player. I gave the basic structure for Stud in Chapter 1, but just to refresh your memory:

- Before any cards are dealt, all players ante a fixed amount of money into the pot.
- Each player starts with three cards (third street), with one faceup.
- The lowest card showing on the table has the bring-in and is forced to bet at least some minimum amount (less than a full bet). In $5–$10 Stud, the bring-in is typically $2. He can elect to bet the full $5 instead of $2, but he is obligated to bet at least $2.
- The other players have the option of folding, calling the bring-in, or completing the bet. For example, in $5–$10 Stud, after a $2 bring-in the other players have the option to fold, call the $2, or complete the bet to a total of $5. After the bet has been completed, other players have the option to raise.
- A total of three additional up-cards are dealt to each player (fourth, fifth, and sixth streets), with a round of betting after each.
- The river—the seventh and final card—is dealt facedown, followed by a fifth and final round of betting.
- The betting limits double on fifth street (the round of betting following the third up-card), unless a player has a pair on board on fourth street, in which case the betting limits double on fourth.

There are many obvious differences between Stud and Hold'em, but let me spell out some of the more important ones.

1. *The lack of community cards in Stud means the rank of a hand has more inherent meaning.* I'll explain. In Hold'em, if I tell you I have aces up, that doesn't say very much. I might have a strong hand like top two pair on a board of A82, or I might have a completely worthless hand like 22 on a board of AA44J. In each of these situations my hand has a very different value, regardless of what the action is. In Stud, aces up is aces up. Of course there are times when aces up will be more valuable than others, but aces up will rarely be obviously worthless, as it can be in Hold'em.

2. *Stud has more information.* Stud players know with certainty a lot more things than Hold'em players do. Specifically, they get to see ten cards before making a decision about their hands, while Hold'em players get to see only two. Stud players also get to know up to four of their opponents' unique cards. Hold'em players see no cards unique to their opponents.

3. *Stud requires memory.* If you're holding a pocket pair in Stud and catch an ace on fourth street, it's nice to know how many aces were folded on third. If there are no aces left in the deck, you probably have to abandon your hand. If you haven't seen an ace yet, however, you probably have an easy raise. Many Hold'em players have a lot of trouble remembering folded cards, as this skill is entirely unnecessary in their game. (By the way, this is one of the many reasons I prefer Hold'em to Stud. Poker is not supposed to be about remembering folded cards—it's supposed to be about analyzing opponents' hands based on their playing patterns and tells. Just my opinion.)

Starting hand selection in Stud is straightforward enough—you want a pair higher than anybody's doorcard, or three big cards to a flush. There is, however, another major factor—how *live* your hand is. If you have three hearts, but there are four hearts showing in other players' hands, you might as well go ahead and fold on third street. But if there are no hearts out there, it is probably worth playing any three hearts at a full table. Similarly, if you start with pocket sevens but see one or more sevens exposed in your opponents' hands, there are very few situations where you will want to play. But if all your sevens are live, you can think about open-raising with a big door card and/or when there is only one overcard left to act behind you.

Although I do understand these basics, I'm really not a Stud player. This might explain why I found myself in a hole early in the 2000 FARGO Stud tournament. I lost about half my stack quickly, and assumed the other half would shortly follow. But then something strange happened. I started to raise in situations where I thought it very likely my opponents would fold—and they did. It didn't matter much what cards I had, if someone raised and I thought they were stealing, I reraised. If the bring-in was a tight player, I would raise with any decent doorcard and usually win the pot. It didn't matter that I couldn't play Stud. I could play tournament poker.

The deeper you get into a tournament, the less game-specific skills matter and the more tournament-specific skills apply. Concepts like stack-size management, stealing and restealing, and survival equity become much more important as the tournament draws near its end. On some level, all poker tournaments are the same after the first two hours, regardless of the game.

At the same time, any tournament is easier when your opponents are playing badly. And that day, even I could tell my opponents were playing badly. Folding to my reraises for one small bet. Failing to protect their bring-ins. In short, they were playing too tight, and that is the easiest thing to exploit at a poker table. All I had to do was bet, and so I bet. I kept betting, and the next thing I knew I was at the final table with a decent stack. To my left was a guy I had met just before the tournament started (Dad and I had breakfast with him, and Dad spilled his drink all over him). He had won several events at the major Foxwoods tournaments, derived some of his income from playing cards, and was a Mets fan to boot. Scott Byron became a good friend of mine in the days and weeks and years following FARGO2K. But on that Sunday, he trapped me by cold-calling my resteal with rolled-up trips, and taking a healthy chunk out of my stack when he made a full house. I ended up finishing fourth, my first ever cashing in an -ARGE event, for a gross earn of $246 (remember, -ARGE events are not about the money). Scott, of course, won it.

I flew back to D.C., pleased with my performance and already looking forward to ATLARGE2K1, just five months away. When the time
arrived, I rode up to Atlantic City as a passenger in Russell's car. From
Baltimore all the way to Atlantic City, we talked poker. Since then,
talking poker with Russell has been one of the highlights of each of
my weeks and most of my days. The next chapter will explain why.

13

♠ ♣ ♦ ♥

Talking Your Opponents to Death

You can't control your opponents. You never know for sure if a person will raise, fold, or call. This uncertainty frustrates the hell out of new players, so much so that many of them quit the game. They just can't stand to make a correct play and still lose the hand. They can't believe people will call with queen-high, or reraise with bottom pair. But bad players do these things all the time, and there is absolutely no way around it. People will play their hands however they want to, and there is nothing we can do to stop them. Or at least, that's what I thought before I met Russell Rosenblum.

Russell made a fortune by founding and then selling an Internet company back when people could make a fortune by doing such things. He put himself through law school and finished first in his class, despite once driving straight from a final exam to Baltimore–Washington International Airport so he could play in the World Series of Poker. Much of his success can be attributed to the way he reads people, the way he adapts his thinking to the individual person he's dealing with—whether that person is a customer, a professor, or a CEO. This ability to analyze people on the spot has obviously helped Russell at the poker table.

Russell is actually able to influence the actions of his opponents, to make them do what he wants them to do. This isn't easy, and it's not something anyone can learn just by reading a few books, let alone one chapter in one book. I will, however, show you how Russell does it and explain the logic behind it. After some practice at the poker table, you too could have opponents folding at your behest.

I sat across from Russell on one of those small, square card tables usually used for bridge, at the Washington, D.C., game in May of 2001. Only three other players had joined us, the rest were sitting at the felt-covered kitchen table where the usual Limit Hold'em game was raging. With an excess of players on this night, however, the host had started a second, smaller poker game—a game of Pot Limit Hold'em.

I fancied myself one of the big boys who didn't need to sit at the kiddy Limit Hold'em table. And I still loved big bet poker. I was fresh off a monster ATLARGE, and I had made a killing at the previous two home games. My confidence was back, and I knew what I was in for (more so than I did at BARGE2K, anyway). I was ready for my next Pot Limit experience.

The key players were Russell and I, the host (a loose-aggressive Limit player, but a more well-rounded Pot Limit player), and a highly aggressive and wild player. Occasionally one or two other people sat with us, but they usually didn't last long. This lineup created a nega-tive EV game for me, and I knew it even then. But this time I accepted it for what it was, and I was comfortable with the amount of money I was risking. Furthermore, I thought playing shorthanded Pot Limit with players of this caliber would be a positive EV play in the long run, even if it wasn't that night. We each had between $500 and $1,000 in front of us, and I was prepared to lose my stack and remain happy.

My first major confrontation occurred when the host was in the middle of a phone call, which wouldn't have been too strange, except that my confrontation was *with* the host. He had limped in preflop, and I raised on the button with ace–ten offsuit. While this was happening, he was trying to give someone directions to his house.

The flop came ten-high, and the host led right out for a pot-sized bet, about $40. Well, there was virtually no way he had an overpair based on the preflop action, so I happily played back at him with a pot-sized raise, $160 total. I got a little worried, though, when he called me. He was not the type of player to call a big bet without at least top pair and a strong kicker. I started thinking maybe he had played a big hand passively preflop, unlike his usual style, because he'd been dis-tracted by his phone call. He was still chatting into the receiver when the turn card arrived. It was nothing of consequence. The host checked. At this point I didn't see any way he could have the best hand, so I bet the pot—around $360. The host thought for a long while, at the same time explaining the minutiae of navigating the residential streets of Northwest D.C. Finally he folded, and I dragged the pot. When he eventually got off the phone, he told me he'd had ace–ten. "Do you want to know?" I said. He nodded. "We would've chopped," I told him truthfully.

"Well played," he said.

Ordinarily, of course, I wouldn't reveal information about my hand. But this was a friendly game, albeit a friendly game for serious stakes. Besides, I figured if everyone, including the other good players at the table, discussed the hands we played, I would probably learn something.

An interesting situation developed a few hands later. I had made a pot-sized bet on the flop with top pair, but two people called me. So I slowed down and checked the turn. It ended up getting checked around, and then the river gave me top two pair—queens and jacks. As the river didn't make any straights or flushes, it seemed to be a perfect card for me. I led out with a pot-sized bet. The aggressive, wild player then made a pot-sized raise. Russell folded, and now I had a decision. The nuts on this board were a small straight, and my opponent would have needed to hold six–four to make that straight. That seemed unlikely. Besides, six–four also would have been the nuts on the turn, so how could he have checked that hand then? If my opponent didn't have the straight, he'd need a set to beat me, another very unlikely holding since he had shown no aggression up to that point.

While all this was going through my head, Russell was talking to my opponent. He didn't seem to be saying anything important, just cryptic things like, "Matt has one of two hands." With Russell still chirping in the background, I finally decided that with this player's level of trickiness I had to call with my top two pair. So I called . . . and got shown the nut straight. Not only did he start with just six–four, he checked the nuts on the turn—allowing both his opponents to see a free river card—in the hopes of winning a bigger pot.

The very next hand the same player opened for a raise of $20, and the host and Russell both called. I looked down at two jacks and reraised the pot—$110 total. The blinds folded, and the aggressive player raised the pot *again*. The two other players folded, and now it was $270 more to me. Well, I didn't think I had much of a decision. For my opponent to raise UTG, and then reraise a player who had himself raised three other people . . . well, I just had to be up against a big pair. So I threw my hand in the muck, but not before showing it to my opponent. He then somehow managed to show me an ace and a jack in his own hand. Never did I imagine that such a holding was possible, even for a highly aggressive player like this one. I had just shown too much strength for him to be making that play, or so I thought.

If my range of hands there was JJ–AA, AK, and I would only fold JJ to the re-reraise, his play was terrible. But if I would fold AK and QQ as well, his play is actually pretty solid. Did he know I would fold a lot of hands for the third preflop raise? I don't know. But there is a Pot Limit Hold'em adage that says the first raise means nothing, the second raise doesn't mean much more, but the third raise is scary as hell. Maybe my opponent was counting on that.

The Pot Limit game broke when the Limit game got shorthanded. As we switched off our Pot Limit brains and moved our chips over to the $10–$20 table, Russell made sure to grab the seat immediately to my left. While it was good for my ego to know Russell considered me his most dangerous opponent, it was bad for my bankroll that I didn't fight harder for a different seat.

It didn't take long for Russell to use his position. I open-raised from middle position with two jacks and Russell immediately reraised. One of the loose players called the three bets cold from the small blind, and I called. The flop came down five–five–four. The small blind checked, and I bet out. I knew from experience that for Russell to three-bet *me* before the flop, and to raise me on this flop, that he almost certainly had two jacks beat. So when he did raise and the small blind called, I was ready to pay $10 (getting 16 to 1 on my money) hoping to spike a jack, and then reevaluate on the turn, giving serious consideration to folding. The turn did not bring a jack, and I checked it to Russell, who went right ahead and bet again. While the loose player pondered his next move, Russell said, "Matt's gonna check-raise." As soon as he said this, the small blind called. If he had mucked, I would have moaned and groaned, but probably paid off Russell with my jacks. With two opponents, however, I decided I could fold with a clear conscience. The river was another blank, and the loose player checked and called one final time. Now I was sure Russell would turn over queens, kings, or aces. But when the hands got turned up, it was ace–queen for the small blind and ace–four suited for Russell. He dragged the monster pot by virtue of the lone four in his hand.

I ended up winning some money that night, but all I kept thinking about over the next few days was how I'd never be as good as Russell—how I could never in a million years three-bet a solid player with ace–four suited and then somehow get the best hand to fold while at the same time earning value bets from a weaker hand. Even when Russell was dragging the pot I said, "There's no way you could have ace–four suited there."

"No, I did. I showed it," Russell kept saying. I'd never be that good.

Today, I am that good. Well, sometimes. At the very least I've closed much of the gap between me and Russell. And of course, I owe my improvement largely to Russell himself, as he slowly revealed to me his secrets over countless e-mails and telephone conversations. Let's analyze that last hand from the start.

First, I raised in middle position. Russell knew this action meant I had a pretty strong hand, therefore he should have folded a piece of trash like ace–four suited, right? Not necessarily. While folding would have been perfectly acceptable, Russell had some reasons to play. He knew I had to have a good hand, but I knew that he knew that, and he knew that I knew that he knew that. Therefore, unless I had a monster like aces or kings, it was going to be very difficult for me to play out of position against Russell's three-bet. I had to figure him for a big pair or ace–king; and Russell, knowing I would have to figure him for these hands, planned to just represent a big pair the entire way.

If the whole thing were that easy, it wouldn't have taken a player of Russell's caliber to pull it off. Let's move to the flop, where three of us still remained. The small blind's cold-call preflop was clearly a disaster for Russell. Loose player or not, the caller's range of hands had Russell crushed. The flop, however, changed things. Russell paired his four, and he knew he had likely moved ahead of the small blind, but may or may not have been ahead of me. When I came out betting, Russell could have chosen to flat-call, planning to raise the turn, or to raise right then and there. The idea, of course, is that he needed me to fold a hand like, say, two jacks. Russell decided to raise on the flop (and he made that decision instantly). He probably did this to get his information cheaper (although a delayed raise on the turn would have also been a fine choice). After both his opponents called, Russell decided he was probably ahead of the small blind, but probably not ahead of me. As he said in an e-mail, "I did not *know* where either of you were, but I had a general idea."

The sequence on the turn is what separates Russell from the rest of us mortals. Again, in his words (with the small blind's name changed), "There was no doubt in my mind that you were playing if Don folded. I really thought you might raise (giving me ace–king). Obviously I needed you to fold, and Don calling was the only way. . . . I basically induced his call to induce your fold."

Wow. Russell knew I would be much more inclined to call him down heads-up than in a three-way pot, although I'm not as sure as he that I was, indeed, calling if Don folded. This was back when I had a "raise or fold" mentality with a made hand in a multi-way pot. This situation, in fact, is a great example of why "raise or fold" is not a good hard and fast rule. It's true that, had I known my opponents' hands, my best play in this situation would have been to raise. But the next best play clearly would have been to call. Calling had a much higher EV than folding did here. Yes, it's rare that calling is the best play from a Fundamental Theorem of Poker (FTOP) standpoint. (The FTOP, formulated by David Sklansky, says that whenever you act in a different way than you would if you could see your opponent's cards, then your opponent gains. Calling with a made hand would rarely be the play you'd choose if you could see your opponent's cards.) Calling is often, however, the second-best play, and can be a very good option when folding and raising both seem like dangerous choices, as they did here.

Russell knew me well enough to know he needed a multi-way pot. That in itself is impressive. But far more impressive is that he knew what to say to make what he needed to happen happen. By saying, "Matt's gonna check-raise" Russell was telling Don to fold. He was saying, "Look out, it'll cost you two bets at least to see the river." So what did Don do? He called, of course. Just as people often act in a way opposite to the strength of their hands (strong when weak, weak when strong), people tend to do the opposite of what people tell them to do. Don's subconscious (or maybe even conscious) mind said something like, "You want me to fold, Russ? Screw you, I'm calling." And that, of course, is exactly what Russell wanted.

Russell surely did a lot of analysis in a few seconds at the table, but his technique had been developed over years of playing the game. Finding the precise nonchalant way of saying, "Matt's gonna check-raise," while still making the comment stand out was part natural Russell chatter, part luck (the play didn't *have* to work, after all), and part the product of many many similar situations Russell had been through at the poker table.

Despite all this subtlety, however, Russell's comment only worked because it followed hours of setup. There are some players who almost never talk at the table. Then suddenly they'll raise and say something like, "Let's see what happens." These people almost always have aces. Or, in the middle of a hand they will say something like, "Do you have a pair?" or "Do you really want to bet?" The other players are usually so surprised to hear anything at all from the Silent Sam of the group that they suspect something is up. They know Silent Sam is looking for a tell, or trying some mind trick, or something. And then all those comments, attempting to gain information, or use power of suggestion, or whatever, will be tuned out and wasted. But everyone was used to Russell's talking. He talks nonstop, so it stops being suspicious very quickly. This is exactly what Russell counts on.

"I am always talking to people in hands (even when I am not in myself). It creates a kind of control group. I get to compare reactions when a real hand is turned over to when one is not," he says.

Russell constantly notices how his opponents respond to his speeches. If one of them rolls his eyes at him all night, and then continues to roll his eyes during a big pot, that person is probably not nervous and usually has a big hand. But if that person suddenly acts very different, there's a good chance he has nothing.

Even more obviously, a player who's been jabbering back and forth with Russell all night, but then suddenly can't form a coherent sentence in the middle of a big pot, almost never has a hand. A player who can't speak properly is almost always bluffing anyway, as we learned in Chapter 5. But you can only get him to *try* to speak if you've been getting him to speak throughout the session. He'll know he'll be giving information away by clamming up, but he'll often end up giving away more information by speaking. A normally silent player, however, gives away nothing by remaining silent. This is why Russell always talks and always provokes people (that's his excuse, anyway).

An example of Russell's information gathering came during my hands with the very aggressive player in the pot limit game. Russell was talking to my opponent, even though he himself wasn't involved in the hands. Russell compared my opponent's reactions when he had the nuts to when he had ace–jack. And he picked up on something. "I may have called him with the jacks," Russell wrote to me. "He seemed a bit nervous." This was something I didn't notice at all—I only noticed the action, which dictated that I had to fold. Russell made a better read than I did, and he did it by talking.

Over the next few months, I tried my best to mimic my mentor's approach. I could never become Russell, but I could at least incorporate some of his weaponry into my game. I won't be able to keep up the chatter at every single poker table I play at, but I've learned there are certain tables where I can provide the noise. Because I want to provide that noise, I almost never wear sunglasses when I play. I don't want to give the appearance of a serious, silent player—I want my opponents to be having fun and chatting me up. I've learned that when they're talking, there are a lot of players out there who will just give me information. Some of them are even famous. Some of them even helped me win pots in one of the most prestigious poker tournaments in the world.

14

♠ ♣ ♦ ♥

The Tournament of Champions

The Tournament of Champions (TOC), when it was still in existence, was the second most respected tournament on the circuit. Only the WSOP main event was a more sought-after title. The TOC was the only tournament where participants had to qualify in order to play. Players couldn't just pony up the $2,000 entry fee—they had to prove their worth by winning a tournament sometime during the year leading up to the event. At the time of its inception, the TOC was also the only multiple games tournament. TOC participants had to play Hold'em, Omaha Eight-or-Better, and Seven-Card Stud to get to the final three tables. Those final three tables then played No Limit Hold'em for the championship.

In one of my initial forays into online poker, I qualified for the TOC through a free tournament on pokerpages.com. Despite Nolan Dalla's concern that the TOC was "a horrible investment," featuring the toughest field of the year, I planned a two-week Vegas vacation around the TOC and BARGE for August of 2001. I just couldn't resist the opportunity to play in the second most prestigious poker tournament in the world. I agreed with Nolan that it was a poor EV decision, but I thought the experience of playing against and learning from the best would be worth whatever I was sacrificing in equity.

The night before the event, I played a **supersatellite**—a smaller multitable tournament whose top prize is a seat in a larger tournament—in an attempt to gain a cheap entry into the TOC. I succeeded. Not only had I qualified for the big tournament, I would be freerolling in it. I had sold 35 percent of myself at face value before the trip, which more than covered the $480 I spent on supersatellites. I was playing for 65 percent of my action with no risk. There are few times in life and fewer times in poker when you truly have nothing to lose. Yet there I was, less than two years after taking up poker as a serious endeavor, with nothing to lose in the TOC.

On the morning of the first day of the three-day tournament, I ran into RGPer and 2000 TOC champion Spencer Sun. I met Spencer briefly at BARGE2K, and we had exchanged e-mails after I'd decided to make the trip to this tournament. As we walked to the coffee shop I asked Spencer, "So, as defending champion, what's the strategy for Day One?"

"Double up," Spencer said. "That's what I did." I asked if I should play reasonably conservatively, and Spencer said yes. "You don't have to take any unnecessary risks."

My first table was right next to the rail, and as I listened to tournament host Mike Sexton make his remarks I was surprised at the number of spectators lining the velvet ropes. And the cameras were everywhere. Would I get to make my first television appearance as a poker player? (I had appeared on a local news show as a "chess whiz" when I was in college—it was possibly the most misplaced label ever applied to anyone.)

I didn't recognize anyone at my table, and this was a good thing. My plan was to play tight, especially for the first hour and a half while I learned my opponents. As I folded, the spectators continued to watch from the nearby rail. I wondered how long they would stay before they got bored—there were ten hours of Day One play scheduled for the 402 entrants.

The TOC was supposed to be the toughest tournament field of the year. Somehow, the quality of play at my table was dreadful. We had a couple calling stations, one maniac, and a few weak-tighties. All this, and the nine seat hadn't arrived yet, putting dead money into pots. I had received a miracle of an opening table—I only hoped I could take advantage.

After about twenty minutes the maniac raised in late position and I looked down at queen–queen in the small blind. I three-bet, and the maniac immediately made it four bets. This time I just called. I checked and called the rest of the way, with the maniac betting every street. When the showdown came, the maniac turned over . . . queen–queen!

After twenty-five minutes of Hold'em, they announced, "We're changing games now, Omaha Eight-or-Better for thirty-five minutes." (There was more time per level for Omaha, because each hand takes longer.) The woman in the six seat asked in a midwestern accent, "What does 'eight or better' mean?" I promise you she was serious. The dealer explained the business about two winners and a low qualifier, and the woman nodded. I think she understood but had never heard the term "eight-or-better" before. Still, who pays $2,000 to enter a poker tournament without knowing the names of the games? Better yet, how did she qualify for this thing in the first place? The funny thing was that she played a poor, but not terrible, tight-passive game. The maniac and the calling stations at my table were playing much worse.

My stack didn't fluctuate much for the first hour and a half. I might have been slightly under the T5,000 we started with for a few hands, but for the most part I maintained a stack size of about T5,400 or so. I loved my table, and I thought my prospects for a productive first day were outstanding. Plus, the nine seat still hadn't shown up. I asked the dealer about this, and he said the seat was sold.

Two minutes later a tall, dark-haired man decked out in ultimate-bet.com gear appeared at our table. And he claimed the nine seat. "Excuse me, we don't want this player," I yelled to the floor. Phil Hellmuth, Jr., smiled. Then he sat down. The same Phil Hellmuth I watched on TV all through college was now on my right in the Tournament of Champions.

Phil wasted no time and, before anyone knew what happened, his stack of T4,000 had become T6,500, about what I had. Phil pressed every minuscule, and even nonexistent, advantage. He raised in early position with ace–eight offsuit. He raised in late position just about every time it got folded to him. On one hand, the maniac raised from the button, and Phil three-bet from the big blind. The maniac called, and Phil bet the flop dark. The flop came five–five–two rainbow, and the maniac raised. Phil reraised, the maniac called, and Phil bet the turn dark. The turn was something like a ten, and the maniac called.

Phil waited to see the river card before betting again. It was an ace, and Phil did bet. The maniac called, and Phil turned over ace–four suited. The maniac had three–three. One can only imagine how many chips Phil would have lost if a three had turned up.

I said something about how much Phil's stack had grown since he sat down.

"I'm just a lucky guy," he said.

In Stud, Phil entered a pot, and I completed the bet with split queens. I got one cold-caller, and Phil called. On fourth street I paired my doorcard queen, giving me trips. I bet the max, and my first opponent folded. Phil thought for a while, and then folded. As I dragged the pot he said, "Raise it." I looked at him, confused. "Just kidding, my cards are in the muck," he said.

I thought for a second, then said, "I wish you'd said, 'Raise it.'"

"Ha, ha!" Phil said. Maybe I was giving away too much information, but I wanted to get Hellmuth talking. I knew Hellmuth liked to give away information himself, and I needed him to start doing it. I felt strongly that Hellmuth would be vulnerable to the Russell chatter attack. Funny that I'd get the chance to try it on Hellmuth before Russell did.

Phil continued to press. In an Omaha pot, there were five players remaining on the river (I told you it was a great table), and Phil was last to act. It got checked to him, and he bet. He got two callers, and his nut-low took half the pot. For his high, he had only a pair of fives.

"Gutsy bet on the river there, Phil," I said.

"I was pretty sure I had the only nut-low," he said. "The question was, Was my pair of fives good enough to win the whole thing?" He raised his eyebrows and nodded. I tried to understand his question. He was pretty sure no one else had the nut-low, yet he was wondering if his pair of fives could be good for high. So what did he think everyone else had, second-nut-lows that couldn't beat a pair of fives, even accidentally? To me, the bet made little sense, as Hellmuth was in serious danger of being **quartered**—sharing the low with another nut-low and thus winning only a quarter of the chips in the middle. But as I said, he had been pushing the slimmest of edges.

A Stud hand came up that really got Hellmuth going. I had the bring-in with 2-6/2 (meaning I had a deuce and a six in the hole, and a deuce as my doorcard). An aggressive player showing a queen completed the bet. Phil called with a nine, and I called as well. On fourth, the queen caught a blank, Phil caught a jack, and I caught a six. The queen bet, and Phil raised. I looked at his board. Could he have made trip jacks? No way, he would have reraised on third. Could he have made two pair? Again, I thought it impossible for him to have flat-called third street with split nines. No, probably he paired his jack and that was it. He might have started with jack–ten or ace–jack in the hole, but I was almost sure I had him beat. So I reraised. To my surprise, the queen called, and Phil called. Fifth brought blanks all around. Checked to me, I bet, and both players called.

"Do you have trips?" Phil asked. "Or just two pair?" On sixth I caught another deuce to make deuces full. No one else caught a pair on board. I bet, and both players folded. "Ahhh!" Hellmuth roared.

"Was my hand no good before that?" I said.

"No, it was good. Two pair was good," Hellmuth said. "But you were a big dog."

"The best hand was an underdog there?" I said. Hellmuth didn't say anything for a few seconds. Finally he burst out.

"I'm not saying any more about it, that's fine. I'm trying to help you out, and you go making a wise comment, so that's it. Nice hand."

"I didn't make a wise comment," I said. Some more time went by, and I added, "You don't have to say anything else, but I didn't make a wise comment."

"Didn't you say something like, 'The best hand is an underdog?'" Phil said.

"It wasn't a wise comment, Phil, I was legitimately asking you. I don't know the odds for that situation. Is the best hand an underdog there?"

"Oh yeah, big dog. I mean you gotta figure you're up against queens over there and jacks over here, at least." Well, at most, actually.

"Right," I said.

"So, you're a big dog, I wouldn't have played your hand the way you did, I'll tell you that."

"Really?"

"I would've three-bet fourth, for sure," he said. "But I would've checked on fifth." This was, of course, utter nonsense. Phil hadn't checked anything resembling a hand all day. And now he wanted me to believe he would have checked two pair on fifth street in a multi-way pot. It didn't matter, I had won my victory, and by that I mean I still had Phil talking. But the pot was nice too.

A few hands later I had split queens and completed the bet. A weak-tight player thought for a while with a king showing. Another king was out there, and eventually he folded. By sixth I had made queens up and won uncontested. As I dragged the pot, the weak-tight player said, "Yeah, I didn't want to play my kings there." I looked at him.

"You folded split kings?" I said.

"Yeah, one of my kings was dead, and if you catch an ace I don't know where I am." I labeled him weak-tight, didn't I?

At this point Hellmuth woke up. "What did you fold?" he said.

"He says he folded split kings," I said.

"What? Oh, I tell you, if that had been me, I would have punished his ass," he said, meaning my ass. "I would have punished his ass, no question."

"They weren't good by the end," I said.

"They weren't good?" Phil said, incredulous.

"By the end," I said.

"Oh . . ." and Phil grumbled something I couldn't make out. I think I had tilted him.

A few hands later I got another queen, the high doorcard, and I raised Phil's bring-in with seven–seven in the hole. (My sevens were live.) Everyone folded to Hellmuth, who flat-called. On fourth we both caught blanks. I bet, and he called. On fifth I caught a blank, and Phil caught one of my sevens. I wanted Phil to prove he had a hand, so I bet again. "Raise it," Phil said, firing two big bets into the pot. Something smelled bad. He had three babies on board, had flat-called until fifth, and then popped me. And he was acting differently. Out of professional courtesy (or something like that) I won't say exactly what I noticed. But I had a read that Phil's hand was very strong—a read based on the principles of tells, and on everything I had observed while talking to Phil for the past few hours.

"All right, Phil, nice hand," I said as I mucked.

"What?!!!!" Phil screamed as he flipped over his pocket aces. "You didn't have the queen?"

"No, just a pocket pair," I said. Phil nodded.

At the first break I went back to my room and left Russell a message on his home phone. "Russell," I said. "I just wanted to let you know I've got Phil Hellmuth on tilt at the Tournament of Champions. Give me a call back if you feel like it."

When I sat back down after the break ended, it was more of the same. Phil returned to his routine of raising many a Hold'em hand. When it got folded to him on the button, he raised it once again. I looked down at ace–jack offsuit in the small blind.

"Reraise," I said as I slid more chips forward. The big blind folded, and Hellmuth called. The flop came jack–nine–two rainbow. "Bet," I said.

"Raise," Hellmuth said. Hmmmm. I had three-bet him before the flop, which I don't think anyone had done yet. Then I bet out on the flop, and he still raised me. And I thought he considered me a dangerous opponent. So he was representing an overpair. I didn't come to the TOC to get into a raising war with a world champion who was representing a bigger hand. But I also hadn't come to let Phil Hellmuth push me off top pair–top kicker. I flat-called, thinking that if I were ahead, he was drawing slim, and I would probably make more money by letting him continue to bet. And if I were behind, I'd lose the least by checking and calling, since I had no intention of folding. The turn was a blank. I checked. Phil bet. I called. The river was another deuce, giving me jacks up, which of course was my RGP screen name.

"Check, Phil," I said. He threw another bet into the pot. "Call, Phil," I said.

"Good call," he said. I flipped my hand over and took the pot. And then came the tirade.

"Aaaaaahhhhh! Now we're playing this game! Now we're playing this game! Three-betting me and calling me down. . . . I think we're gonna play some pots, yeah I have a feeling you and I are gonna play some pots! I'm gonna have aces and you're gonna call me down with ace-high."

"If you do that, it would be a great play," I said.

"They always call me down with ace-high, makes the game easier."

"I imagine it would."

I had him right where I wanted him.

After an orbit, it got folded to Phil in the small blind and he raised.
I had a hand I didn't want to play in the big blind, so I folded it. "You
should three-bet," Phil said. "It's good strategy." He then flipped over
ace–queen offsuit. "It was gonna be four bets that time," he said. I
wasn't sure if I was supposed to be scared by that. I was actually glad
he had decided to start four-betting me out of position with ace–queen
offsuit. It was great news!

It didn't matter, though. The floorman soon came over to our table,
presumably to high card a player. "Anybody rooting for anyone?"
Hellmuth said, staring at me. He didn't get the response he'd intended.

"Yeah, you, Phil," a woman who'd taken two pots from him said.

"You're all going," the floorman said. It was sad but true. They
were breaking our table—my beautiful fishy table where I had position on the only troublesome opponent, an opponent I had tilted.

As we got up to find our new seats, I walked over to Hellmuth.
"Phil," I said, and he turned to me. "I really enjoyed it," I said, shaking
his hand. He just smiled.

When I moved to my new table I had about T9,000 in chips—great
shape. But five hands at the new table convinced me that my miracle
was, indeed, over. Only one player even resembled a calling station.
Then there was one weak-tight player. And that was it. There would
not be nearly as many spots to grab chips. The best strategy would
probably have been to play uber-tight for the last few hours until Day
One ended and they redrew the tables.

Instead, I lost two pots on steals gone bad and went down to about
T6,000. I'd spent all day gathering chips only to lose a third of them
on two hands. By the last break I was down to about T4,500. With the
blinds at T150 and T300, and the betting at T300–T600, I would soon
need to start taking chances for chips.

Throughout the TOC I had this wonderful habit of coming back
from break and getting a monster in my first or second hand. The last
break of Day One was no exception. On one of the first hands, a tournament pro, Warren, raised from the cutoff. The button cold-called,

and I looked down at pocket kings in the small blind. Earlier in the day I would have raised with no hesitation. But now I was trying to accumulate some chips, and I wanted some deception. So I smooth-called. The big blind called behind me.

"Jeez, did anybody call?" Warren said. The flop came three small cards and a two flush. I checked, figuring one of the three players must have improved on the flop and I could get a check-raise in. Then all three players checked behind me. The turn brought the third flush card. I had trapped myself. But I bet . . . and all folded.

"I probably would have won it with a bet on the flop," the big blind said. I tried not to laugh. At least I had him completely fooled, even if I only won one bet from him. As the hand played out, I probably would have made more money if I'd reraised preflop. And that's what I should have done. It builds a pot, so the late position players will be tied to the hand if they flop anything. If my aim was to take a chance to grab some chips—and it was—reraising was clearly the best play.

But I did win a few chips, and now my stack was out of danger. I planned to play it cool the rest of the night, just stealing blinds and antes here and there.

The problem was those steals got expensive. In Stud, four players had folded to the bring-in, a weak-tight player, and I raised with next to nothing, hoping to pick up the bring-in and antes. An opponent on my left called, and the bring-in called. Fourth brought no apparent help to anyone. I bet, and both players called again. On fifth I caught a king and my opponents caught blanks, but I was done bluffing this multi-way pot. I checked, and both opponents checked behind me. On sixth street I caught open kings, the guy on my left caught a blank, and weak-tight caught a spade for three spades on board. Now I bet, because I thought it likely I had the best hand, and I didn't want to give my opponents a free river. The guy on my left called . . . and weak-tight raised all-in. Oh, no. He must have made his flush. Furious at myself for pushing this hand, and not so happy to be staring at a flush, I whipped my cards facedown and sent all six airborne into the muck. As I did so, a pro who was at the table (but not in the hand) nodded at me.

The other clown called—he had a low pair and a straight draw (how I didn't get more chips from this guy I don't know). Weak-tight, of course, had his flush. Someone asked the other player how he could have called. "I didn't think he had the flush," he said.

"I did," I muttered.

"Me too," the pro said.

"The guy hasn't bet without the nuts yet," Warren said.

While this was true, I was now down to T4,000 in chips. We only had about fifteen minutes before we finished for the day. I couldn't believe I would end up shortstacked after being in fine chip position for eleven hours.

It appeared my stack would dwindle some more when I got the bring-in with a four as my doorcard. I threw in my T100 and then looked at my hole cards . . . pocket fours. I was rolled up. All folded to an aggressive player to my immediate right, who raised. I flat-called, hoping to turn this into a big pot. I check-raised fourth, as I wanted to both disguise and protect my hand. My opponent called. He caught a card that might have given him a flush draw on fifth, and I caught a high card. I bet and he called. By sixth street he might have had a straight draw, a flush draw, or both. He called my bet again. The river gave me no help. I still had the same trip fours. I thought my opponent could easily have a small two pair, so I value bet. He thought for a while, and then mucked.

A few hands later Day One was over. I had T6,600 in chips—no monster stack, but 50 percent more than I'd had twenty minutes earlier. Still buzzing from my rolled-up trips, and "knowing" I would be at a different table the next day, I spoke to the guy on my right.

"You know I had rolled-up fours that last hand."

"Mmm, I had a big draw," he said. "A flush draw and a straight draw."

"Yeah, I figured you were drawing, I was just hoping to fill on the end."

"Did you?" Warren said, butting in. I shook my head. "And you bet the river anyway?"

"Yeah, was that a bad bet?" I said.

"Horrible," he said.

"Really?" I said. "I thought there were a lot of worse hands he might call me with."

"Is that really how you want to end your tournament? Throwing in your last six hundred against a guy who might have drawn out on you?"

Technically, it wasn't my last six hundred, as I would have had a (very) few chips remaining even if he had raised me.

"Yeah, I guess you're right," I said. "The bet makes sense in a ring game, but not in a tournament."

"Absolutely," he said. "The idea in Stud is to make them pay on sixth and check it down on seventh. Unless you have the nuts. Or if you don't have anything." And he was, absolutely, correct. I had made a hideous value bet for the situation. Sure, I might have squeezed out another six hundred if he had caught some weird two pair, but the risk of losing twelve hundred (most of my stack) if he had made his draw was far too great. I vowed not to make the same mistake the next day.

The floor personnel passed out plastic bags and labels. We were responsible for counting out our chips, writing our chip count on the label, and sticking it on the bag. It was a labor of love. A floorman came by and verified my stack. I then put the chips in the bag, and another floorman sealed and stapled it shut. It was cool.

My hotel roommate, John, was waiting for me outside the poker room. He congratulated me on getting through the day, and introduced me to his buddy Louis, who played regularly at Foxwoods with John. Louis was still in the tournament, and he said he'd had T30,000 at one point (the chip leader didn't even have that many). On the way back to the room John told me Louis was the nicest guy I'd ever meet, but one of the wildest card players. I'd find that out myself the next day.

Before I flew to Vegas, I told my friends my goal was to reach Day Two of the TOC. So if I'd been on a freeroll the day before, then Saturday morning felt like playing for the gold bracelet after I'd already made a deal to divide the prize money.

Between sleeping, showering, calling the family, and eating breakfast, I was running late. When I got to the poker area I had time only to check my seat assignment and find my seat. I did, and my chips were there waiting for me in their plastic bag. I ripped it open and counted my stack. I still had T6,600.

I looked to my left and laughed as I greeted my opponent there. It was the guy from the rolled-up fours hand the night before. I should have thought twice before telling him what I'd had. Then the player to my right spoke up.

"Matt, how you doing?" he said.

"Good, good," I said, trying to place him.

"You remember me, right? Louis?"

"Yeah, yeah, how are you?"

"Good, funny we're at the same table, huh?" It was funny. It might also have meant good things for my stack size. If Louis was as loose as my roommate John had said, I would get chances to pick up a few chips, as I had perfect position on him.

Louis got involved in a lot of pots early, usually for a raise. He seemed to be playing like a maniac, just as John had suggested. But he wasn't turning over total junk—I think he had at least ace–queen every time.

So I had him pegged as a loose player, but as someone who wouldn't raise without some kind of hand, when he raised in early position. I looked down at pocket eights. There was a decent chance Louis had an overpair, but if I flopped a set on him I knew he would pay me forever. I thought I could outplay him after the flop, and I needed to take a chance to get some chips. So I cold-called the T800. The small blind cold-called as well and we took the flop three-handed. It came . . . eight–six–five with two to a flush. Oh baby. The small blind checked, Louis bet, and I raised (no sense letting the flush or a seven draw cheap; besides, Louis would pay me off, or even reraise). The small blind made it three bets! Louis, of course, called. I made it four bets. Both of my opponents called. The turn was a ten. They checked to me, and I bet. The small blind folded!? Louis called and said, "I need the river."

"Good luck," I said. My plan was to check behind him if a four, nine, or a flush card came. Anything else I would value bet. The river came five, giving me eights full. Louis checked, and I bet. He called, and my boat beat Louis's pocket queens. I had vaulted to almost 14,000 in chips, completely out of danger.

At the first break I told myself not to get involved in too many confrontations—to protect my stack. But that, as usual, didn't happen. Instead I won another big hand. I had a flush against trips in Stud, and I checked the river when I knew my opponent had been drawing for the boat, avoiding my mistake of a day earlier. By the next break I had around T22,000.

Then I really did go into stack maintenance mode. (By the way, I would never do this today. My philosophy now is to keep accumulating chips until the tournament is won. This was *not* my philosophy when I played the TOC.) I played tight for the next few hours, until the blinds got to be just enough where I needed to steal them every once in a while. I picked up ace–queen–queen–eight in late position in Omaha. It got folded to me and I raised, hoping just to take the blinds. The small blind, a loose player, and a lunatic besides, called, and the big blind folded. Even though my hand was no monster, I didn't mind the call. The flop came jack–nine–three with two spades, and the lunatic bet right out. I raised, thinking my queens were likely good. The lunatic called. The turn brought the king of spades. The lunatic looked at his hole cards, and then bet. Wasn't this interesting? I knew he didn't have a real flush or he wouldn't have needed to check his hole cards. He might have been betting a baby flush, but he might have been betting a pair of jacks. This player had earlier *value bet* me on the river twice without being able to beat a pocket pair. I knew he was capable of having nothing. Crazy as it may have seemed to the casual observer of my hole cards, I called. The river was a ten, and now I had to call his bet with my broadway.

"I just have a small flush," he said, turning over the five–two of spades with, I believe, a jack and some random card.

"Unfortunately, that's good," I said, and mucked my hand. If I could have replayed one hand in the tournament, this would have been it. Sure, my opponent could have been bluffing, but there were too many ways he could have been bluffing with the best hand (which was essentially what he had done). Now I needed chips again.

The blinds went up to T500 and T1,000 for the last level (Hold'em) before dinner. I picked up king–ten offsuit on the button and open-raised. The small blind, a player I had pegged as weak-tight, reraised. The big blind folded, and I called. The flop came ace–ten–four, and the small blind bet. I decided to find out how much he liked his hand and raised. I found out he didn't like his hand. He groaned and muttered and looked frightened. Then he called. The turn was a blank, and he checked. I felt pretty certain he had a pocket pair of picture cards.

Normally if I put my opponent on a big pair I don't try to move him off it, especially in Limit Hold'em. But this player was tight, and I really didn't think he wanted to call T2,000 with a pair of jacks (or even queens or kings) here. So I bet. The player thought for a minute. Then he showed me ace–eight . . . and folded. Weak-tight, indeed. I nodded, dragged the pot, and shot my cards into the muck. If the ace–queen–queen–eight was the hand I wanted back, this hand was my shining moment.

By dinner break there were about 90 players left out of the 402 who had started the tournament, and the 201 who had started Day Two; 45 would finish in the money, and get at least $4,000 for their trouble. The winner would get $203,722.

John, even though he hadn't played the event, snuck into the lounge for the players' complimentary buffet, yielding to the peer pressure I'd applied. We didn't talk much strategy, just enjoyed the food and grabbed free hats from Planet Poker. The day before, Planet Poker had given me a free T-shirt; but I'd also given them twenty bucks in exchange for *Mike Caro's Book of Tells*.

"Kamikaze is still in the tournament, surprisingly," John said. Kamikaze, a player I didn't know, was apparently a maniac's maniac.

I wasn't in immediate chip danger after dinner, and I didn't get involved too much during the first Hold'em round. I did get to spend some time watching two new players at my table. One was a guy two to my right named Freddy, who played a wildly loose-aggressive game. The other was four or five seats to my left. He was the man John called Kamikaze. Kamikaze raised with about 40 percent of his hands. He always did it with a sneer, and he was always really upset when his flush draw didn't get there or when his hand was no good or when anything at all didn't go his way.

I was still in fine shape when we moved to Omaha, where I picked up ace–four–king–jack with a suited ace. I raised, and got called by Kamikaze (who could have had anything) and a loose player in the big blind. The flop came king–seven–two with two of my suit. The loose player bet, I raised, Kamikaze called two bets cold (I actually liked this call), but the loose player reraised. The loose player was overly aggressive but not a maniac. I couldn't think of a hand he'd be reraising with besides a set. The other possibility would have been the nut flush draw, but I had that in my hand. I flat-called and so did Kamikaze. The turn brought an offsuit jack, which gave me top two pair. The loose player bet out, and I just called, still feeling I needed a flush card, a king, or maybe a jack to win the high. I thought any low card other than a four would give me the low. I prayed for a flush card three on the river, but instead I got an offsuit six. The loose player bet, and I called with my second nut low and top two pair. Kamikaze overcalled. The loose player turned over K–K–xx (two irrelevant cards)—the nut-high on the flop which was still the nut-high on the river. I turned over my ace–four, and Kamikaze looked, disgusted, at his hand. This was beautiful, I would get half of a monster pot and I would be in great shape. But then Kamikaze turned his cards over, and he had an ace–four! It was the most painful slowroll of my life. Instead of getting half the pot, I would get a quarter of it. Since I was nearly all-in after calling the river, my stack would be about half as large as I'd anticipated.

This pot started a downward trend, and my chips were bleeding away. By the next break we were down to about 55 people, but I was shortstacked. I would need to make some kind of move, or I was certain to be eliminated just out of the money. I saw Phil Hellmuth, who was still very much in the tournament, and without preface I said, "I'm shortstacked."

"How much do you have?" he said.

"About fourteen thousand," I said. He nodded. He knew, as I did, that I was in trouble.

When we returned from break the game was Hold'em, and the limits were T1,000 and T2,000. I couldn't expect to receive a big hand right after every break ended, so I figured I'd have to pick a blind to go after. The first hand was dealt, and I looked down at queen–queen in early position. The break gods hadn't abandoned me yet.

"Raise," I said, and all folded to Freddy in the big blind. He started thinking. That he was thinking got me praying for a call. This man would have called instantly with any kind of hand, so I knew he had nothing. He seemed about to fold, and I did my best to appear nervous. Maybe it worked, because he threw another T1,000 into the pot.

The flop came jack-high with two rags. Freddy checked, I bet, and

Freddy raised. I reraised, and Freddy made a short reraise all-in. We turned our hands up and he had jack–five suited. The flop didn't contain a five, or a flush draw. No jack or five came to save him. Freddy was out, and I had moved back up to T20,000.

On the other side of the table, Kamikaze had lost some big pots and was down to about T6,000. When he had sat down he had a mountain-sized stack. Now that he'd lost it he seemed unsure of where he was. Kamikaze didn't know any way to play except raise, raise, raise. He still tried to raise every once in a while and even survived some confrontations, but I knew his chips weren't long for the tournament. I waited for a slightly better than average hand to take against him and go for his remaining chips.

Sure enough, I picked up ace–ten offsuit in late position on Kamikaze's big blind. I raised, all folded to him, and he called immediately. I was pretty sure he had at least two cards, but the dealer might only have given him one. The flop came queen–jack–two, and Kamikaze bet right out. I raised, and Kamikaze made a short reraise all-in. I called, and we flipped the cards over. He had king–ten. The straight draw was Kamikaze's only out as a king would have given me broadway. None of his seven outs (I had one of his aces) came, and I had busted not one, but two lunatics. We were down to fifty players.

The scene as we approached the money was chaos. As the fiftieth, forty-ninth, and forty-eighth place finishers were eliminated, more and more players would go to the floorman to make sure of the situation. There was one guy who must have asked how many players were left every two minutes. I know, because he was at my table and sitting in my seat.

Many top players were still alive, and most had big stacks. Hellmuth had a big stack, Scotty Nguyen had a big stack, and T. J. Cloutier had a big stack after starting the day with under T2,000. Reigning world champion Chris Ferguson was hanging in with the shortest stack of anyone. Tournament pros Daniel Negreanu and John Bonetti each had monster stacks earlier in the day, but both were eliminated just a few spots away from the money.

When the forty-seventh place finisher busted, the action stopped and it was time to go hand-for-hand. As you might remember, this means that each of the six tables would start dealing a hand at the same time, and they wouldn't deal another hand until every table had finished the first one. When I play a tournament, I play to maximize my expectation, not sneak into the money with no chips. This time, however, a part of me was praying that I'd find a hand I could fold every time.

Perhaps to ease the tension, tournament host Mike Sexton announced which nations were still alive for the international trophy, awarded to the country represented by the foreigner who places highest in the event. When Sexton finished, Scotty Nguyen yelled, "What about Vietnam?" Sexton explained that in order to be eligible for the international trophy, a nation had to have a card room that hosted poker tournaments. Scotty's home country was thus ineligible. As the agony of hand-for-hand went on, Scotty jumped from his chair, his trademark Michelob in hand, and said, "Anybody want to go to Vietnam for a tournament?"

At one point I tried to steal some blinds, but I got caught and became a true short stack. It wasn't yet a crisis situation. I figured I'd wait until someone got knocked out, which had to happen soon, and then start gambling.

Except after about twenty-five minutes of hand-for-hand play, the only players who had gone all-in had doubled up, and we weren't any closer than we had been after losing player number forty-seven. The tournament director got on the microphone and said, "There has been a proposal that we stop playing hand-for-hand and instead return to normal dealing. Does anyone object to this?" If he had taken a closed ballot vote, I'm sure several people would have preferred to continue hand-for-hand. But it's one thing to cast a private vote, and another thing to raise one's hand as the lone objector when forty-five other players seem unified against you. Incidentally, I would not have objected even in a closed ballot vote. I wanted to get this over with as soon as possible.

No one raised a hand in objection, and the director asked, incredulous, "No one objects to this?" Still no hands. "Okay then, dealers, shuffle up and deal normally."

Our dealer, a young, chubby guy from Kentucky, said as he shuffled, "Man, imagine that guy who finishes forty-sixth?" I glared at him.

"Imagine him?" I said. "You're looking at him." I believed it too. I'd been telling myself all day that I would finish forty-sixth. I would take some risk to pick up chips when everyone else was playing tight, and I would get knocked out by a big stack playing sheriff. I knew it would happen. But I forced myself to *un*know it as I folded hand after hand.

As more time went on, a forty-sixth place finish for me seemed even more likely. First, at the table behind me, Chris Ferguson had been forced to go all-in with some lousy Omaha hand that happened to contain a deuce. On the flop he was drawing next to dead, but the turn and river both were deuces, and Jesus's trips kept him alive. Then, a player went all-in with a pair of eights in Stud. He was against aces up. As the river card was dealt, one of the many players standing by to watch the action raised his arm in anticipation, but the all-in gentleman caught one of the two eights in the deck to remain in the tournament.

The "normal" dealing did allow more hands to be played, but it only increased the madness. Every time a player went all-in, half the players from the other tables would jump up to watch the action. Every time they would return to their tables, disappointed that we still had forty-six players left.

"We've got a player all-in over here," the table in front of me announced.

"He probably has the nuts," another player yelled. I don't think that guy had the nuts, but he too survived.

Eventually the director had to announce that all players were to remain in their seats until we knocked out one more person. It was that much of a mess.

By this time the T400 ante had taken a chunk from my already small stack. I realized that if I didn't go for some chips soon, I would have almost no chance of winning the tournament, even if I did sneak into the money. I decided, as I knew I eventually would, to go for some chips, one away from the money or not.

I got a four of clubs as my doorcard, and I had the bring-in. I looked at my hole cards—the queen and ten of clubs. Two other queens were out there, so although one of my overcards was not so live, it was also unlikely that either of the players with queens was paired up. The only other big card out there was an ace. And I hadn't played a hand in an hour. And everyone had heard me whining about how I didn't want to finish forty-sixth. So I brought it in for a full bet, thinking there was a good chance my opponents would fold, and I would pick up the antes.

Both of the queens did fold . . . but the ace raised. Okay, the play didn't work. But my clubs were live, and I was getting about 6 to 1 on a call. I decided to see fourth street and go to the river if it was a club. Fourth street came, the ace caught a baby, and I caught the six of clubs. Lord, this was everything. I couldn't get away from the hand now. All my chips would go in, and I would finish one out of the money, just as I knew I would. The ace bet and I called, knowing I didn't have enough chips to get my opponent to lay down his hand. The dealer burned a card and tossed me the most beautiful three of clubs I've ever seen. For all I know, my exhalation was audible. My opponent bet his T4,000, and I didn't bother to make a short raise all-in. It went in on sixth anyway when my opponent had a pair of fours showing to go with his ace. I called all-in for the first time in the tournament. My angry opponent had pocket sixes.

I stood up and waited. I had one of his sixes and one of his fours, but that still left him with two outs—two more than my heart could take. Mike Sexton came to the table as the river card was dealt. "Okay, he needs a six or four," he said, obviously rooting for the card to come. I didn't blame him, as we had been at forty-six players for about forty-five minutes, but it didn't endear him to me either. The dealer put out the river cards, and my opponent was still muttering about the flush (out of curiosity, what hand did he give me on fifth that he could beat?). I guess he thought that when someone else has a flush it's a good idea to take your time sweating your card, because that's what he did. He sat there for what seemed like hours without touching his river card. I thought I would have an aneurysm if he didn't reveal it soon, so finally I yelled out, "Sir, please turn the card over!" He did . . . and it was a deuce. I had doubled up. And before we even finished our next hand, two players at other tables (one of whom was Ferguson) busted and split the $4,000 forty-fifth place prize. I collapsed in my seat. It was over. I hadn't finished forty-sixth.

The kind directors gave us a break, and I called some of my backers (specifically, my parents and one friend) to give them the good news. Then I saw Spencer and asked him if he had any advice.

"How many chips do you have?" he said.

"About twenty-two thousand."

"And what are the blinds and antes?"

"Right now we're anteing four hundred and the bring-in is six hundred, but then we'll be moving up to Hold'em with blinds of one thousand and three thousand."

He thought. "See, the problem is you're a medium stack," he said.

"Yeah, so what do you think?"

"If you want to steal, do it in Stud, there's more value," he said. "And if you get shortstacked, pick a hand you like and go all-in with it." It sounded good to me.

We redrew seats for the final five tables. As we did, the directors announced, "Congratulations players, you have all qualified for next year's Tournament of Champions."

"I'll be here," I yelled out. Unfortunately, that tournament never took place. The TOC folded a few months after its 2001 event. That's what happens when tournaments try to exist independent of a sponsoring casino. Sexton, however, did eventually get to bring poker to the mainstream, when he became the commentator for the World Poker Tour two years later.

As far as I remember, only one of the players from my old table was at my new one. It was the loose-aggressive guy who had the set of kings against my kings up in Omaha. He was now to my immediate left.

Quickly I got dealt an ace for a doorcard, and after four or five players folded, I looked down at eight-eight in the hole. I raised, and my friend to my left called. The rest of the field, including the bring-in, folded. On fourth I caught a king, and my friend caught a blank. I bet, and he called. At this point I was ready to shut it down if I didn't improve—but I did improve. On fifth I caught another king, and my opponent caught a blank that was suited with his doorcard. I bet, and he called again. I now felt strongly that he had a flush draw, because I was representing aces up and he wasn't folding. But he was a loose player, and he might have just been calling me down with two small pair. On sixth street I caught a blank . . . and my friend caught a third card in his suit. I checked, and he bet. I thought my hand was too good to fold against a player like this one, and I called quickly. Did I have to call? The pot was laying me 7 to 1, but if I would face a bet on the river my effective odds were 4 to 1. There was probably at least a 20 percent chance I had the best hand, plus a small chance that I would improve (though one of my eights was dead). And I would still have about T6,000 left if I called twice. I think I had to call. At the same time, the hand I thought most likely for him was a flush, and this wasn't a ring game. My tournament survival was at stake. It was a close decision, and at the very least, I don't like that I decided so quickly.

The river brought me an ace, which was a very slight improvement that almost certainly didn't change anything if I was behind on sixth. I checked again, and my opponent bet. I called (this was forced after I called sixth). As you probably guessed by now, he did have the flush, and my three pair were worthless. I looked up at Spencer, who had been watching from the rail, and he shrugged his shoulders.

A few hands later a player immediately left of the bring-in completed the bet with an eight showing. I had split queens, and I raised after everyone folded to me. The bring-in folded, the eight called, and fourth street brought no help to either of us. I checked, looking to keep some chips if by some miracle this hand got checked to the end and my queens were no good. But my opponent bet, and I called all-in. We turned the cards over and he had split eights. "Oh, you had the queens," he said. No, you idiot, I raised an early position player, pot-committing myself and risking elimination from the Tournament of Champions, without a queen in the hole. On fifth I was still ahead, but sixth brought him a third eight, and I was drawing mighty slim. I looked up and shook my head. I think they caught my expression on camera. The dealer dealt seventh, and my opponent turned his card over first to see if he filled. He hadn't, so I still had a shot. The other times I'd been all-in in Stud tournaments, I'd taken my time sweating the river. But I didn't hold out much hope for this card so I looked at it quickly. It was a good card, as it gave me two pair. But two pair doesn't beat trips. After twenty-two hours of poker over the course of two days, I was out of the TOC.

I walked away from the table, and Mike Sexton shook my hand, saying something about how I had done well to recover from my all-in and finish in the money. I wanted to tell him to go fuck himself. I'm very glad I didn't.

I walked to some place where I had to produce my driver's license. I'd been paranoid the entire trip because my license still had my previous address on it. The worrier in me thought this inconsistency would somehow keep me from getting paid. But when I pointed out that I had a new address no one cared. I was handed forty $100 bills for my thirty-ninth place finish.

When I got to the rail, Spencer greeted me. "You had the best of it both times," he said.

The next day I slept till noon and watched the final table of the TOC from the bleachers. The late Brian Saltus played some truly inspired poker against the more experienced Scotty Nguyen and T. J. Cloutier (who both played brilliantly as well) to take the title and the $203,722 first prize.

I missed out on the big money, but still I was satisfied. I had taken what I'd learned about implied odds (the Louis hand), effective odds (the aces up versus flush hand, even though I lost it), semibluffing (the king–ten hand), and table talk (Phil Hellmuth) and turned it into $4,000 (well, I netted $2,820 after supersatellite costs and paying my backers). It was the second biggest tournament on earth, and I had been able to compete. I knew then that I could play this game, and play it well.

15

♠ ♣ ♦ ♥

Heads-up Theory

Kitchen table poker players often make inane statements like, "You need at least six guys for a poker game," and "Poker's no fun with just two or three people." This belief is not just confined to the kitchen. A lot of the crotchety types in low limit casino games refuse to play shorthanded. They somehow reason that with fewer people the pots will be smaller, and therefore it isn't worth it to play.

I love shorthanded games. You can play a lot more hands, the game goes much faster, the rake is smaller, and the skill factor is much greater than in a full game. This logic applies to even the shortest of shorthanded play—heads-up.

One-on-one poker is completely different from any other form (yes, even three-handed poker). In Limit Hold'em, for instance, any two cards are playable from the button because you are *always* in position against just one random hand (the button is the small blind in a heads-up game and is first to act before the flop). The world's leading poker authority would have a hard time convincing me that even two–three offsuit is unprofitable getting 3 to 1 immediate pot odds in position against a random hand. And against an opponent who folds too much, it is clear that any hand is playable in virtually any form of heads-up poker.

The adjustments needed to become a great heads-up player, however, go way beyond simply "play more hands." Your opponent will also be playing more hands, so you'll have more opportunities to observe and counter his playing patterns. You should know his play intimately. Does he cap the flop with any pair or draw? Only draws? Only pairs? Middle pairs and flush draws? Does he ever fold to a check-raise? Does he fold on the river in big pots? Does he call down with any ace-high? Does he fold preflop for one bet? What does he think my bets mean? You should be able to answer all of these questions after playing one opponent for a hundred hands or so.

The questions I ask myself tend to be more specific and more nuanced in heads-up matches than in full ring games. It's much harder to anticipate the actions of four or five opponents than it is to anticipate the action of one. In full games, then, there is not as much room for subtlety. I make much fancier plays (bluff-reraising the river, checking the turn and river in the hopes of check-raising, value betting king-high on the end) in heads-up matches than I would ever dream about making at a full table, and it's because I have much more information about my opponent to work with.

It is impossible to know too much about the enemy. It's not even enough to know that your opponent bets the flop whenever you check, because if he does, with what hands do you call? With what hands do you check-raise? What hands do you fold? It seems we have enough information to formulate exact answers to these questions, and we could . . . if this opponent were all-in. In that case, the solution would be to call with almost all your hands on every flop because of the pot size. But when both of you have plenty of chips, we need even more information about your opponent—specifically, how will he react to your check-raise or check-call? All auto-bettors are not created equal.

And, of course, you should know what to *do* even when you have a very precise read on your opponent's range of hands. In heads-up Limit Hold'em, it is often correct to call down with ace-high and, conversely, to value bet with bottom pair. It is often correct to play top pair as though it's the nuts, and to play extremely aggressively with draws and overcards. All the knowledge of your opponent in the world won't help you if you don't understand how his play affects the value of your own hand.

It might surprise you to learn that I much prefer heads-up Limit Hold'em to heads-up No Limit Hold'em. There are a lot more decisions in Limit Hold'em, as No Limit Hold'em often comes down to all-in or fold. Along those same lines, Limit Hold'em allows for more play. If my opponent and I both flop strong hands in No Limit Hold'em, there is almost no way to avoid getting all the chips in, and one of us is going broke. In Limit Hold'em it's much easier to minimize the damage in this situation. For this reason, Limit Hold'em matches rarely come down to who gets the better cards. The more skilled player wins far more often than he would in a No Limit heads-up match.

The downside to Limit Hold'em matches is that they take forever. It is impractical enough to have a heads-up tournament of any kind. Almost no casino in the world will spread a heads-up tournament where each match will take an hour or more, and I've never seen a heads-up Limit Hold'em tournament even at a home game (although such tournaments are possible through the beauty of online poker). So how do I get my real-world heads-up fix? I get it at FARGO.

Greg "Fossilman" Raymer hosts a self-dealt invitational No Limit Hold'em heads-up tournament in his home during every FARGO weekend. Or I should say, the event used to be held at his home. In the summer of 2004, Greg won a poker tournament that ended up changing his life. I can't understand why—the event was only the World Series of Poker championship, and first place was a paltry five million dollars. I am proud to count Greg as a friend, and offer my most heartfelt congratulations to the Fossilman, who is still touring the country with a champion's media following at press time. Understandably, Greg has moved the heads-up tournament, which has grown tremendously in popularity, away from his place of residence.

As a newcomer to the scene in October of 2000, I wasn't presumptuous enough to try to snag an invitation to Greg's event. But one year later, with four -RGE events under my belt, and having played a shorthanded tournament with Fossilman and four others in a hotel room minutes after I busted out of the TOC, I felt comfortable asking Greg for an invitation. I got one.

This wasn't like being invited to Augusta National for the Masters or anything, but I was eager to play a strictly heads-up tournament, my first ever. As the reader knows by now, I had played plenty of heads-up poker with friends from school, at home games in D.C., and at the end of satellites. But I'd never experienced an entire tournament of heads-up play.

Greg's was another impressive house—far too big for the three people who lived there. It didn't have any worm-shaped coffee tables on its floors or paint-splattered circular objects displayed on its walls, but in most other respects it was like the house from the home games in D.C. Unlike in D.C., however, this home game would require the entire ground floor, as we needed ten playing locations, one for every two people in the tournament.

The format was a stroke of genius—four flights of five people each, everyone in the flight played everyone else in the flight, and the winner of each flight advanced to the semifinals. Everyone was guaranteed to play at least four matches. I've yet to see another heads-up tournament with this structure, but I encourage online card rooms like PokerStars.com to incorporate it.

The draw was announced . . . and Russell and I were in the same flight.

"Find someone in your flight and start playing," Greg said. Russell and I looked at each other at the same time and said, "I'm not playing you first."

People found their ways to coffee tables, TV stands, or one of the three full-sized tables Greg had graciously set up for the occasion, and started dealing their matches. Russell and I found other people to play and went to separate parts of the house.

My first opponent was a very nice guy, around my father's age, who played way too tight. This was obvious from the first few hands. In a No Limit match, tight play is not as big a sin as it is in Limit. When the stacks are deep, tight play is a great strategy against an opponent who is consistently overbetting. You let him keep moving all-in, and you fold and fold until eventually you trap him with a strong hand. But I wasn't overbetting. In fact, I was underbetting the pot most of the time. And he wasn't playing "*good-tight*," folding early in an effort to lose the minimum. He was playing "*bad-tight*," often calling on the flop and/or the turn, only to fold on the end. All I had to do was bet.

His play was so exploitable that I actually wasn't sure what to do when he raised me on a flop with three low cards and I had two kings in my hand. Ordinarily, an overpair on the flop is a clear reraising hand in a heads-up match, even a No Limit match. With an overly tight opponent, however, it might have been best for me to just fold and let him continue to bleed his chips away until he was broke. Why should I ever bring about a showdown when I could continue taking his chips with no risk?

I didn't fold, though. I moved all-in. This play was certainly reasonable as well, especially since he might have just folded again. I guess he decided he'd had enough, though, because he called me with a pair and a gutshot. When he hit neither, I had won my opening match of the night.

I found Russell, and he too had won his first match. We avoided each other again, and I sat down to play against a tournament player whose game I respected and who had a Russell-like ability to table talk. My white-haired opponent billed the match as "the young punk against the old hippie." I didn't know about all that, but I knew I had a tough game ahead of me.

I dug myself a hole when I called a big river bet with ace–queen on a board containing a king and a queen. My opponent did indeed have a king, and I was crippled. Russell, who had already won his second match, walked by and couldn't believe I had called. "I'm not sure I call with ace–king there," he said. Today, Russell would not have been so incredulous. A huge part of heads-up success (especially in No Limit) is taking advantage of an opponent's aggression by calling him down with reasonable hands. Second pair–top kicker is certainly a reasonable heads-up hand. It's not a raising hand on the river, nor is it even an automatic call, but calling one pot-sized bet with it is not the head-spinning play Russell seemed to think it was.

I fought my way back, stealing some pots, getting paid off on some others. Eventually I had taken the chip lead, and the blinds started to get big. My opponent open-raised on the button, and I chose to reraise with ace–king. We got all the chips in, and I was up against pocket nines. My opponent dealt three babies on the flop and prospects weren't so good. Then he peeled the turn card from the top of the deck, looked at it, and set it facedown on the table. He dealt a blank on the river and started cheering, "Woohoo, I win!" Enjoying his act only a little, I flipped over the turn card and revealed an ace, winning me the pot and the match.

I was proud of this victory, not proud that I spiked an ace to win, but proud that I had recovered from a crippled stack against a good player to put myself in position to get lucky. I faced my next opponent with confidence. I confidently called his raise with five–four offsuit, "knowing" he had a big ace in his hand. So when I flopped a pair we got all our chips in, and he turned over . . . two queens. Whoops. Except when I spiked a second pair on the turn, I had scored another win and improved to 3 and 0 in my flight. "Sorry, I thought you had a big ace," I told my opponent.

"Yeah, I could see you thinking that," he said. This is still one of the stranger comments I've heard at a poker table.

Despite my win, this match was a failure. I had failed to learn anything about my opponent. I went in and made a read based on what kind of player I thought he might be. This kind of superficial judgment is inexcusable when you're heads-up, and you have plenty of time to study your opponent's tendencies. These days, I almost never win or lose a No Limit heads-up match in just a few hands. I want to gather information before I commit a serious amount of chips. I learned this lesson that night—funny, I learned it while *winning* a heads-up match.

Russell, meanwhile, didn't make this mistake. He waited out his opponent (the white-haired "hippie") and moved to 3 and 0 himself. The stage was now set. Teacher against student to see who would go undefeated through the flight and advance to the semifinals. "I just need a quick break," Russell said.

"Take your time," I said.

Russell taught me most of what I knew about poker. He was also the best reader of people I had encountered. I paced around Greg's kitchen wondering how I could play against someone who would always know what I had, and what I would do when I had it.

"I don't think I can beat him," I said to a friend who happened to be standing nearby.

"He doesn't think he can beat you," she said.

As tough an opponent as Russell was, my plan for the match was the simplest one yet—attack, attack, attack. I knew Russell wouldn't want to commit a lot of chips before the flop, when it's relatively hard to be a sizeable favorite. Russell would want to take flops cheaply and try to outplay me on the later streets. Since I didn't want him to outplay me on the later streets, and I knew he could outplay me on the later streets, my counterstrategy was straightforward. I would raise often before the flop, and come out swinging on a lot of flops. I would risk getting trapped by a big hand, hoping Russell would fold often enough to make this risk worthwhile, and I would force Russell to commit a lot of chips if he wanted to try to start bluff-raising me. And I would call him with anything resembling a hand if he *did* play back at me (you can't just commit a bunch of chips and then routinely fold). This is a brute force, hyperaggressive strategy, and I almost never use it. But my usual approach of taking flops and waiting for my opponent to make a mistake just wouldn't work against Russell. I thought my best chance was to lower the skill factor and increase the luck factor, which is essentially what the brute force strategy does.

We finally started dealing, and my approach worked. I raised my button almost every time, raised a bunch of times from the small blind, and folded the few times Russell raised. If Russell ever called, I would lead out on the flop and usually take down the pot. Russell just kept folding. Soon I had built up a 2 to 1 chip lead. I was surprised Russell hadn't played back at even one of my raises. He told me later he was completely card dead early in the match. While I'm sure that's true, Russell was still more than capable of reraising with nothing. I hadn't expected to take the lead so easily.

Then a strange hand happened. Russell limped from the button, and I checked on the big blind with the ten and eight of clubs. I liked the flop of ace–ten–five with two clubs, and I led out for a pot-sized bet. Almost immediately Russell said, "I'm all-in." It was a sizeable overbet, but Russell knew anything less than an all-in raise would pot commit him anyway, and he didn't want to give himself the chance to fold.

"Well, Russell," I said. "I may not have the best hand, but against you I have to call."

"No, you're ahead," Russell replied.

"Really?" I said. I flipped up my hand, and Russell was sick—rightly so, as he had ten–six without the six of clubs. With only two outs in the deck, Russell had about a 6 percent chance to win the pot (although his equity was about 17 percent, as there were many ways we could have ended up splitting). Of course, Russell had played his hand fine. As aggressive as I'd been playing, middle pair was plenty to play back with. The interesting thing is that my strategy had made

Russell do something very uncharacteristic of him, namely put in all his chips with a mediocre hand. I had forced Russell to play my style ("I'd just had enough," he said later), which was really all I could have hoped to accomplish. And I guess it was nice that I had him all-in with only 17 percent equity.

Russell was in even more trouble when the turn brought a low card that failed to pair the board. He had five outs to chop and two outs to scoop going into the river . . . and scoop he did when it came an offsuit six. Russell whooped and cackled. I moaned with a smile on my face. The sizeable (for a tournament held in a living room) rail just seemed stunned.

I managed to shake off this beat and retake the chip lead through more aggressive play. Russell, however, would not let himself get run over again. This time he played ram and jam poker with me. We exchanged raises, and the chip lead went back and forth. Raise, fold. Raise, fold. It went this way for a solid twenty minutes. With neither of us willing to commit all our chips, the blinds got all the way up to $10 and $20 (we only started with $100 each).

Finally we both found hands we liked. Russell made an all-in reraise, and I called quickly with pocket tens. Russell had an ace–king, and it was off to the races for 90 percent of the chips in play (I had Russell slightly covered). Before he put up the board, Russell shook my hand for a fine match. Whoever won this hand would almost certainly be the winner. It didn't really matter how the cards fell, though. I'd had a plan, implemented it well, and it had worked. I had played a strong match against my mentor (who happened to be one of the best players around), and probably deserved to win. That was more than enough.

When the cards came up, Russell did hit his ace. He then won the match on the next hand when I was forced all-in on the blind.

Let's review some of the basic ideas of heads-up strategy that came up over the course of these four matches.

1. *You're playing one specific opponent—figure him out.* It's impossible to say whether I should have moved in against my first opponent when I had KK without knowing how he had been

playing up to that point. Against Russell, moving all-in would've been beyond automatic. I'd been betting so many hands, an aware opponent like Russell would have to start raising with less than premium hands, and I would therefore have to reraise with a big overpair like KK. Against an opponent who had given every indication he would continue folding, however, the reraise made much less sense. The two kings could easily have been the worst hand! Hand values are always relative, and this is more true in heads-up poker than any other form. Be sure to learn your opponent's tendencies before committing a serious amount of chips without the nuts.

2. *After you've figured him out, adjust.* Make the plays to beat your opponent instead of waiting around to play his game. Against a tight-passive opponent, make a lot of small bets and fold to any aggression unless you have a monster. Against an overbettor, check and call with all your reasonable hands and let him bet them for you. And against a superb player like Russell, force the action by playing very aggressive. An expert can only counter naked aggression by playing back (or calling down) with his decent hands. His edge is much less than it would be if both players were forced to limp in for the flop. But whatever strategy you choose, it should be chosen to exploit your opponent, not because it happens to be your favorite way of playing.

3. *Use the bluff.* You'll be easy to play against if you have a strong hand every time you make a decent-sized bet. In my second match, I moved all-in on the river against the tournament pro with six-high. He folded instantly. If your gut tells you your opponent can't call a big bet, it's usually a good idea to make the bet. If you have the nuts whenever you bet, your opponent will stop paying you off. Sometimes you just have to bluff.

4. *Use the value bet.* Conversely, you can't bluff every time or your opponent can always call. Don't be afraid to make big bets with your big hands. You'll be amazed at how often some opponents will call. My favorite heads-up opponents are the ones who fold to all my small bets but call my big ones. This strategy is about the most exploitable strategy possible (besides folding every hand). I can just bluff with little risk and get enormous value

from my real hands. Too many players make the mistake of underbetting their big hands in a heads-up match. They reason that, heads-up, their opponent probably doesn't have anything, so they might as well sell the hand as cheaply as possible. What they fail to consider is that, heads-up, players are more inclined to call, thinking their opponent is bluffing. My least favorite heads-up opponents are the ones who, when they move all-in, could have the nuts or could have absolutely nothing. Be one of those players.

5. *Use the check-call.* I didn't employ this strategy in any of the four matches I just described, but checking and calling is a powerful tactic against overly aggressive opponents, especially ones capable of folding. Think about it. If I bet my small pairs and my opponent always folds, I win a tiny pot. If I check and call down an opponent who will bet with virtually any two cards, I make a lot more money in the long run. The downside is that I'm never giving my opponent a chance to fold, but this is more than made up for by the increase in my expected value. In the 2002 version of the Fossilman tournament, my lone loss (in the semifinals) came against a game theory expert who check-called me to death.

There is a book to be written about heads-up play (and maybe after a few thousand more matches I will write it), but the essential strategy can be summed up in one sentence: use every weapon at your disposal to exploit the weaknesses in your opponent. Don't be locked into any one style, and don't eliminate any particular play as something "you just don't do." The more ways you can counter an opponent's style of play, the more opponents you'll have an edge over.

16

♠ ♣ ♦ ♥

Analysis

Poker hands happen quickly. Every decision must be made in a minute or less, and most decisions are made in seconds. An entire hand takes just a few minutes, during which time thousands of dollars may get moved around. Unless, of course, you're playing in the World Rec. Gambling.Poker Tournament (WRGPT), in which case none of the above is true.

WRGPT is a poker tournament conducted entirely over e-mail. This is not to be confused with online poker (which we'll discuss in depth next chapter), where players bet and raise, and their actions are instantly transmitted to opponents all over the world. WRGPT is e-mail. Participants get a personal e-mail telling them what their hole cards are. They can then send one of the predefined commands, like MAKE $2,400 (raise to a total of $2,400), CALL (call any bet), or simply JAM (move all-in) to act on their hands. There is even an option to chat. To follow what's happening, the entire table gets an e-mail giving everyone's stack sizes, the button position, and the most recent action. When the last action for the hand takes place, everyone gets a summary e-mail.

In WRGPT, you usually have a day or more before you're required to act on your hand. (Most of the time, though, I just send an immediate response of FOLD.) The pace is excruciating. Blinds double every two weeks, which sounds slow but actually translates to only about six or seven hands on most tables, so the blinds actually go up *quickly*. The tournament still takes almost a year, as more than a thousand people play in it. And for the winner? Well, he or she gets the title of WRGPT champion. No money is involved.

I was skeptical when I entered my first WRGPT in 2000. How much fun and how worthwhile could it be? I couldn't win any money, I had to wait hours or days for my opponents to act, and a lot of those opponents weren't even taking the tournament seriously, at least in the early rounds.

I soon learned. There are a lot of fantastic things about this super-long tournament with the fast structure. As an RGPer pointed out, one of the fun things about WRGPT is that when you have aces, you have them all day, unlike in real poker when you only have them for a few minutes. In WRGPT, wherever you go—meetings, classes, sporting events, whatever—you still have those aces. Another great aspect of the tournament is that world class players enter it. Spencer Sun, 2000 TOC champion, Andy Bloch, two-time WPT finalist, and a former world champion whom I'll mention again soon all played in 2002. But what makes the WRGPT one of my favorite tournaments is the amount of time I have to analyze my hand while I'm still in the middle of it.

To improve as a player, it is vital to be able to analyze a hand away from the table, long after it has taken place. Doing a good postmortem analysis is not as easy as it might sound. It's tempting to find mistakes in every hand you lose, and brilliant decisions in every hand you win. The reality is that the result of a hand has no impact on how you played it. The most brilliant poker play ever made might have cost the guy who made it thousands of dollars. And atrocious plays win pots all the time. There is no surefire way to know whether a hand was played correctly. All we can do is think hard about what play has the highest EV, and discuss the situation with other players whose opinions we respect.

This is where the WRGPT comes in. It's the only tournament where you can do thorough analyses of hands *as they happen*, so there is no risk whatsoever of being influenced by results. In theory you can play your absolute best game in WRGPT, because you can consider every factor before acting. You can weigh your options for hours instead of seconds. I learn more in any given WRGPT than I do in probably four or five regular tournaments. I know I probably shouldn't learn more in a free tournament than I do in money tournaments, but in

WRGPT I have written records of all the action, an inordinate amount of time to think through my options, and Russell's input just by forwarding an e-mail. These things naturally lead to analysis ad nauseam. A lot of people dislike the WRGPT for its slowness and its number-intensive interface. I am a WRGPT junkie for those exact reasons.

I talked my roommate Ben into signing up with me for the 2000 version of the event. We started getting e-mails from dealer@elvis. warmfuzzies.com, and the tournament was underway. As we got to see a few hands, it became apparent that Ben would have the not-so-unusual experience of dealing with a maniac at his opening table. I'm talking about a true WRGPT maniac—someone who would move all-in preflop around 90 percent of the time. At the same table as this guy, Ben had no choice but to get involved with him at some point.

The test came when Ben raised with pocket nines and the maniac moved all-in behind him. The rest of the field folded, and Ben asked me what to do. It was obvious Ben was a favorite over his opponent's range of hands, but was he a big enough favorite to justify calling for all his chips when he might be able to find a better spot? I said that either play (calling or folding) would be reasonable. He would have to pick one on his own.

If I were approaching this situation today, I might tell Ben something like this: Your opponent is moving in with around 90 percent of his hands. So let's just say the maniac would move in with every hand except offsuit hands containing a deuce or a three with a kicker nine or lower (92o, 82o, 93o, 83o, etc.). In that case, he would be moving in with 88 percent of his hands. Against that range of hands, pocket nines have 70 percent equity. (I did this calculation, and all other range of hands calculations in this chapter, through a computer program called PokerStove, downloadable from www.pokerstove.com.) Is that enough to call? Hell yes. The maniac probably isn't long for the tournament, and against a reasonable range of hands people would move in with, you need aces or kings to have the 2.3 to 1 edge you have here. There is no question in my mind that this situation is a must-call in any tournament with a normal payout structure. The only time you should pass up an edge like this would be, for example, in the later stages of a super-satellite when folding every hand would virtually guarantee you a top prize. Of course, technically the WRGPT has no payout structure, but the idea is to play it as if it were the main event at the World Series of Poker. With T10,000 in starting chips, calling in this situation has an EV of T4,000. You increase your stack size 40 percent in the long run with a call here. Do you risk elimination? Of course you do. But I promise you'll have to risk elimination at some point in the event. Forty percent is not a marginal edge; it's a huge edge. Let me put it one other way—holding pocket nines in this spot is *better* than holding pocket kings against an opponent whose range of hands is 99–AA, AQ, AK.

When Ben played this hand, I didn't realize he had so much equity, and I didn't realize the importance of getting chips into the pot when you're more than a 2 to 1 favorite. I wasn't sure then if survival was more important than chip accumulation. Now I know, nothing is more important than chip accumulation. You need to increase your stack size by a factor of 100 in a 900-person tournament to have an average stack at the final table—and if you want a serious shot at the real money, you *need* an average stack at the final table. The question is, what is the best way to accumulate chips? Well, there are few better ways to accumulate chips than to call as a 2.3 to 1 favorite. It's automatic. Ben did call, and doubled up when he beat the maniac's monster 96o.

My own big decision came several rounds later. I was down to T7,150 in chips when I opened in early position for a standard raise with AQs. The player to my immediate left, "Action Bob," made a reraise that would set me all-in if I called. I had played with Action Bob at ATLARGE, and my impression was that he played like his name—loose, aggressive, giving action. But still, AQ was not a hand I ordinarily liked to call with for all my chips (these days, against an opponent I consider loose and aggressive, calling an all-in reraise with AQs for any kind of price would be close to automatic). I decided to consider what Action Bob might have. I ruled out aces or kings, figuring he would slowplay those hands. I thought he could have any big ace or medium pair, so I tried to calculate my equity against those hands with a pen and paper. It turns out that if I gave Action Bob a range of hands that included pairs from QQ–66 and big aces from AK–AT, my AQs had 52 percent equity. Not only was I getting a decent price, I was a favorite. This was the first time I can remember really thinking through my opponent's range of hands and determining my exact equity in a pot.

I called. Loose-aggressive Action Bob had two kings, and I got knocked out. I have since learned that "Action Bob" is one of those clever misnomers. Action Bob is as tight-solid a player as they come. He was more than capable of holding kings or aces in that situation, hands I hadn't included in his range. In fact, he happens to be one of the few WRGPT players against whom I might not have been correct to call in that spot. Does that mean I played the hand badly?

Absolutely not. We can only make decisions based on the information we have. I played the hand correctly based on the read I had on my opponent. It turned out I had a bad read, but I had no way of knowing that. My "read" was the *a priori* information I had about Action Bob. My "play" on this hand was what to do with that information. There is a difference between a bad read and a bad play. I played the hand correctly. It would've been easy to say I played the hand incorrectly, because I called with the worst hand and lost. But that is results-oriented thinking. The play was correct because it was the proper action based on the range of hands I gave Action Bob. The cards he actually held (in his E-mail) were irrelevant.

One year, three -ARG events, one TOC, and hundreds of conversations with Russell later, I considered myself a much better hand analyst. It turned out I would get the chance to test this theory. My first table of WRGPT 2001 included two strong players—RGPer friend Steve Landrum, and a guy named Chris "Jesus" Ferguson. Chris, the 2000 world champion, remembers his roots of free-play Internet poker and continues to play WRGPT every year, even as he consistently wins big money on the tournament circuit. He's one of the true class acts in the game.

Early in the tournament, I got dealt one of the trickiest No Limit Hold'em hands—two queens. To make my life even more difficult, Steve made a minimum raise to T100 from under the gun, and Jesus called behind him. Let's take our time and analyze every possible option for my action.

Fold—This is ridiculous. If I decide to only put additional money in the pot if I flop a set, I could still make money by calling here. Obviously we're not going to consider folding.

Call—Not quite as ridiculous, but I don't love this play either. By calling, we gain no further information about Steve's hand. It will be extremely difficult, therefore, to maximize our expected value when the flop brings low cards. Against a good player like Steve, it probably wouldn't be a great idea to raise such a flop—risking too much to win too little—because we'll usually have to fold to a reraise (giving him credit for KK or AA). If, however, we call on a flop of low cards, waiting to see the turn, we run the dual risk of folding the best hand on a later street *and* calling down the whole way, only to be shown a bigger overpair or set.

A truly disciplined player might be able to only play on if he flops a set of queens. But since there is almost no way this strategy maximizes our EV, it is only natural to try to make the difficult postflop decisions after calling preflop. Although we could fluke into the best strategy in this way, difficult decisions usually lead to losses in equity, in my experience.

Reraise—If we want to avoid all those excruciating postflop decisions, we need to reraise before the flop. We're not looking to get our entire stack in with this hand against a good player when we have T10,000 and blinds of T25 and T50. But it will be much easier to make the correct decisions after the flop if we gain some information preflop. The downside is we run the risk of getting blown off the hand without giving ourselves a chance to flop a set. That's a risk we probably have to take with QQ. Postflop play is just so difficult; we have to do something to make it easier.

So the next question is, how much should we reraise? I like to look at this by asking, what does my opponent least want me to do? Steve has a hand he was willing to play from under the gun. This means if we offer to let him see the flop for a few hundred more, he almost certainly won't fold based on the implied odds alone (we know Steve doesn't have a junk hand here; even his worst hands will have significant implied odds). Similarly, we know Steve will love it if we reraise to some absurd amount like T2,000. He'll be happy to move in with kings or aces, and he'll be happy he didn't get trapped into playing with anything else. A raise to T2,000 risks too much to win too little, and a raise to T400 offers Steve too good a price to play. It stands to reason, then, that the ideal raise should be somewhere in between, to something like T700 or so. When met with this raise, Steve should feel uncomfortable. He won't be getting enough of a price to call with his hands that need implied odds, and he'll still likely need kings or aces (and possibly ace–king) to reraise. If we were in Steve's seat, this is the raise size we'd least want to see, in my opinion. Therefore, that's the raise we should make.

I really like the argument I just gave, and faced with this situation today I'd definitely follow its logic and make it something like T700. The only problem is, most of this argument came from a conversation I had with Russell *after* I'd already acted. When I sent my message to the E-mail server, I'd typed MAKE $500, meaning I'd only be raising $400 more and offering Steve decent implied odds. Back then, I always reraised to four or five times the initial raise. With smaller stack sizes in relation to the blinds this reraise is not a bad play. The implied odds wouldn't have been nearly as big if Steve and I each had, say, T3,000 in front of us. With T10,000 each, though, the reraise to $500 has the problems I've already described.

The action got back to Steve, and he reraised another T1,150?! Jesus folded, and it was down to just the two of us. Let's look at the options for this stage.

Fold—A reasonable choice. Steve's play is screaming KK or AA. Why put in 12 percent of our remaining chips in an attempt to outrun such a big hand?

Call—Another reasonable choice. If Steve does have kings or aces, we will probably bust him on a queen-high flop. After committing 16.5 percent of his chips preflop, it will be extremely hard for him to get away from an overpair. Therefore, our implied odds are something like 9.28 to 1 (10,675 to 1,150). It's only about 7.5 to 1 against our flopping a set. It seems we make money by calling here.

Reraise—Hmm. Seems scary, since Steve is representing aces or kings. But let's put some numbers to this. A reraise should be an all-in reraise, because any other reraise completely pot commits us anyway, and we want to discourage him from calling if he happens to have AK (suited or not). If Steve's range of hands is only aces or kings, reraising is obviously a bad idea. What if he could also have AKs, and fold AKs to our reraise but call with AA and KK? Then our equity from moving in is $(.25)(T2,325) -$ $(.75)(T5,816) = -T3,781$ (there are four ways he can have AKs and twelve ways he can have kings or aces—so we win the pot 4/16 of the time, when he folds his AKs, and we lose T5,816 on average the other 12/16 of the time, when we get called by aces or kings). Not so good. What if we throw in AKo to his range hands and still assume he'll only call our reraise with AA and KK? Our equity is then $(.57)(T2,325) - (.43)(T5,816) = -T1,172$. Better, but still pretty bad. Since this range of hands is already bigger than the range I gave Steve (KK and AA), it's pretty clear that reraising is not a profitable play. Let's rule out this choice.

This is the analysis I would make now, and it was also the analysis I made then. I called, and the flop came king-high rainbow, uncoordinated. Steve then led out for an underbet—a bet significantly smaller than the size of the pot—of T1,500. This part of the hand doesn't require much analysis. Time to fold. Steve's range of hands crushes us to pieces.

I like to think I would've folded even on an eight-high flop, the correct play based on my read. We'll never know if I would've had the discipline to actually do it.

What did Steve actually have? I never found out, but I suspect it was KK, based on his preflop play combined with the underbet on the king-high flop. But maybe he was in WRGPT screwing-around mode and completely outplayed me with something like JTs. It doesn't really matter. I made what I thought were the best plays based on what I thought his ranges of hands were after each of his actions. Notice that if I had followed Russell's advice about making a bigger reraise preflop, Steve would've been forced to make a bigger re-reraise, and I could've folded my hand, saving chips compared to the way I played it. Of course, if a queen had flopped I'd be telling a different story, but the fact is that Steve got me to commit 16.5 percent of my stack preflop. That's not an ideal result of the preflop action if I was up against a big pair.

A few weeks later, as I struggled on in the tournament with the T8,350 I had left, my coworker and fellow WRGPT participant Kevin Maurer came by my cubicle. "I have a WRGPT question," he said. It was either answer it or do job-related work, so I told him to go right ahead. "Okay, blinds fifty and a hundred, twenty-five-dollar ante. Under the gun player limps for a hundred, next guy folds, I make it nine-hundred to go with pocket queens. The small blind calls, the limper calls. The flop comes jack–jack–jack. What do I do?"

Wow, the scariest full house you can flop with QQ! (Next to KKK or AAA, that is.) Although we have to be somewhat cautious about a slowplayed KK or AA in this situation, we're going to play this hand pretty strongly, and we're not going to fold in a heads-up pot. There are several reasons for this. One is that this is a good flop for QQ, and we can't go fearing monsters under the bed just because trips have flopped. Another is that typical players highly overvalue small pairs on a flop like this. They reason, "I've flopped a full house, only a jack can beat me," when in fact many other hands beat them. Unless we know something about our opponents (and Kevin didn't know much here), QQ has to be treated as pretty close to the nuts on this board.

Given that philosophy, let's look at Kevin's options after both opponents checked.

Check—Not a terrible idea. The downside is that it gives a free card to anyone holding an ace or a king, and it costs us EV against a player who would call down with a small pocket pair until the end. The upside is that it might induce a bluff on the turn, and it might save us money against an opponent who would call with an ace once but not twice (against such an opponent we could see the turn for free and bet if it wasn't an ace, making the same money when we're still ahead, but saving money when our opponent catches up). To me, the downside outweighs the upside. I don't really like checking here.

Bet—This lets us get value from smaller pocket pairs and even some aces, and makes our opponents pay if they want to draw out on us. This play costs us money against an opponent with total junk (like T9s or something) who would fold to our bet but possibly could have caught something or bluffed at the turn. Given the ranges of hands that would call our raise preflop (our opponents shouldn't have total junk), I like the betting option here.

Kevin did bet, T2,500, which was just under the pot size of T3,050. (Incidentally, Kevin's preflop raise size and flop bet size were both pretty reasonable, in my opinion. The preflop raise was a similar situation to my hand against Steve Landrum, and the flop bet was big enough to cut down his opponent's odds, but small enough not to be an absurd overbet.) The small blind then proceeded to raise the minimum, another T2,500. The limper mucked and the action was back on Kevin. What now?

Fold—No way. A minimum raise often means a monster, but so many players think 88 is a monster on this board. There's just no way we can fold getting 4.22 to 1 on our money here.

Call—A decent choice. The minimum raise is somewhat scary, and we're not *that* worried about free cards in a heads-up pot. If our opponent has a smaller pocket pair, he's essentially drawing dead. If our opponent is making this play with ace-high, he has at most six outs and probably fewer. And if our opponent has us beaten, we certainly don't want to be raising.

Reraise—To consider this option, we need to know how deep the players are. Kevin had T10,525 left, and his opponent barely had him covered. A reraise charges the maximum if our opponent has outs against us. But again, he probably is either drawing close to dead or has us beat. In that situation, raising is rarely the right play. And since Kevin does have a substantial amount of money behind, a player with KK, AA, or even a jack might leave him alive if Kevin just calls down (people like to milk their big hands and often forget to go all-in with them). Raising here seems to cost us money. We can always value bet later if our opponent checks to us. Calling is my preferred play.

Kevin did call. The turn card made Kevin's life much easier—it was a queen. We just moved ahead of AA and KK. Take all the arguments I made for calling on the flop, and they are doubly true on the turn. We're hardly worried about any free cards, and we could be drawing to one out ourselves. When Kevin's opponent bet T1,500, Kevin called. And when Kevin's opponent moved all-in on the river (which was an eight), Kevin called again. He had to. Our philosophy was to be cautious about someone holding AA or KK, but not to be scared silly into thinking someone flopped quads. Well, now we had AA and KK beaten. We probably weren't laying the hand down anyway, but we definitely weren't laying it down after the queen hit.

Unfortunately, Kevin got shown KJo and was eliminated from the WRGPT. You should be able to see, however, that he played his hand very well. Sometimes we play a hand as well as we can and still go broke.

This idea of just calling with a huge non-nut hand is one that Mike McDermott should've incorporated in that first scene of *Rounders*. On the river, KGB bets $15,000 into a $5,200 pot. This is a large overbet. Recall that the board is A♠9♠8♣9♥3♠. Now KGB is a good player, and Mike knows it. Further, Mike is a good player, and KGB knows it. So what hand does Mike hope to get a call from when he raises all-in for another $33,000? A nine? Highly unlikely, especially since Mike's check on the turn reeked of a trap. A flush? Also unlikely, for the same reason. It's doubtful KGB has 93, because he probably would've folded that preflop; and it's unlikely he has 98 because he probably would not have flat-called a large flop bet with that hand, preferring instead to raise. Even if KGB has 88, he will have a tough time calling as he could easily put Mike on the exact hand he has, namely nines full. So most of the time, the only hand that will call Mike's river raise is the hand KGB has—aces full of nines. Frankly I'm surprised KGB calls as fast as he does with that hand. If he gives Mike credit for making the same analysis we just made, he has to think there's a reasonable shot Mike has quad nines. I'm not saying KGB should fold (in fact I don't think he should), but I think he should think about it longer, especially if he believes Mike's raise is a value raise and not a bluff. Mike's best play when facing the enormous bet on the river is to just call. His hand is a huge underdog to the hands that call his value raise. In the final analysis then, Mike did not need to lose all his chips to KGB. He in fact made a $33,000 mistake by raising. Good thing it was just a movie.

I hope this chapter has illustrated the kind of thorough analysis a good player should go through when thinking about a poker hand, and how the WRGPT is a useful place to work on such analysis. You won't always be able to do it alone. You should discuss hands with other players you respect, post to the newsgroups, use PokerStove, and keep an open mind to different playing styles. Let logic, not results, prevail in your conclusions, and you'll improve as a player a lot faster than you ever thought you could.

17

♠ ♣ ♦ ♥

Online Poker

In the summer of 2003, a twenty-seven-year-old accountant from Springville, Tennessee, stunned the poker world when he won the main event at the World Series of Poker, capturing a gold bracelet and some $2.5 million. Incredibly, his name was Chris Moneymaker—he had the driver's license to prove it. But even more incredibly, Moneymaker had won his seat to the $10,000 tournament by entering a $40 buy-in supersatellite . . . on the Internet.

Online poker is exactly what it sounds like, poker played by real people sitting at their computers, in real time, for real money. Anyone who wishes can open up an account on an online card room, much as one would for a bank, and play poker under some screenname (as you know by now, my screenname is "jacksup"). There is no *requirement* to play for real money. Players can begin with **play money** games, where there is no real money at stake. I recommend playing for real money as soon as possible, however. Sites like PokerStars.com—host of the World Championship of Online Poker (WCOOP)—offer games as small as $.02–$.04. I know anyone reading this book can afford the 20¢ buy-in for those stakes.

Playing poker online is pretty straightforward for even the most novice computer users, and extremely intuitive for anyone who spends all his working days at a computer (as I do). Players click buttons to fold, call, and raise. Let's look at an example of an online poker interface.

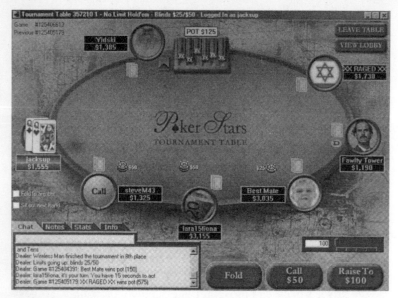

My Action

In this shot it's my turn to act in a No Limit Hold'em tournament (a satellite, actually), so the numbers below each player do not represent real money but tournament chips. Since it's my turn, there are buttons in the lower right-hand corner which read "Fold," "Call $50," and "Raise to $100." In order to raise more (which I should do), I have to type my raise amount in the box above the action buttons or use the scroll bar to the box's right. The circle with the "D" on it in front of "Fawlty Tower" is, of course, the dealer button, and you can see from the virtual chips that there has been one limper for T50. (In this actual hand, I raised to T250, and all folded to the limper who called. The flop came ace-high, and the limper led out for T300. I folded, and the limper clicked his button to "Show Cards" and revealed an AJo.) The current pot size is displayed at the top of the interface, and the virtual chips are moved to the center of the table at the end of each betting round.

The "N" under "steveM43"'s name indicates I have notes about that person's playing style. The displayed "N" is actually an invaluable feature that was unique to PokerStars for a long time. With the

"N," I know instantly if I have notes about a player, even when he first sits at my table. At some other sites, I either have to drag my mouse over a player to get my notes, or worse, right-click on his name and select the notes box. It's hard to remember to repeat this process for every new player who sits down.

Below is a situation where it is my big blind, and not yet my turn to act:

Not My Turn

This is from a $10–$20 Hold'em ring game, so the numbers below each player represent real money. Notice that instead of action buttons, I have checkboxes in the lower right-hand corner. These are called **advance action** checkboxes. I can click them now, and when the action gets to me I will automatically take whatever action I have checked. In this case, I could hypothetically click "Check/Fold." I could do that, but I would never. It is easy to spot an advance action check, because it occurs instantly. If the small blind limps, and I check instantly, he knows I probably don't have a hand I would've called a raise with (very few players use the "Check/Call Any" option). That's valuable information, and I'm not about to give it up to my opponents. Use of an advance-action box is the most classic example of an online tell.

Notice the chat box on the lower left-hand corner of the screen. This is where players can "talk" to their opponents by typing in comments, or things like "nh" (nice hand), "ty" (thank you), and "gg" (good game—this one is used when someone busts out of a tournament). Click the tabs on top of the chat box to instead view your notes on your opponents, your statistics for this poker session (flops seen, showdowns won, pots won without showdown, etc.), and information (in tournaments, this gives your chip position, the average stack, and the number of players left). The statistics are more a measure of the cards you've been seeing for one particular session than they are any kind of indicator about your play. We'll discuss how to gather and interpret statistics later in the chapter.

To pick your table, you must browse through the various options in the lobby, which looks something like this:

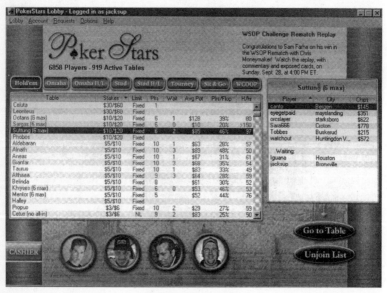

Poker Stars Lobby

This interface might look intimidating at first, but it's easy once you spend a few minutes familiarizing yourself with it. You probably recognize the names of the various ring games in the green bubbles (although the selected bubble, Hold'em, is brown) which I'll call "tabs." The "Tourney" tab is a listing of multi-table tournaments. The "Sit & Go" tab contains one- and two-table tournaments, plus heads-up matches. These start whenever enough people register for them, not at any particular time (hence the name "Sit and Go"). Finally, the WCOOP tab is for World Championship of Online Poker events.

In this screen shot, you can see there are plenty of Hold'em games going. To join one, you can go directly to the table by highlighting and double-clicking it (although you won't be able to play unless there's an empty seat). If the table is full, you can join its waiting list (notice that I am on the waiting list for table Suttung). But before picking a table, make sure you gather some info about it. The lobby tells you the average pot size (Avg Pot), percentage of players who see the flop (Plrs/Flop), and the average number of hands per hour (H/hr) for any given table. Bigger average pots and many players seeing the flop are generally better, because these things usually mean people are playing too loose and the game is good (although an ultratight game can, of course, also be profitable). And the last thing you want is a slow table. Anything under sixty hands an hour is totally unacceptable for online poker.

Finally, to play for real money, you'll have to get real money into your account. The most surefire way to do this is through a company called Neteller (www.neteller.com). You will have to create a Neteller account and use it to make a deposit to your online card room account. Neteller will ask for your bank account number, and you'll need to re-veal it. (Note: you do this anytime you write anyone a check.) Also, to establish a Neteller account in the first place, you'll have to give them your social security number. In essence, you'll have to trust them as much as you'd trust any company you'd work for, any school you'd attend, or any state that uses social security numbers on its driver's li-censes. Once Neteller is all configured, it takes a few days for money to actually move from your bank account to Neteller. Transferring from Neteller to online card rooms is done in minutes.

So now you know *how* to play poker online. Let me tell you *why* to play poker online.

1. *Shorthanded games.* There are only six players in the $10–$20 game shown on page 209. That's because only six are allowed at that particular table. As you know, I love shorthanded play. Online is the only place you can get a guaranteed shorthanded game—and you can get one anywhere. Every site has tables limited to five or six players set up specifically for five- or six-handed action. It's a beautiful thing.

2. *Speed.* A typical brick-and-mortar dealer will churn out 35 to 40 hands an hour. A typical online game gets 70 hands an hour, and shorthanded games can deal out 120 hands per hour or more. On top of this, you can play two or three tables at once. If you're playing three tables, all shorthanded, you might see 300 hands an hour and take the flop with 125 of them! This is much more exciting to me than a brick-and-mortar game where, on the average, you'll expect to see the flop three or four times during an hour of play. And, obviously, if you're a winning player, the more hands you see per hour, the more money you make.

3. *Accuracy.* There are no misdeals, illegal raises, string raises, accidentally mucked hands, floor decisions, ambiguous hand motions, dealer mistakes, misread hands, miscalled hands, incorrectly awarded pots, or exposed burn cards in online poker. There is no acting out of turn or shortchanging of the pot in online poker. Try to find a brick-and-mortar card room that can say any one of these things.

4. *Cost.* The rake online is less than it would be at an equivalent table in any brick-and-mortar card room. The reason for this should be obvious—who do you think has a bigger overhead, the Bellagio or PokerStars.com? And there is no tipping online. Keep track of how much you spend toking dealers and waitresses on your next casino trip. It adds up.

5. *Convenience.* Online poker is played from your home. You don't have to drive, you don't have to go to the ATM, and you don't have to adjust your schedule to play. You also never have to deal with drunken idiots, body odor, an annoying dealer, or a boring

sports game on television. You can play in your underwear while listening to They Might Be Giants if you want to (not that I've ever done that).

6. *Game selection.* You can scout out hundreds of games and get all the relevant statistics on them before deciding where to sit. This fact alone makes online play far more appealing than real-world poker.

7. *Heads-up matches.* Online poker is the only place where you can always find a heads-up match. You can play for any stakes, with anyone, at any time, and the rake is minimal (5 percent juice for the entire match, so $50 + $2.50, $100 + $5, etc.). I never play a full table online, except in multi-table tournaments. Otherwise, I am a shorthanded and heads-up specialist.

Having given these seven outstanding reasons why you should play poker online, let me briefly discuss some of the perceived draw-backs.

1. *Collusion.* It's easier to collude online because all you have to do is call up your buddy on the phone and tell him what cards you have. But a signaling system will get this done just as easily in a brick-and-mortar card room. Some would argue that the casino has cameras to catch colluders using such a system. That may be true, but online card rooms know the hole cards of every player in every hand they've ever been dealt. Armed with that informa-tion, online card rooms are at least as likely, and probably more likely, to detect collusion than their brick-and-mortar counter-parts. If you're still not convinced, talk to the PokerStars.com support team. They've snuffed out teams of colluders and re-funded thousands of dollars the colluders had stolen from honest players.

2. *Hacking.* Some people worry that hackers will break in to an on-line card room's system and learn the flop, or the hole cards of every player. If someone really could do this, and I think there are few if any people who could, don't you think that person could make a lot more money using his talents elsewhere, like by robbing someone's online bank account? Again, if you're not

convinced, contact the support team of your favorite online card room.

3. *Cheating from management.* Some fear that online card rooms rig the deck. The different conspiracy theories are numerous. Some say the software deals more big hands (straight flushes, quads, etc.) so that games are more fun. Some say it causes more bad beats so that bad players stay in action. These theories are fun. The only problem is, none of them make any sense. Online card rooms are a gold mine. They are guaranteed to make money with every hand they deal. If the managers of such a room got caught rigging the software, the room would lose all of its business. Why in the world would they risk such a disaster, when all they have to do is let their software run legitimately to rake in money hand after hand, hour after hour, day after day?

4. *Absence of body language.* Okay, yes, there are fewer tells in on-line poker than in brick-and-mortar poker, so as a player you are operating with less information. I promise that a good player still has plenty of edge just knowing poker fundamentals. Besides, part of the fun of playing online is picking up online tells, tells unique to that form of poker. If the only thing you love about poker is staring at your opponent's eyes, then online poker probably isn't for you. If you love anything else about the game, I strongly recommend giving online poker a shot.

5. *Legality.* It is unclear (to me, anyway) whether it is legal to play online poker in the United States. But to the best of my knowledge, no one at the time of this writing has been charged with, prosecuted for, or convicted of playing poker online. If the government decides to turn online poker into a legal battlefield, players should know about it in plenty of time to get their money out and stop playing before any of them are charged. The way I see it, until an authority figure declares online poker illegal and actually prosecutes someone for it, online poker is legitimate in the eyes of the law.

I began playing online during the last few weeks of 2000. I started out with the freerolls on PokerPages.com (which, of course, is how I qualified for the 2001 Tournament of Champions). By the spring of

2001, I had graduated to real-money online poker at ParadisePoker. com, then the only real place to get a game on the Internet. A lot of people, myself included, believed that Paradise essentially had a monopoly on the online poker world, and that any new site was competing for only a small fraction of the market.

We all couldn't have been more wrong. Over the last two years, online poker has exploded. Paradise is now the *fourth* largest online card room (in terms of average number of real-money players), behind PartyPoker.com, PokerStars.com, and Ultimatebet.com. There are plenty of other places to play, and having learned my lesson, I won't put it past any of them to break into the fray and emerge as one of the more popular sites. A good listing of online card rooms, complete with live reports on their activity, can be found at www.pokerpulse.com. As I write this, it is estimated that $43 million has been wagered in online poker rooms over the last twenty-four hours.

Here is a quick review of the Big Four online card rooms as of early 2004.

PartyPoker

has established itself as the biggest of the Big Four. Its signature event is its annual PartyPoker Million Limit Hold'em tournament, a World Poker Tour (WPT) event held on a cruise ship. Players on PartyPoker can win a cruise for two plus entry into the PartyPoker Million through satellites held online. In fact, I accomplished this feat in 2003.

What Matt likes: Party has the softest games you'll find anywhere, and the most players. In fact, every online player should have an account on Party simply because it's such a great moneymaking opportunity. Party's player base expanded exponentially as a result of the WPT. You won't find better game selection anywhere.

What Matt dislikes: The software and the technical support are terrible. I've tried to play many tournaments on Party that have either been delayed or canceled because of technical problems. I've also had a ton of trouble communicating anything to their technical support team. Network problems that I know are solvable have prevented me from playing on Party from my dorm room at Sarah Lawrence College. I still play at Party when I'm at a computer that can access it, but I will be forever leery of receiving any help from their side should things go wrong.

PokerStars

also experienced a meteoric rise through the online poker world. It offers great prizes throughout the year, including a trip to Australia and several seats in the Main Event of the World Series of Poker (WSOP), as Chris Moneymaker could testify. PokerStars also has its own cruise, complete with its own WPT event on board. Finally, PokerStars has the WCOOP, which has been a smashing success and will only get bigger. In 2003, an astonishing 891 entrants played the $1,000 buy-in WCOOP main event. Many of these people had earned their way in through the satellites and supersatellites that had been running constantly for the previous month. The total prize pool for the eleven-tournament series came to a whopping $2,716,100.

What Matt likes: Just about everything. The software is the best and the most reliable. The technical support team is light years above anyone else's. They add features to their games as players ask for them, whereas most other sites rarely change even the smallest things about their interface. The "N" signifying player notes is a great example of the adaptability and creativity of PokerStars. And PokerStars is the *only* place to play multi-table tournaments, in my opinion. Their tournaments go around the clock, and they are the most well run of any site. Nobody else could pull off something like the WCOOP, and PokerStars does it easily, complete with a floor supervisor monitoring the final table in case the players want to make deals.

What Matt dislikes: The ring games tend to be tougher than at any of the other Big Four, but the rise in popularity of online poker has made even Stars's games highly beatable. The truth is, I have no real complaints with PokerStars. I can play on Stars from Sarah Lawrence (because support fixed the same technical problem that still prevents me from playing on Party), and I enter four to five tournaments there a week. PokerStars is the primary site where I currently play.

UltimateBet (UB)

has name players like Phil Hellmuth, Jr., and Annie Duke stomping for it, even hosting tables online. Its signature event is a No Limit Hold'em World Poker Tour event held in Aruba. Players can win a trip to Aruba for two, plus entry into the event, through satellites on UB. I won this prize in 2003 as well.

What Matt likes: The interface is the best of the Big Four. UB always seats you in the center of a round table, which is nice. And even better, UB has Mini-View, one of the greatest features of online poker. Mini-View shrinks a Hold'em table so that it only takes up a small fraction of your monitor. I find Mini-View absolutely essential for playing two or more tables at once. Finally, UB gives hand histories instantly at the click of a button, so you can use this information in your very next hand. On any other Big Four site, hand histories must be e-mailed.

What Matt dislikes: UB's tournaments aren't as big or as reliable as Stars's. Also, the ring games are usually on the tougher side. And while the instant hand history is great, there is no easy way to have a hand history e-mailed. E-mailed hand histories are vital for statistics purposes. So, although UB is the most pleasing site to play at from an aesthetic standpoint, you won't find me playing there very often.

ParadisePoker

is an oldtimer in the Internet poker world, going all the way back to 1999. When PokerStars and PartyPoker started out, they borrowed a lot of features and ideas from Paradise. How the virtual tables have turned. Paradise got complacent, in my opinion, and they are no longer the best online card room for any one thing. Paradise does, however, remain a great place to play.

What Matt likes: The games are still good, and the fact is Paradise has been doing this longer than the other members of the Big Four. When you play at Paradise, you know you're playing on software and hardware that have been through everything a million times, and you know you have an experienced support team behind it in case anything does happen to go wrong.

What Matt dislikes: Paradise has been a real disappointment. Instead of being the pioneer for multi-table tournaments, high limit ring games, and satellites into WPT events, Paradise has had to follow everyone else—and they're not even doing a good job at that. I was still doing beta testing for PokerStars in the fall of 2001, when Paradise was a well-established site. Now Stars has a better interface, better tournaments, and better support than Paradise does. What does that tell you? I keep no money in my Paradise account at the moment.

As you can see, there are good reasons to play at all four of these sites (I have accounts on all of them), and I would recommend that all players try them out and form their own opinions. Be sure to get a **deposit bonus** when you first put money into your account. A deposit bonus is a gift—a thank you from the online card room to you for putting real money into play on their site. Typical deposit bonuses are 20 percent, up to $100, meaning if you deposit $500, you'll get $100 added to your account after you've played a certain number of hands (usually 500 or so). This free money is possibly *the* best feature of online poker.

So now you know how and why and where to play online poker. Let's talk about what strategy adjustments you need to make to succeed there.

My first piece of advice is, if you're prone to tilting do *not* play online poker. Online play lends itself to tilting. Clicking a button is just easier than reaching for real, physical chips from a stack and throwing them into a pot. The few seconds longer it takes to grab those chips might allow a tilting brick-and-mortar player to reconsider his actions and fold his hand. No such luxury online.

The buttons have other effects, too. It's more tempting to bluff. You don't have to worry about appearing calm or handling your chips evenly—all you have to do is click "Bet $10." I know this betting impulse was difficult for me to control when I first started playing online poker. I bet far too many hands for about a year before I got it right.

Another tricky aspect of playing online is learning when *not* to pay off an opponent's bet. Brick-and-mortar players schooled in the "strong-when-weak" theory of tells sometimes have trouble interpreting bets online. I know I did when I first started. Every bet online makes an emphatic sound of chips hitting the pot. Well, this is a sound of strength, so intuitively I think my opponent must be bluffing. The problem, of course, is that the opponent had nothing to do with the sound the software made. Online players *do* bluff more often (see below), but that doesn't mean you have to pay off with every last ace-high on the end. If you find yourself paying off too much, don't start folding to every bet on the river as an adjustment (we know that's a bad strategy). Instead, you might want to try turning off the sound at your table.

Because of the bet-button phenomenon I described earlier, and because online players tend to take the game more seriously than brick-and-mortar players, online games tend to be more aggressive than brick-and-mortar games, especially shorthanded. In a three-handed pot, I can check-raise from the small blind almost any time I want to, as the button will bet nearly 100 percent of the time if two players check to him on the flop. Check-raising and inducing bluffs should be major weapons in a successful online player's arsenal.

Online poker requires a higher level of discipline than brick-and-mortar poker. The temptation to play will be there twenty-four hours a day—don't fall into the trap of playing right before you go to sleep, or "just for a few minutes before work," or at any time when you don't feel 100 percent committed to playing your best poker. And don't be afraid to leave a table when you have a lousy image, when you're on tilt, or when you realize you just don't feel like playing anymore. Online games will *always* be there for you—and no matter how good a game is, I promise you'll find a game that good again. With the post-WPT boom in full swing, it's hard to find a bad poker game anywhere these days.

In addition to strong discipline, an online player needs strong money management skills. It's not the same as in a casino, where if you run out of cash in your pocket you can just hit the ATM. As I've already described, depositing money into online card rooms can be a tedious process. You'll want to make sure you have enough bankroll in your favorite online poker rooms to withstand more than just one bad session. At the same time, I don't recommend keeping more than a few thousand dollars in online card rooms at any given time, just in case something truly disastrous happens. I trust online card rooms with my money, but I'm not naïve enough to think those card rooms offer the same security as a bank. I don't trust *myself* to hold more than a few thousand dollars of my money.

While tells are not as prevalent online as in real life for obvious reasons, there is plenty of information to be gained by observing your opponents' online play. Here is a list of online tells to watch out for. The first five are based on the time it takes a person to respond. The last three are based on what players type into the chat window.

1. *The advanced-action boxes.* As already mentioned, players who use the check-in-turn advanced-action box usually have nothing, while players who bet or raise instantly usually have some kind of hand.

2. *The brief delay.* A delay of three or four seconds, followed by a bet or raise, usually indicates a very strong hand. The bettor/raiser is afraid that a quick response will give away his hand.

3. *The long delay.* A long delay, ten to twelve seconds or more, usually means your opponent is legitimately thinking about whether to call, fold, or raise with a weakish hand.

4. *The time request, followed by raise.* This is unique to Poker-Stars, the only site that allows players to request "Time" to consider their options when playing a hand (though every site *should* have this feature). A person who requests time, runs ten or fifteen seconds off his time bank, then raises, almost always has the nuts.

5. *The quick call.* Just as in real life, a person who calls a bet very quickly is usually on a draw. With a made hand, most players want to consider all three options (fold, call, or raise). With a draw, players don't want to show weakness by hesitating, but they don't want to raise either, so they usually call right away.

6. *The unprovoked chat.* Again, just as in real life, when a normally quiet person suddenly perks up in the chat window in the middle of a hand, that person almost always has a very strong holding.

7. *The hand revelation.* A person who types in, "I have JJ" usually has JJ, or something very close to it, like TT or QQ. This tell, by definition almost, would have to come from one of your less intelligent opponents.

8. *The angry chat.* Someone who types in "moron" or "lucky ****" or "amazing" is about to go on tilt. And usually this person isn't a very good player to begin with.

These tells all follow the same principles as real-life tells—players act strong when weak, and weak when strong. Pay attention and I'm sure you'll find even more tells on your own online opponents.

Online poker offers a unique opportunity to learn about your game. Through pieces of software like PokerStat (www.pokerstat.com) and PokerTracker (www.pokertracker.com), you can keep every hand you ever play in a database and analyze it later. This data keeping capability is useful for so many reasons. Yes, you can find out how tight or loose, or aggressive or passive you are playing and make adjustments based on the numbers. But you can also find out exactly how much money you earn every time you get dealt T9o, QJs, ATo, or any other hand. You might find you're doing better than you thought with some hands, and worse with others. This information is a huge help both for plugging leaks in your game, and for finding opportunities to add a few hands for profit. When I first started using PokerStat for short-handed play, I found that I was losing more money with A4o than any other hand. Before I kept statistics, I had reasoned that any ace was playable in a five-handed game. I was wrong. I now believe that A8o should be the minimum offsuit ace to raise with UTG five-handed. PokerStat helped me come to this conclusion.

Possibly the *best* part of your statistical database is the ability to keep track of your opponents' play. Wouldn't it be great to know how often each of your opponents see the flop, raise, win showdowns, bet the river, or raise the turn? Well, play often enough with the same people and you'll get this information through PokerStat or PokerTracker. The latter software in particular is very nice—it has a feature called "game time" that allows you to see statistics on each of your opponents *as you play*. PokerTracker also can request your hand histories for you, *and* retrieve them from your e-mail inbox on its own. These things make life incredibly easy. I now use PokerTracker exclusively.

One downside to these programs is the cost ($65 for PokerStat, $40 for PokerTracker, as of this writing). But you can try each of them out for free, they just stop working after a certain number of hands. And if you do get the full version, I promise either will pay for itself quickly.

Internet poker is the greatest thing since the electric guitar. It has helped me expand my game, and it has expanded my bank account in the process. I hope it does the same for everyone else reading this book, so long as you're not at my table.

18

♠ ♣ ♦ ♥

Running Bad

There is a difference between losing and being a loser. I might lose a hand, or have a losing session, or even have a losing weekend, but I still wouldn't be a loser. Losing is something that happens every time we play—no one has ever played a meaningful session of poker and won every hand. *Losers* are people who lose not just once in a while, but whose bankrolls are being steadily, inexorably depleted by the game.

From the time I started playing poker seriously until early 2002, I had never experienced a prolonged losing streak. I had never been a loser. Sure, I had a swoon at BARGE 2000, but that was just one bad trip. I got back to my winning ways as soon as I returned home.

When I booked nine winning sessions in my first nine tries online in 2002, I thought I had guaranteed another winning year. I was up $1,228—no way would I give that much back, right? I gave it all back and then some by the end of January. By the end of February I was stuck more than $3,000.

At that point I still wasn't worried. I'd lost $1,800 in ten tournaments, a totally insignificant sample size, and $1,200 in 115 hours of ring games, an amount easily attributable to luck in shorthanded $10–$20 and $5–$10.

By March, I was worried. I was stuck more than $5,600. I had never experienced more than a bad weekend or two of results before. Now, suddenly, I was digging deeper and deeper into the red, and I had become convinced it would be impossible for me to post a *winning* year. I was losing. But more than that, I was a loser. There was no way to argue the point. I was losing in the same D.C. game I'd spent the better part of two years crushing. I was losing in the online games that had looked so promising as the year started. I was losing during my Atlantic City trips. And I sure wasn't cashing in any tournaments.

I had told myself for a long time that such an extended bad run was possible. Other good players had warned me it would happen, and on a purely intellectual level I believed it would happen. It's simple statistics. A person who wins one big bet an hour with a standard deviation of 10 (a normal figure) has about a 5 percent chance of getting stuck 150 big bets after any given point in time. Throw in a few tournaments, where the best players in the world are underdogs to cash, and you've got a vicious losing streak. If you play long enough, it is inevitable.

I knew these facts, but just as I hadn't been truly prepared to dump $2,365 in one weekend at BARGE, I hadn't been truly prepared to lose $5,600 over a few months and continue playing. I didn't know how to react. I started e-mailing Russell dozens of hand histories, trying to figure out what was wrong. I kept telling myself I didn't need the money, but that failed to make me feel a whole lot better.

At some point in March, after a truly disastrous $10–$20 session in D.C., I decided I'd had enough. I wasn't going to quit poker (God forbid). And I wasn't going to whine that I kept getting unlucky. Instead, I decided to completely reconstruct my game from the bottom up. I would question every aspect of my strategy—what hands to play, when to open-raise, how aggressive to be after the flop, how often to pay off on the end—everything. I was losing too much money to not ask these questions and still live with myself. If I was going down, I was going down confident that I was playing a solid strategy and following that strategy at the table. No one wants to be a loser, even if he understands it's sometimes unavoidable.

Most people don't bother to work on their games when they're winning. They don't sit down and think about what hands are truly profitable from what positions, in what situations semibluffing is most useful, when to pay off with a marginal holding, how best to maintain and increase stack size in a tournament, or when to look to game theory to find the best play. They think, "Man, I'm running great! I'm going to sit in the biggest game I can afford and mop the floor with the tourists there. Then I'll go smoke a cigar." While it is a serious detriment to bring a losing image to the table—inviting your opponents to raise you where they would normally call or even fold—a losing streak can be the best thing that happens to a player.

I can say that because I was cocky when I was winning. Whenever I sat at the table I was confident I would take everyone's chips. I played like a winner, bold, aggressive, tough to read. Most of my opponents didn't want to mess around with me, which of course led to more winning. But I don't remember ever opening a poker book during a winning streak. Only twice do I remember having a winning session and then analyzing hands from it when I got home. A winning image is a powerful image to bring to a poker table, but a winning player is at great risk of becoming complacent.

Not only that, it is easy for a winner to go overboard with what he thinks are winning techniques. I was making money with razor-thin value bets in the five-handed games on Paradise Poker at the beginning of 2002. As I started reconstructing my game, one of the first things I noticed is that my value bets had gotten thinner and thinner until finally they weren't value bets anymore. They were stone bluffs.

More specifically, I had adopted a strategy of following through with my preflop raises by betting the flop, the turn, and the river virtually every time, in heads-up and even three-way pots. Betting the flop after raising preflop is generally correct, and you need to follow through with your semibluffs on the flop by betting the turn. But although betting the river with something like king-high will usually not have positive EV, I was betting even then. I did this so that my opponents wouldn't think they could call the turn and get a free river card. If this play increased the chances my opponents would muck the turn on future hands, then I would improve my overall EV at the expense of this particular hand.

The logic seemed sound. Here's why it was wrong.

While it is important to bet the flop after raising preflop, it shouldn't be done every single time. Something like 90 to 95 percent of the time is probably more appropriate. If I bet every time, my opponent might as well check to me every time—he'll be able to check-raise whenever he pleases. But betting the flop too often was probably the smallest leak in my play. Far more problematic was my strategy on the turn and river. It's important to follow through on a lot of flop bets with bets on the turn, especially with marginal hands that may still very well be best, like an unimproved AK, AQ, AJ, small pair, or even KQ. But continuing to bet my weakest holdings here was a serious mistake. Once my opponent calls the flop bet, I should need at least a draw to continue firing. Hands like 98 on a board of KJ26 should certainly be checked behind. Further, the idea of playing suboptimally on the river in the hopes of having a better overall strategy only works if it's done occasionally. I can't play suboptimally on the river every hand—how can that help my overall equity? Sklansky has written that good players should bet many hands on the flop, fewer hands on the turn, and even fewer hands on the river. He is right. I was staying aggressive with far too many hands on the later streets.

I was also overaggressive preflop. I never open-limped. I still never open-limp, as I believe it is correct for a good player to always raise when he's first into the pot. But I had a policy of never limping on the button, even when several people had limped in front of me. I was open-raising with about the correct frequency, but I was destroying my own implied odds when I raised three limpers with hands like 65s and Q9o. My logic had been that I never wanted to let the blinds see a flop for free. The problem was that I had to beat all the other hands as well. I wasn't increasing my chances of winning much by raising (because the blinds often called), and I was putting more money in the pot at a point when I didn't have positive equity if the action ended. This is not a good combination. The reason to play the so-called speculative hands on the button is to see a flop cheap and make up the equity through superior postflop play. There is little reason to force the issue by raising preflop. After thinking through this logic, I started limping more and raising less, and things improved.

Toning down my aggression in the appropriate places was the most noticeable adjustment I made in the restructuring of my game. The other adjustments were more mundane, but important nonetheless. For one, I found I had to play tighter. This was a simple finding for sure, but it certainly wasn't obvious to me at the time. From the first days of my Hold'em education I had been expanding the number of hands I played as I got better and better. Eventually, though, I was just playing too many hands. I'd play 24s on the button, 54o in late position, and

87o in middle position. I question whether anyone is good enough to play these hands for a profit in Limit Hold'em. I finally figured out that I wasn't, and reverted back to an extremely tight preflop starting strategy. I added hands one by one and didn't add another until I felt comfortable. Eventually I reached the point I'm at now—loose, for a good player, but much tighter than all the fish.

By the way, this flip-flopping from tight to loose and back is not an uncommon experience. Many thinking players start out tight, play looser and looser until they are playing close to optimally, continue to play looser and looser until they realize they've gone too far, and then start tightening up again. At some point they settle into the perfect spot on the loose-tight scale. Readers can try to avoid this meandering on the tightness scale in their own learning process, but it will be difficult and not necessarily even helpful. Playing too loose for a few months can make you a better player in the long run. You'll have better insight into how your loose opponents think, and you'll have experience for those situations where you might actually need to play junk hands. Remember, we're playing one long game of poker. The goal is not to maximize profit in today's session, but to maximize profit for life.

The last adjustment I made in reconstructing my game was mostly psychological. I simply had to execute my strategy better. I found that sometimes I would know the right play, but make a different play anyway. In my case it was usually that I would bet when I knew I should check. A byproduct of losing, for me, was that I grew less confident at the table and found myself not trusting my strategy. My knee-jerk reaction to this mistrust was to just bet whenever I wavered about a crucial decision (your reaction might be different). It took Russell to say to me, "I don't know what the fuck you're doing," before I actually realized I'd been deviating from good strategy at the table. Losing had blinded me from making an honest analysis. I had to force myself to stay disciplined enough to carry out my strategy, something that only comes by putting in the hours at the table, and being conscious of the problem. Eventually, I learned to always have reasons for my plays before I made them. This lesson may sound obvious, but it's easy to fall back into routine reactions like betting, and then come up with justifications for them after the fact. Question every play as it's being made. It worked for me.

The reconstruction of my play didn't take place over a day, a week, or even a month. I had to reanalyze every aspect of my game—a game I'd spent three years building, tweaking, rebuilding, rearranging, and adjusting. The changes I just discussed didn't come about in one moment of divine inspiration. I struggled along the way.

I "only" lost about $1,000 in April as I continued to go through my reconstruction period. I dumped another $1,600 in May, and yet another $600 in June. Still, I knew things were getting better. In April I had won a seat into the main event of the New England Poker Classic, and in June I had won a seat into the main event of the WCOOP. Even a small cash in either of these events would've turned around a lot of my losses. And I knew as I analyzed hands that I was playing better. I was sure my results would eventually turn around.

I did not finish with a winning year in 2002—far from it. But I'm happy to report that I recovered every penny I lost during that difficult year by the end of the next year. In fact, for the two-year period of 2002 through 2003, I made an amount in the five-figure range, and safely so. Not a bad comeback, for a grad student at least.

The thing is, I didn't find any of the leaks in my game until I started losing. The cards were good to me in 2003, but I also played much better than I did in 2002. I know I capitalized on my good cards because of the work I did during the losing streak.

Think what could happen if, as players, we analyzed and fine-tuned our games, not just during the bad times, but when we were running great. Could we avoid prolonged losing streaks entirely? Probably not, but I bet we would cut down on them. These days I constantly assess my game, instead of waiting to lose money first, and it has showed in my results.

We all know people who fail to show a lifetime profit in this game, yet insist they are just unlucky. They refuse to acknowledge that maybe there are gaping holes in their games, that maybe it isn't just bad luck that keeps costing them their chips, that maybe, just maybe, the other players are simply better than they are. These people, the ones who won't put in the effort needed to improve, are the real losers.

19

♠ ♣ ♦ ♥

Televised Poker and Me

The World Poker Tour (WPT) is the next huge thing in poker. I loved seeing poker on TV before the WPT came into existence in 2003. Now even I consider the pre-WPT broadcasts unwatchable. The WPT does something every televised poker tournament before it should've done—it plants cameras along the rail of the table so that viewers can see the players' hole cards. Where broadcasts of pre-WPT events showed few hands and offered little explanation, the WPT makes a conscious effort to let the audience follow the action. Many more hands are shown, and the specifics of every situation (blind sizes and bet sizes) are given. Viewers really can play along at home.

Since the WPT's inception, many of the casual acquaintances in my life—my barber, my next-door neighbor, people in the Student Affairs office at school—have flooded me with questions about the game. People hear I'm a poker player, and poker becomes the only topic of conversation for the next hour. They tell me who their favorite pro is, which one is the most scary, which one is the most arrogant, and it's all based on the WPT and WSOP shows (the latter are ESPN's contribution to the televised poker explosion). The effects of the series are also obvious in card rooms across the country. The Tuesday night tournament at Foxwoods, which only filled two or three tables when I was in college, now draws two hundred or more entrants every week.

The WPT seems like a gift from the poker gods, but rest assured, the WPT is not perfect. Vince Van Patten, who is one of the announcers along with Mike Sexton, spends much more time trying to make inane statements (I swear that's what he's trying to do) than actually discussing the poker. The WPT has also instituted a "no deals" policy for its tournaments, which I think is a mistake. Deals are a part of tournament poker because the players are the ones putting up the money. If I get heads-up with a very good player and there is $400,000 at stake, why in the world would I want to gamble for that kind of cash? I took the risk by buying in; I should have the right to lock in my equity if my opponent and I can reach an agreement.

There are those who say the WPT has diminished the game by forcing players to reveal their hole cards, and thus their style of play. They reason that normally hyperaggressive players like Layne Flack have been intimidated by the cameras into bluffing far less often. Well, that's their problem. Why should a player ever be too intimidated or embarrassed to make what he feels is the correct play? If I ever make a WPT final table broadcast, I will probably be nervous and possibly even make some hideous blunder, but I won't be changing my strategy. I will make the best possible decision I can, given the edgy state I am sure to be in.

A final beef some players have with the WPT is that it glamorizes poker in a way it was never meant to be glamorized. Poker should be played in dark smoky rooms, they say, the way it was in the Old West. As any reader who has come this far in the book could guess, I completely disagree with this opinion. I think the more poker is looked at as an intellectual exercise, free of cheats, **angle-shooters** (players who, while not technically cheating, engage in unethical behavior in an effort to gain an advantage at the table), and other unsavory types, the better the game will become. Today's players are mathematicians, game theorists, and dedicated poker professionals. Once this becomes clear to the public, more people will play, games everywhere will get better, and our collective theoretical understanding of the game will increase. Everyone will win.

The first tournament on American television to reveal the hole cards on every hand was the Ladbrokes Poker Million in 2000. Ladbrokes had cameras underneath the table surface, cameras that caught the hole cards on film before the players even looked at them (in the WPT, the cards are revealed only when a player lifts them off the felt). The final table was broadcast *live* across Europe and considered a success. The producers of other televised tournaments must have taken notice, because soon every televised tournament included some way of revealing a player's hole cards.

The WSOP producers decided to reveal the hole cards for its 2002 broadcast, although the method wasn't quite as sleek as the Poker Million's. The WSOP had a camera next to the dealer's rack, and as players turned their cards in, the dealer would flash them to that camera. The players' hole cards would then be spliced into the TV show during editing. This method didn't lend itself to a live broadcast of the tournament, but it was better than nothing.

Coincidentally, my mentor Russell decided to play his first WSOP main event in 2002. Naturally, I was a huge supporter of this decision, and even bought 1.5 percent of him. At some point during our many conversations on poker theory, Russell must have decided he respected my opinion on the game, because he called me during every break in the five-day tournament to talk strategy. The story of his experience deserves a book in its own right. For now I'll just show how being Russell's coach prepared me for big-time televised tournaments.

Russell spent the first three days of the main event playing brilliant poker, winning a ton of chips without showing down a hand, and always taking the best of it when he did get called. He twice had to come back from dire short stack situations, and each time he picked all the right spots and recovered to a healthy stack. Through fantastic play, and through his hands holding up when they were supposed to, Russell survived the first three days and got into the money at the Big One. We celebrated over the phone, ecstatic at the comebacks Team Russell had made.

But on Day Four, we had to do it again. Russell got all his chips in with ace–queen, calling twenty-two-year-old British phenom Julian Gardner's re-reraise. Julian had ace–king, and Russell by all rights should've been out. He knew he'd made a bad call and was furious at himself . . . until he flopped two pair and turned queens full to double up. He was then sitting on about T150,000 in chips, more than an average stack. A few hands later, he made a standard raise with two jacks, and the same Julian Gardner called him. The flop came down ten–ten–four and Russell led out for T15,000. Julian made it T50,000. Russell made it T100,000. Julian moved all-in. In a post to RGP written later, Russell says about this moment:

"I am now sick. If I fold I still have maybe 55,000 in chips (I started with 83,000 and believed I could still come back with this much). I completely tilt and leave the table. I go where nobody can see me. Twenty minutes ago I felt the same feeling when I thought I would get knocked out with the ace–queen. I want to avoid that sick feeling at all costs. I put him on queen–queen, and I don't want to go home. I don't want to feel that sick feeling. Not with jack–jack. I scream, 'Kill it, fold it, I am out.' I say this from a good fifteen feet away from the table, behind the wall, for cocktail waitresses. I was *gone*. I have never *never* been that tilted in my life. When I come back to the table they again ask what I want to do, but the dealer has now restacked Julian's chips, and I only have to call about 35,000. Wait, he can't bust me, I will call. Matt Savage says my fold from the rail is binding. Matt made the correct ruling, and I respect him for it (as I told him ten times afterwards). Julian then turns up six–six and takes the huge pot."

When Russell told me this story over the phone minutes after it happened, I halfheartedly told him to forget the hand and get his chips back. I then hung up and went out for drinks. I thought we were done. Had Russell called and had his hand held up (which it would have about 92 percent of the time), he would've been sitting on more than T300,000 chips—almost three times as big as an average stack. Instead, Russell was shortstacked and had to battle his way back with just T55,000. I don't know anyone else who could've done it without getting really lucky. To suffer a once-in-a-lifetime disaster hand, and still make a recovery; it seemed almost impossible. Yet Russell did it. And he didn't just go on tilt and catch a run of cards. Russell somehow calmed himself down and realized where he was—at the final five tables of poker's world championship. "I just kept thinking," Russell wrote, "I may never get back to the final forty-five again. I have to make the best of this and get back to my A game."

Russell did just that. He picked the right spots to move-in and win pots uncontested. He survived an all-in confrontation with two kings against ace of diamonds, king of diamonds, even after two diamonds flopped. He kept his head. "I just had one disastrous hour," he told me during the dinner break. Amazing that he could have simply catalogued it as such and then moved on.

For me, the rest of Day Four was a perverse sweating session from across the country. I played a Stud Eight-or-Better freeroll on Poker-Stars to pass the time between hitting refresh on PokerPages (which had tournament updates about every fifteen minutes) and talking on the phone and over instant messenger to various Russell followers. When they got down to twelve players and Russell was still alive, I booked a flight to Vegas. I'd told Russell many times that if he made the final table, I would be there.

Soon, PokerPages was reporting there were only ten players left. Nine would make the final day. A few minutes later, my phone rang.

"Hello?" I said.

"Final table," Russell said. I howled or yeehawed or something. He had to survive a coin toss with jack–jack against ace–king suited to make it, but he made it. "Don't fly out here, dude, it's crazy. Keep doing the phone thing, save your money."

"Whatever," I said. Russell told me to talk to Bruce Kramer, a mutual friend and another person thinking of making the flight to watch Russ. I called Bruce, who was still on the fence. "Russell says it's crazy to do it," he said.

"It's crazy *not* to do it," I said.

Throughout the tournament I'd been e-mailing Russell scouting reports on his opponents (table draws were posted on pokerpages.com). When Russell made the final table, I was giddy, but not so giddy that I couldn't send one last E-mail before driving to Baltimore-Washington International Airport on no sleep.

Those who have seen the broadcast of the 2002 World Series of Poker final table on ESPN know only part of the story. They know that Russell lost nearly all of his chips when he moved all-in on the button with the jack–six of diamonds, only to have Julian (yes, that same Julian) wake up with aces in the big blind. That's probably all anyone who watched that TV show will remember about Russell. A lot of what Russell did well did not make it on the air.

For two hours, no one busted. Russell pretty much maintained his stack, but he wasn't the talkative wacky person (and player) he usually is.

"See if you can find me some chicken soup," he said to me during the first break.

"They have matzo ball soup at the deli downstairs," Bruce, who had also been smart enough to make the last minute Vegas trip, said. Russell snapped his fingers.

"Matzo ball soup!" he said. "That's perfect."

"I'll get it," I said.

The action at the table had already restarted as I made my way downstairs. The line at the Horseshoe deli was short but immobile. It must have taken the one person behind the counter an average of five minutes to make each sandwich. I had come all the way to Vegas to stand on line and watch the patron in front of me drink a beer, which he finished before he ordered, while my friend and poker mentor was playing the world championship final table a few hundred feet away.

After waiting a solid half hour, I finally got to order Russell's soup and a sandwich for myself. When it came, I went back towards the tournament area, soup in hands. I got past security and negotiated my way to the bleachers.

"Is Russell in this hand?" I asked the contingent of Russell followers. Russell's wife, Anne, and Russell's friends Greg "Fossilman" Raymer and Kevin "Blind Stealer" Maurer each independently said he wasn't. So I entered the final table area carrying Russell's soup. And I saw him look down at his hand!

I froze, praying Russell would fold. He did. But I still had a problem. I was halfway between the crowd and the players, holding a hot bowl of matzo ball soup. I didn't want to interrupt the action, I didn't want to drop the soup, and I didn't want to walk back to my seat and wait for the hand to end. Then it occurred to me. Russell wouldn't care if I burst into the final table with a bowl of soup. In fact, that would be to Russell's benefit. The interruption could very well tilt the other players, but it would never tilt Russ. Russell's game revolves around loosening up the table, chatting, confusing his opponents. Matzo ball soup fit.

"Russ!" I yelled. And he (and presumably everybody else) noticed me standing there holding his soup. He looked at me, took a second before he realized why I was there, then shrugged as if to say, "Okay, now what do I do with this?" He looked over to a member of the tournament staff, who then whisked a chair over to the table. I guessed that would be his tray. I set the soup down, pleading with the fates for it to stay upright.

I left the area and went back downstairs to retrieve my sandwich. As I did, I noticed Russell's matzo ball soup in close-up on the TV monitor, to much laughter. This had to be a good thing.

When I returned with my sandwich, I had the pleasure of watching Russell win two pots with reraises before the flop (neither hand was shown on ESPN). As he raked in the second one he looked in my direction and yelled, "It was the soup, Matt!"

Few could have realized he wasn't kidding. Russell later wrote on RGP: "My soup started things getting a bit wacky. This is how I like it. My goal was to appear wacky, and then shut down for a couple of rounds (absent cards)."

The one Russell victory ESPN did show came on a blind-on-blind hand against John Shipley. Shipley, another pro from the United Kingdom, had entered the final table with over 2 million in chips and seen his stack whittle away to about 1.5 million. He limped in the small blind, and Russell checked his option. The flop came down ten–five–two, all spades. John checked, and Russell bet about the size of the pot. Shipley said softly, "Two hundred thousand," and slowly stacked his chips. Russell later told me he contemplated saying, "Keep counting." Instead he just said, "I'm all-in," and shoved forward his entire stack. John folded quickly, and Russell took the pot. As ESPN's cameras showed later, Russell had ten–two.

Just before the next break, Russell raised under the gun, only to have Robert Varkonyi make a small reraise from the small blind. The flop came down jack–jack–four and Robert checked. "Two hundred thousand," Russell said with emphasis. Unfortunately, the next words out of Robert's mouth were, "All-in." Russell folded instantly, and Robert turned over two aces. Over 300,000 in chips had just left our (Russell's) stack. In this hand, also shown on ESPN, Russell had ace–queen.

There were still eight players left at the second break. Russell had been waiting for other players to get knocked out, but it hadn't happened. I said to stay in his game, be patient. We couldn't control that the all-in players always seemed to survive. I told him it wasn't yet move or muck poker—he had about 600,000 left, and could still make it 100,000 and fold to a reraise. I wasn't emphatic about this. I didn't say, "Whatever you do, don't risk all your chips—these guys aren't playing back at you today." I could have said this. I should have said this.

It wasn't too much later that Russell moved in with the jack–six of diamonds, a hand that left him crippled (although the jack and two diamonds on the flop had given us brief hope). On the very next hand, Russell was eliminated (an automatic play—Russell moved in with ace–eight and got called by ace–king).

Russell finished sixth, which earned me $2,250 for my 1.5 percent stake in him. Do the math and you'll see that Russell made $150,000. But more important than the money was the experience. Not only did I get to see my poker mentor at the final table of the world championship—a televised, high-pressure event—I also had firsthand knowledge of his strategy, and his emotions, throughout. The success of Team Russell gave me confidence to compete in big-time tournaments, perhaps even more than the TOC did.

World Poker Tour events typically have buy-ins between $4,000 and $10,000—money I wasn't about to put up. But to my surprise, I won my way into three WPT events in 2003. I did it all through supersatellites, two online, and one of the brick-and-mortar variety.

My first event would be the PartyPoker Million (PPM)—the only Limit Hold'em event on the WPT. Party Poker was my online card room of choice for the last half of 2002 and the beginning of 2003. I would take breaks from the $5–$10 shorthanded games to play $25 single-table satellite qualifiers for the PPM. I won several, earning entries into online supersatellites whose top prize was a cruise for two and entry into the PPM, a $5,000 buy-in tournament that takes place on the cruise.

I struck out in the first six supersatellites I played. But in my last one, just two weeks before the cruise, I waded through a four-hundred-plus player field and got one of eleven trips. I did it. I was on the boat.

When I actually, physically, got on the boat, I ran into my friend and fellow RGPer Andy Bloch. He was checking out the ship's Internet connection (something I was stunned existed). A tall, fit man sitting next to him was busy calculating the value of playing the $80–$160 game on Ultimate Bet while paying the absurdly high onboard rate for Internet access. He determined he could still make a tidy profit. I wondered who this $80–$160 player and friend of Andy Bloch was. I would find out later.

My PPM got off to a lousy start. I lost a third of my stack before the first break, and was down to T1,000 out of my starting T5,000 before the second. I was in serious danger of being the very first person out of the tournament. I was looking for any reasonable hand to play when it was three bets to me (not at all unusual, almost every hand was raised and reraised at this insanely aggressive table) and I looked down at aces in the small blind. I wound up making aces full and winning a monster pot. By the end of Day One, I had T8,900, exactly in the middle of the field. It was a complete recovery.

When I checked my table assignment for Day Two, it turned out I had two big names with big stacks for opponents—Chris Bigler with T19,100 on my left, and Erik Seidel with T14,600 on my right. Erik is a multi-bracelet winner, and Chris is one of the more respected players on the tournament circuit.

Bigler made it known from the start that he'd be involved in a lot of pots. In one of the first hands, he limped UTG, something no one had done during my entire first day of poker. I called from the small blind with eight–seven offsuit, and we took the flop three-handed. I flopped nothing but a straight draw, and there were a dangerous looking two spades on board. So naturally I check-raised Bigler. The big blind folded, Bigler called, and I led out at the pot on the turn. Bigler called again. I was ready to bet the river no matter what hit—if I caught my straight I would value bet, if not I would bluff. Except the river came six of spades, making my straight but also bringing in a flush. Bigler's play had been very consistent with a flush draw, and I thought if he didn't have a flush he would probably bet it for me if I checked. So I didn't see the value in betting. I checked, and Bigler checked right behind. His check probably meant he was planning to call down all the way with something like a medium pocket pair, and that I'd missed a bet after all. I announced my straight, and it was good.

A few hands later I open-raised in late position with ace–jack, and Bigler defended his big blind with pocket eights. He led out when the flop brought small cards, but I sensed weakness and raised (whoops). Bigler called . . . only to lose more chips when I spiked a jack on the turn. "That's twice I sucked out on you," I said after the hand.

"Yeah, I know," he said.

Soon Bigler's T20,000 had disappeared and he was out of the tournament. On the other hand, I had built my own stack to T20,000 and was feeling confident. Meanwhile, the tall, fit guy I had met in the Internet room joined our table. He played a very aggressive style, but he seemed to think through every bet and raise before he made them. He also made some unorthodox folds—laying down hands in big pots on the river after check-calling on the turn. I got the sense that he was trying to find every piece of equity he could, not afraid to make strange plays if he thought they were best.

In my first encounter with this opponent, he open-raised in early middle position, and I defended my big blind with ten–eight offsuit. The flop came ten-high, and I check-raised. He called, and he called again on the turn. The river brought a king, and I decided to check. My opponent wasted no time in reaching for chips and firing them into the pot. I clearly had to call, as I couldn't give this guy a king, and I had no reason to think I was behind before the river. So I called . . . and he showed me queen–ten offsuit. I was stunned that he had (1) opened with this hand from an earlyish position, and (2) value bet the river with it on a king-high board.

During a break in the action my friend Oz, who had been moved two seats to my right about half an hour earlier, asked that tall, fit guy what his name was. "Howard," he said.

"Oh, you're Howard," Oz said.

No. It couldn't be. I had seen pictures of the high-stakes player Howard Lederer, and he looked nothing like this guy. Lederer was much bigger and had a beard. And yet, from everything I'd heard about the way Howard played, and the stakes Howard played, it was a perfect match. As I looked at him again, I imagined the Howard I saw in pictures minus a lot of weight and clean-shaven. *Oh my God*, I realized, *I'm playing Limit Hold'em against the best Limit Hold'em player in the world.*

Ever the poker player, I still considered my information incomplete. I mean, I didn't *know* this person was Howard Lederer, and I didn't know what I was supposed to do differently if it was. I'd seen enough of Howard's play to know he was dangerous. I wasn't going to change my game plan just because this Howard might have been *the* Howard.

I open-raised in late position with pocket fives. Howard cold-called my raise from the button, and the big blind defended. The flop came jack–four–two with a two-flush, and after the big blind checked, I decided to take another stab at the pot. Howard coolly flicked out two chips, indicating he was raising. The big blind folded, and I had a decision. I was running low on chips, so I didn't have the luxury of reraising or even calling for information purposes. I had to decide then and there, did I have the best hand? Howard would've almost certainly reraised preflop with ace–king. His cold-call probably meant something like a middle pair, ace–queen suited, ace–jack suited, king–queen suited, queen–jack suited, or jack–ten suited. Of those hands, the only ones he was likely to raise with on that flop were the pairs and the flush draws—and he was much more likely to have a pair than a flush draw, given his range of hands. I didn't like my fives, and I threw my cards in the muck. Months later, I asked Howard about this hand. "It sounds like that flop hit me," he said, almost embarrassed.

The two pots against Howard had whittled away my chips. Soon I found myself with a piddling T3,000, while the blinds were T500 and T1,000. But I still wasn't ready to give up. I never give up. It got folded to me on the button, and I had an easy raise with king–nine offsuit. The small blind folded, but Howard reraised out of his big blind. I threw in my last T1,000 instantly (getting 5.5 to 1, I had to call with any two cards). Howard groaned as I flipped up my hand, because he had only king–five suited. I watched the flop for a five or flush draw, but neither came. There was no five on the turn either. When the river also came not a five I inwardly cheered, but only for about half a second because I heard everyone else at the table groan. I feared I had missed something, so I rechecked the board. One diamond on the flop. Another diamond on the turn. A diamond on the river. Howard had the king–five of diamonds. I was out.

I said "nice hand" and quietly got up from the table. I had finished 37th in a field of 177. Not good, but not bad considering I nearly finished 177th. Howard, the man who took me out, went on to win the whole thing. And yes, it was Howard Lederer.

* * *

Winning my way to Ultimate Bet's tournament in Aruba was probably more satisfying than winning the PartyPoker entry. First, the super-satellite gave out one seat for every sixty people, rather than one seat for every forty like Party's. Second, Ultimate Bet's supersatellite was No Limit Hold'em. Most of my early tournament success had come in Limit events. The Aruba tournament entry was my most substantial No Limit success at the time.

The trip to Aruba got off to a great start, although not because of anything related to poker. My buddy Gavin Smith (a guest of another online winner) decided he'd seen enough of wide-eyed WPT fans asking players for autographs and getting their pictures taken with the "pros." So Gavin asked our mutual friend and two-time WPT finalist Andy Bloch if he would sell Gavin his Ultimate Bet T-shirt for $20. Andy happily took the $20 and signed Gavin's new T-shirt right under the Ultimate Bet logo. "I'm gonna get all the stars of poker to sign it," Gavin said. "And then I'm gonna sell it on eBay." For the rest of the night, every time we saw a "name" poker player, Gavin had that person sign his T-shirt. By midnight he had several dozen signatures. I wonder what percentage of the players realized it was all just a big joke (I'm confident Phil Hellmuth didn't).

As for the tournament, I only survived it for four hours. Early on, I check-called for a third of my stack against a psycho who had gone all-in for T3,225 into a T175 pot. I called with top pair and one card to come, figuring I was probably way ahead. Unfortunately, my psy-chotic opponent had the nuts (yes, he bet T3,225 into a T175 pot with the nuts), and I was drawing dead.

I built my stack back up to about T8,500, but then spent a few thou-sand when I open-raised with eight–eight, got called by a tight player, and had to fold to his all-in raise on a flop of jack–jack–two. Then one of the more aggressive players at the table opened in middle position, and I moved in on her from the small blind with ace–queen suited. She had just won the previous pot, and she'd been raising often enough that I felt ace–queen suited to be a sizeable favorite over her range of hands. In addition, I felt she would lay down hands as big as two jacks and maybe even ace–king. She thought for a while, and then grabbed her cards to throw them in the muck. But then, without looking at me (so I'm confident she didn't pick up a tell), she put her cards back down and said, "Oh, that's why they call it gambling," and put in enough chips to call my raise.

"What are you gambling with?" I said.

"Big slick," she said.

And my Aruba tournament was over.

At least I got to party with the champ, because Gavin's friend Erick Lindgren ended up winning the whole thing. It also turned out Erick and I had logged quite a few hours together at PokerStars. It was encouraging to see one of the best online players succeeding in the "real" poker world.

Foxwoods came up with an ingenious system for getting players into its 2003 WPT event. They had satellite tournaments that they called "Acts." Act One was a $30 buy-in single table satellite with two winners who advanced to Act Two. Act Two was a $115 single table satellite with one winner who advanced to Act Three. Act Three was a $1,060 supersatellite, giving away one seat to the WPT event for every ten entrants.

By promoting the Acts with lines like "for as little as thirty dollars you could win hundreds of thousands of dollars and appear on TV," Foxwoods drew an incredible turnout for their supersatellites. In the end, more than one hundred people won seats into the big event through the Acts.

My first Act experience was, well, noteworthy. I got into Act Three by making a deal heads-up in an Act Two. I caught some cards in the Act Three and reached the ten-handed final table in sixth position. Three players were extremely shortstacked, and eight of the final tableists would get seats. I estimated my chances of winning a seat to be around 98 percent. Unfortunately, the three short stacks doubled up three times each. One of them finally busted, but then another one doubled up again, and suddenly I was the short stack. I went out next, forced all-in on the small blind and unable to win the showdown. It was the worst thing I've ever experienced in poker.

The next day I got right back in the saddle and played an Act One, advancing easily (the Act Ones were largely populated by total rookies, most of whom had never even played poker before). I played my Act Two at FARGO, won that, and returned to Foxwoods the next week for another Act Three. Again I reached the final table in sixth chip position. Again the shortest stack seemed to double up every time he had to. With eight players left and seven seats up for grabs, I had T3,500 left. The *ante* (not the big blind) was T1,000. But another player was forced all-in on his small blind on the very next hand. Despite having fifteen outs on the turn, the small blind busted. And I won my $10,200 seat after all.

Two months later I was back at Foxwoods, this time for the real thing. I avoided major confrontations for the first few hours. Then, right before the dinner break, I went from having T10,000 to T2,500 and back to T9,000 in the span of just a few hands. First I called a large check-raise all-in on a flop of eight–nine–ten with two aces. It was a bad read on my part, as my opponent took down the pot with a set of nines. But soon after that, I limped behind several limpers with six–three suited, and doubled back up to T7,000 when the flop came jack–six–three and the first limper went to war with *his* pocket aces. I took down one last pot uncontested. And then it was time for dinner.

Over steak, I told Russell that something about this particular tournament was more excruciating to me than even the other WPT events I'd played. I never think about the money when I'm playing poker, but I was thinking about the million-dollar first prize often during the Foxwoods tournament.

After dinner, I doubled up when I shoved in with ace–king and got called by ace–queen suited. But then I started running into a lot of hands. I would open-raise, and someone would reraise. I would fold, and they would show me aces, or queens, or some other big hand. Still, I got up to T18,000 when I opened with two jacks, got reraised (of course), and finally put my opponent to the test by putting in the rest of my chips. He called with ace–king suited, and my jacks held up. I never got my stack any higher, though. I continued to run into hands, and I was fittingly eliminated when I moved in with king–queen and ran into aces one final time. I finished about 90th in the 313-person event.

* * *

I don't know when my next WPT event will be, but I'm confident in my ability to get back there. And it is only a matter of time before we see a WPT event with a $2 million or even $3 million first prize. I like to think *that* will be the one I'll win—that the poker gods were just keeping me in abeyance these first three times.

20

♠ ♣ ♦ ♥

Cashing Out

Believe it or not, you will not become a world-class poker player just by reading this book. Poker is a never-ending learning process. There are so many ways to improve your game—books, software, essays, newsgroups, game theory problems, discussions with other players—there's never an excuse to stop. You must take the time to study the concepts, read the books, and play as much as you can. But be careful. Don't let the results of hands or even sessions dictate the way you think about the game. Play your hand in a way that is logical, not in a way that would have worked best the last time you had it.

I've mentioned recommended reading along the way, but here's a refresher.

For Beginners
Winner's Guide to Texas Hold'em Poker by Ken Warren
Winning Low Limit Hold'em by Lee Jones

For Stud Players
Seven-Card Stud for Advanced Players by David Sklansky and Mason Malmuth

For Everyone
The Theory of Poker by David Sklansky
Tournament Poker for Advanced Players by David Sklansky
The Complete Book of Hold 'Em Poker by Gary Carson

The Mathematics of Poker by Bill Chen, Jerrod Ankenman, and
   Andy Latto

Honestly, these seven books are the only ones I recommend without any reservations. There are some other books, however, that I think have some interesting things to say, even if I don't agree with all the advice in them. My caveats are in parentheses.

Other Interesting Books
Hold'em Poker for Advanced Players by David Sklansky and
   Mason Malmuth (Be sure to ignore the advice on shorthanded
   and loose games in the 21st century edition.)
Super/System by Doyle Brunson (The No Limit Hold'em section is
   pretty solid, but the rest of the book is largely outdated.)
Pot-Limit & No-Limit Poker by Stewart Reuben and Bob Ciaffone
   (I think this book errs on the weak-tight side, so be aware of that
   going in.)

Read any other books at your own peril. I don't want to name names, but there are some well-known poker authors whose books are conspicuously absent from my list. While I do not recommend those authors (in some cases because of the writing style, in other cases because of the poker advice), I encourage everyone to read as much about the game as possible. Just remember that poker authors are often only giving their opinions. Don't take any poker advice without thinking it through on your own, especially after you've familiarized yourself with the game.

As for me, I received my M.F.A. in fiction writing from Sarah Lawrence College in May of 2004, and am now dividing my time between writing fiction and playing poker. I play mostly online: shorthanded games, No Limit Hold'em tournaments, and heads-up matches. Of course, I still attend FARGO and ATLARGE, and am in Vegas during BARGE. I still play plenty often at Foxwoods and in Atlantic City.

I've been thinking lately about how to maximize value by inducing bluffs, when to get hyperaggressive during tournaments, and how to balance my play to avoid being exploitable. The details on these things

I'll keep to myself for now. I've shared plenty of strategy already in this book—anyone reading it should have the tools to be a winning player. You didn't think I was going to tell you how to beat me, did you?

My website, www.mattmatros.com, is up and running, so if you want more poker strategy through my experiences as a player, feel free to stop by. The site has polls on how to play hands, discussions of recent hands I've played, and a section on the mathematics of poker. Basically it's like this book, only on the Web.

I look forward to building on the three World Poker Tour events I played in 2003 with some big money scores in the future. I don't ever see myself retiring from poker completely, but I think if someday I've won enough money and I no longer find the game interesting, I might move on to another full-blown passion. For now, though, I want to see how good I can get. Just like Mike McDermott in *Rounders*, I want to find out if I can compete with the world's best players. As long as that motivation is there, I'll be doing everything I can to improve. There are, of course, ancillary benefits. Master this game, and you master nothing less than logic, psychology, relationships, economics, and self-sufficiency. Most people who think a career in poker is a waste of time just don't understand that.

I hope you enjoyed learning poker vicariously through me. I know I enjoyed relearning the game while writing this book. I tried not to tell many bad beat stories, and the ones I did tell all had some point or lesson to them. But I think you've heard enough of my hands to last quite a while. Now it's your turn. Get out there and play, and I'll see you at the tables. I won't be wearing sunglasses, but I will be keeping the game friendly, and secretly scheming to get every last dollar out of my opponents. If you see me you can mention that you read my book, but I would also understand if you don't. Poker players are expected to hold back information.

Still, my best friends in poker are the ones who do not hold back information, the ones I discuss hands and strategy with for hours. My last piece of advice is to become one of those knowledge sharers. Don't be the old guy at the end of the table who refuses to engage any of his opponents. Be the person at the snack bar everyone wants to come to for advice. Not only is life more fun this way, but you really will learn the game by talking about it, telling stories about it, reliving every decision of your crucial hands. I hope I've convinced you of that, if nothing else.

21

♠ ♣ ♦ ♥

Postscript

A funny thing happened after I finished writing this book. It started when I was sitting at home in Westhampton on spring break, and I decided to take a crack at winning some real money. I went on Party-Poker and entered a tournament whose entry fee was $109, and whose prize was a flight to Las Vegas, hotel accommodations at the Bellagio, and two entries into supersatellites for the World Poker Tour Championship, a $25,300 buy-in event. I won.

It was a chore to fly out for those supersatellites. I can almost say I didn't even *want* to do it. It was April 16, 2004. I had just been to Vegas two weeks earlier for a bachelor party, and my M.F.A. thesis at Sarah Lawrence College was due two weeks later. Yet there I was on a plane, hoping I could somehow play in the WPT Championship. It was going to be a reach. First, I had to win one of the two supersatellites. A supersatellite awards as many seats into its main event as possible, so in a $2,600 supersatellite for a $25,300 event, there would be roughly one seat given away for every ten players. If, for example, two hundred people entered, there would be about twenty top prizes, meaning twentieth place would be just as good as first. Figuring I'd have an edge over the field, I estimated my chances of winning a seat in either of the given supers at 15 percent. So even after beating out ninety-seven other people on PartyPoker to win the supersatellite entries, I still only had about a 28 percent chance of getting into the big event. That put my chance of getting *into the money* in the WPT Championship at somewhere around 4 percent. In other words, I was flying to Vegas knowing there was about a 96 percent chance I'd be coming home with no money. It certainly wasn't my most optimistic of poker adventures.

I landed in Vegas around midnight on a Friday night, waited an hour for a cab, and finally got to sleep in my Bellagio room at 2 A.M., also known as 5 A.M. Eastern time. I got up the next day, hoping to use adrenaline to get me through the event. I wore my PartyPoker hat and ran into Russell right before the super was starting. "What table you at?" I asked him. He told me and I felt sick. "No!" he said. There were 442 people entered in the super, creating by far the biggest prize pool in supersatellite history, and Russell and I were at the same table. The good news (for me) was that I had Russell on my immediate right. We had both taken a bad beat, since we each knew the other's game so well, but Russell had taken the ultimate 441 to 1 bad beat of drawing me on his immediate left.

Sipping my coffee and hoping not to tangle with Russell in a big pot, I picked up ace–king offsuit on one of the first hands. A player raised and another reraised before the action got to me. I had my first decision of the trip. The opener could have had anything—he'd raised the first few pots. Because of this, the reraiser, a tough player I knew from Aruba, didn't necessarily need a monster either. I decided to re-reraise, sliding T1,600 out of my T5,000 into the pot. I didn't have to sweat long. Both of my opponents folded quickly.

My table was one of the first to break. We drew seats for new tables . . . and Russell and I were at the same table again! At least this time we were at opposite ends, with neither of us having a positional advantage.

Big slick, this time suited, played a role in my next big confrontation. An unconventional player minimum-raised from middle position, another player called, and I made a real (that is, pot-sized) reraise from the blind with ace and king of hearts. *Both* my opponents called. The flop brought junk. I had no pair and no draw. But I had the sense neither of my opponents had very much, so I bet right out. The first opponent folded, but the other guy reluctantly called. The turn was another blank. I had the strong sense that my opponent wasn't committed to his hand, so I bet another T2,000, essentially setting him all-in. I would've been crippled if he called, and I didn't improve. But he mucked, saying out loud, "He has a big pair." The guy who folded first said, "Yeah, I figured that out earlier." Nice detective work, gentlemen.

I got a bunch more chips when a highly aggressive player put in a lot of money with king–queen on a queen-high board. The two aces in my hand were just enough to beat him. Needing only to finish forty-second to secure a seat, I avoided major confrontations the rest of the way. I went all-in against an opponent who had me covered only once during the entire super. The opponent, Tom Jacobs, folded before the flop. We got down to forty-four players, and with nightmares of the Foxwoods Act Three fresh in my brain, I was sweating with my slightly-below-average-but-still-perfectly-safe stack. Then, two people on different tables were all-in on their big blinds. Miraculously, they both busted. Without ever having to win a showdown for all my chips, I had won a seat in the 2004 World Poker Tour Championship.

The next day I had a bankroll decision to make. Since I'd already won my entry into the big tournament, PartyPoker.com didn't care whether I played my second supersatellite. Party's (and every other online card room's) agenda for running satellites to major tournaments is to get their players into the big events, have them win a lot of money, and generate tons of exposure for the company's business. Therefore it made no difference to Party whether I played yet another super, or simply took the $2,600 entry fee from them. If I chose to play, I would be playing for a prize of $25,300 in cold hard cash, since I already had a seat in the WPT Championship. That was a major incentive to play, but having $2,600 in my pocket was a major incentive not to play.

I compromised (sort of). I took the $2,600 in cash, and decided to play a smaller, shorter tournament. I went back to my room, sat in the comfort of a plush Bellagio chair, and played the $215 buy-in Sunday tournament on PokerStars. I finished in the money and made about six hundred bucks.

That night, Russell and I had dinner at Prime, one of the best restaurants in Bellagio. We talked logistics (how to get food when there was no food break until 9 P.M., how to find medicine for my flaky stomach, how much PartyPoker gear I should wear) and strategy, mostly about what adjustments to make for the super deep stack sizes we would start with. Players in the WPT Championship start with

T50,000 in chips, with blinds of T50 and T100. There is no other tournament where players start with five hundred big blinds—not even the WSOP championship. In general, deeper stacks mean a higher skill factor. This is one of the reasons I consider the WPT Championship poker's world championship.

Soon enough I was alone again in my room, trying to sleep—trying to talk myself into thinking I could be competitive in what was the biggest poker tournament in history. More than three hundred entries were expected, which meant first place would be more than the $2.5 million Chris Moneymaker had won just a year earlier at the WSOP. Everyone who made the final six could expect to earn more than $200,000 in cash. I'd say I was feeling a little pressure.

The tournament area was roped off and surrounded by placards reminding us we were playing a World Poker Tour event, and that filming was in progress. Still, on the surface nothing distinguished this tournament from the other three WPT events I'd played. There was no championship banner, no coronation for the rest of the season's winners, there wasn't even that much more of a media presence. It's called the WPT Championship because it's the last event of the season, it has the biggest buy-in, and every Tour winner from the year competes in it. Other than that, I guess it's just another tournament.

I drew a Day One starting table which featured Paul Darden, Erik Seidel, Toto Leonidas, and Jeff Shulman, all very tough professionals. The strange thing was that most bets on this table were getting called down. I felt that if I ever picked up a hand I would've been paid off. I never got anything. I made some aggressive plays to win a few pots, and I made at least one tough call that worked out in my favor. I thought I was lucky to end Day One with T33,850, having "only" lost T16,150 from my stack. I was way down in the chip count standings, but at least I had found some ways to stay afloat. Russell ended Day One in even worse shape than I was in, sitting at a paltry T29,275.

I won the first pot of my new table on Day Two and thought maybe it was a sign I'd turn things around. Soon, however, I found myself down to one T25,000 chip, and I had even less after I anted away for a few hands. I was getting desperate when a middle position player opened, and the player to his left reraised all-in for about T21,000. I looked down and found two queens. It was by far the best hand I had seen in the tournament to that point, and I felt I had to go with it. I moved in on top of both players (though I had the reraiser covered). The initial raiser folded, and the all-in player looked sick, claiming he hadn't looked at his hand (I didn't believe him). He rolled over ace–nine offsuit, and despite his catching a nine on the flop, my hand held up. I had knocked out a player, and was almost back to my starting stack size.

Then, after blinding away a little, I played what ended up being, in my opinion, my most crucial hand of the entire tournament. Seated to my left was a tournament professional. She was super-nice, engaging in conversation from the outset, and I had every indication that she was a tough, solid, experienced poker player. I had yet to tangle with her before *the hand*. With blinds of T400–T800 and a T100 ante, I opened for T2,600 in late position with jack of hearts–eight of diamonds. Then the pro to my left said, "Raise. Make it five thousand." It was a minuscule reraise, and it scared the hell out of me. I figured her for kings or aces, and thought it almost impossible that she could have anything else. The blinds folded. I called for several reasons, one of the most important being that I didn't want to have people reraising me for the rest of the day. The flop came queen–jack–seven, with two diamonds. I checked, fully intending to fold my middle pair-no kicker to any bet from my opponent. Except she only bet T2,000 into the T12,100 pot. So I called again, thinking I was now getting a price to draw out on king–king or ace–ace. The turn brought the ace of diamonds. I felt this was one of the best cards I could hope for. If my opponent had two kings (especially without the king of diamonds) she might well have given up the hand to a bet, and even with a set of aces she had to be worried I just made a flush. I led out for T6,000, thinking there was a chance my opponent would fold, and that it would be almost impossible for her to raise. "Raise" was the next word out of her mouth. *Damn*, I thought, *so much for making a play at this pot.* And then something strange happened. My opponent tried to make it a total of T4,000. It was then she realized that I had bet T6,000—a T5,000 chip and two T500 chips. I had not, as she originally thought, bet T1,200—a T1,000 chip and two T100 chips. "But I said 'raise,' " she said. "I raise, I make it twelve thousand." With some players I would've been worried. Less than scrupulous folks might have done something like this as an angle with the nuts. But I had played with this woman long enough to be confident she wasn't angling. She was a stand-up person and player. I was equally confident my opponent didn't have two diamonds in her hand. So what to do about this? I could have folded, of course. I was sure my opponent had a much bigger hand than I did. I could have called the T6,000, accepting the price she was offering for my eight-high flush draw. Or, I could see how much she really liked her hand. Did she really want to call an all-in reraise from me with two kings, with or without a diamond? Hell, did she really want to call with a set of aces? I decided she didn't, and that if God forbid she did call me, I still had some outs against her likely holdings. "I'm all-in," I said, raising her T25,000 more. When my opponent failed to call instantly, I knew there was a chance the play would work. This knowledge didn't make me any less petrified as I sat there, for minutes, with all my chips in the middle, as she deliberated. I didn't dare say anything. I didn't dare look at her. I try never to do those things anyway, but this was the only time in my poker career I was actually *scared* to do or say anything. I had never put a player on a range as strong as king–king/ace–ace and tried to move that player off the hand, and now I was doing it in the WPT Championship. Finally, my opponent took her protector off her cards. She waited a few more seconds, just to be sure . . . and she slid her hand into the muck.

We had a break shortly after this hand, during which my opponent apparently revealed her hole cards to several other players at the table. In one of the first hands following the break, she got all her chips in on a board of queen–eight–two, saying out loud, "Here we go again." She turned over eight–eight for middle set but was sent packing when Joe Cassidy's ten–nine caught a running six and seven for a straight. My opponents at the table told me her "Here we go again" comment referred to the fact that she had just made another set—because she'd folded a set of queens against me.

After the jack–eight hand, things started clicking. I got it all-in with king–king from the button against the small blind's ace–king offsuit, and doubled up to more than T100,000. I called down two large bets from *CardPlayer* publisher Barry Shulman with those same two kings, and Barry mucked his hand on the river without showing. Then, as Day Two wound to a close, with blinds at T1,000 and T2,000 with a T300 ante, I opened for T6,000 with eight–six of clubs against the tightest player's big blind. He had been folding, folding, folding all day, and was now down to T19,500. All folded to him. He thought for a second, and then moved in on me for T13,500 more. I did a little quick math. I had to call T13,500. There was T19,500 (his all-in raise) + T6,000 (my initial raise) + T1,000 (the small blind) + T2,700 (the nine antes) = T29,200 in the pot. So I was getting 2.16 to 1 (I didn't figure it that precisely at the time, but I knew it was more than 2 to 1) on my call. Given how short he was getting, and how often I had been raising, there was just no way I could've been more than a 2-to-1 dog against his range of hands. So I called. I certainly wasn't a 2-to-1 dog against the hand he had—ace–jack offsuit. In fact, I wasn't even a 3-to-2 dog. The flop came ace–nine–five. But it was all over for my opponent when the turn brought a seven, giving me a straight.

I ended Day Two with T239,400 in chips, in seventeenth place out of the 122 remaining competitors. Russell, meanwhile, had vaulted all the way up to T291,800. His pots were less exciting—kings versus aces, a set versus two pair, those kinds of things—but his stack increase was even more impressive than mine. We had dinner at Olive's to celebrate one of the best poker days of both of our careers. Even as we ate, though, I said, "I want to enjoy this for a while, but tomorrow it's back to work."

I woke up on Day Three knowing that by the end of the night I would either have made $33,266 (the prize for finishing fiftieth, the first paying position) or more, or I'd be out of the tournament with nothing to show for my tremendous Day Two performance. I played some loud music in my hotel room—The Murmurs, Rufus Wainwright (had to turn up the volume for that one to qualify)—and busted out the door high on adrenaline.

I wasn't crazy about my table draw. I had Jennifer Harman, one of the best ring game players in the world, on my immediate left, and Foxwoods WPT event runner-up Mohamed Ibrahim two to my left. Despite this horrid position, I managed to increase my stack size by flopping a big hand against an unfamiliar opponent. I started to gain some confidence. *I can play in this seat, no problem* I told myself. That was about the time Howard Lederer moved into the seat to my right.

Howard and I, the reader will remember, had a history from the Party Poker Million, where Howard knocked me out and then went on to win the event. After that tournament, when I asked him about my play, he described it as "aggressive; you were annoying to play against." I asked him if that was a good thing and he said, almost exasperated, "Yes." The point of this story is that Howard had played with me before, had labeled me as an aggressive player, and certainly remembered it. I don't think Howard ever forgets anything.

Up until this time, no one at my table had received a walk in the big blind. Every pot had at least been called, and much more often raised by the time it was the big blind's turn to act. The very first time Howard posted his big blind, *everyone else at the table folded*. This was a bad sign. Howard's opponents were cowering in fear, telling him he had a green light to run them over as he saw fit. Sure enough, when everyone folded to Howard in late position, and the tightest player on the table had the big blind, Howard opened for T12,000. I reraised to T35,000. I didn't have a pair, or even a picture card, but I *didn't* want Howard to start running over the table. Everyone passed to Howard, who also threw his cards in the muck.

On the next orbit, Howard opened in late position again, for the same T12,000. I planned to be a little tighter with my reraise this go around, but just a little. I looked down and found two sevens. Once more, I put T35,000 into the pot. If Howard chose to play back at me for his last T75,000, I was committing to the hand. I knew Howard wouldn't let me reraise him forever, so I was prepared to take a stand with my medium pair.

Everyone folded back to Howard, but he didn't move-in on me. He decided to just call. The flop came down five–five–four. I was more committed to my hand than ever. The action was on Howard, and he sat there for at least two minutes without moving. Thinking I might have missed something, I finally said, "It's on you, right, Howard?" "Mmmm-hmmm," he responded, without moving his hand from his chin. Finally Howard rapped the table, checking. I waited about ten seconds, then fired four T25,000 chips in the pot, more than enough to cover Howard. "Call," he said instantly. Yikes. "Do you have a big pair?" I said. "No," Howard said. I turned over my hand, and Howard turned up his . . . pocket sixes. The turn and river brought no help, and I had eliminated the two-time World Poker Tour champion.

Incidentally, I think Howard played his hand perfectly. There was no way he could win the pot without a showdown, and there was no way he could fold on the flop after he'd called preflop. If he was behind, he was going broke anyway. If he was ahead, he was getting the maximum value from his hand. Unfortunately for Howard, sometimes the perfect play will still get you broke.

The next few hours felt like treading water. Mohamed was a constant irritation on my left, and he gave me little room to make any moves. The next thing I knew we were down to fifty-three players, just three away from a $33,000 payday. And for some reason, we were going hand for hand. I jumped out of my seat to figure out what was going on. It turned out one player had been stalling every hand, and tournament director Jack McClelland made the decision to go hand for hand early. This was excruciating for those of us to which $33,000 meant a great deal. I got back to my seat and tried to focus on both accumulating chips *and* not busting in fifty-third, or fifty-second, or fifty-first place. The money just meant so much to me that I had to sacrifice some chance of winning the tournament in order to cash. I lost some chips. I raised on the button with ace–five and was pot-committed to Lee Salem's reraise. He had aces. I got some of it back by stealing a set of blinds. But mostly my stack diminished. Minutes and minutes and minutes went by. Finally we got to fifty-two players, then quickly we got to fifty-one. I folded a few hands, praying for some good news. It came. "The guy who was stalling just busted on the bubble!" someone yelled. I've never seen a group of poker players so singularly happy about anything. I joined in the celebration of poetic justice and found Russell, who had also made it through to the top fifty. And then it hit me. "Did I just win thirty-three thousand dollars?" I asked him.

Indeed, I had. I called my girlfriend, Ivy, and she couldn't quite believe it either. Thirty-three thousand dollars is, after all, a lot of money. Cashing in the World Poker Tour championship was an achievement I hadn't even let myself consider until it actually happened.

Before I could consider it for very long, however, it was back to poker. My stack had diminished, and I knew I needed to get a hold of some chips if I wanted to make a run at the final table. An aggressive player open-raised, and I called in the small blind with two tens. The flop came seven-high, and I check-raised. My opponent then moved all-in on me. I thought for not too long and called him. He cursed when I called, always a good sign. The funny thing was he had two nines in his hand. He must've given me credit for being a tight player, to assume there was no way his nines could have been good after I called. He didn't improve, and suddenly I had busted a player and was back among the tournament's chip leaders. When Day Three play ended shortly thereafter, I found myself with T714,000, in ninth place among the thirty-one remaining competitors, and having already locked up forty-one-thousand real dollars.

For some reason, I thought the pressure would be off after I'd made the money. I can't remember the last time I was so completely wrong about anything. There is actually a big difference, I realized, between $41,583 and $2.7 million (the prize for first place). The next day of my life would determine whether I had enough money to pay rent for a while, or enough money to buy real estate and not worry about a "real job" for the near future.

The cards were kind to me to start the day, but not as kind as Ivy and my father, both of whom had hopped on last minute flights from the East Coast to watch me in action. I picked up queens on back-to-back hands. The first time, I reraised poker author and all-time tournament leading money winner T. J. Cloutier and took the pot. The second time I got it all-in against a former WPT finalist holding ace–king. My queens held up, and I found myself in the top five in chips.

One of the other chip leaders was at my table, sitting almost directly across from me—a short, talkative guy, whose style was very similar to mine. He was a lawyer from Maryland . . . and his name was Russell Rosenblum. It was surreal, unreal, beyond real. Russell and I were the chip leaders of the biggest tournament in history.

It got even less real.

With both of us sitting at about T1.1 million in chips, Russell opened from UTG, and I called him with two sevens. Everyone else folded, and we were heads-up. Russell and I are friends, but we're competitors at the table, especially when we're playing for millions of dollars. The flop came eight–seven–three, and Russell led out for T75,000. I thought for a while and made it T225,000. Russell looked pained, but that meant nothing. I hated the position. I was either going to be taking a bunch of chips from one of my best friends, or worse, losing my chips to him. Russell finally reraised, firing a total of T500,000 into the pot. It was T275,000 to me. Russell's small reraise worried me. I knew Russell's game enough to know that if I moved in, he would have likely only called with a set, and possibly not even bottom set. The problem was, Russell could have very easily had top set. I knew I couldn't fold. There was too good a chance Russell was trying to move me off an overpair, or top pair, or a straight draw, or something. Calling was equally pointless. Russell wouldn't put in another dime unless I was beat, in which case I would double him up. I finally did what in the back of my mind I knew I had to do from the beginning. "I'm all-in," I said.

"You flop a set?" Russell said instantly. I almost shrugged. It was that much of a joke. Russell *knew* I had a set, and I knew he would know I had a set if and when I moved in. When stacks are that deep, and with a nonthreatening board, and when going against the other big stack, it's just hard to get *that* many chips in with anything else. Russell folded.

"Aces?" I said.

"Tens," he said.

The exchange was painful (though, as it turned out, more for him than me), but after it was over I looked around and realized something. I was the chip leader of the World Poker Tour championship. This got confirmed when Jack McClelland walked around the tables and read the chip counts of the leaders. He had to ask me how to pronounce my name (it's May-Tros).

My stack stayed right around T1.5 million for a while, and pretty soon I wasn't the chip leader. I was fine with that, but I wanted some more chips. So when Ricky Grijalva, an aggressive twenty-two-year-old player, raised in late position, I reraised from the small blind with king of diamonds–jack of diamonds. To my dismay, Ricky called me. There was more than T400,000 in the pot, and Ricky had about T500,000 behind. When the flop came king-high with two hearts, I felt I had little choice. "I'm all-in," I said. Ricky thought for maybe three seconds. "I call," he said, quickly turning up his hand. He too had king–jack . . . of hearts. "You're freerolling," I said. I held my breath as the turn brought a blank. But the ace of hearts on the river was one of the ugliest cards I'd ever seen. "Yes," Ricky grunted, and who could blame him. I counted out his money and paid him. I was suddenly down to about T600,000, and in danger of busting out of the tournament at any time.

We went on break, and Russell told me to try to regroup, that the Ricky hand was long over, that my style of play lent itself to large swings. I knew he was right, but I also wanted my chips back.

On one of the first hands after the break, I opened for T100,000 with ace–jack of clubs. My old friend Mohamed Ibrahim, who had taken some horrific beats to become shortstacked, moved in from the big blind for about T400,000. I'd played with Mohamed enough so that I gave him a wide range of hands in this spot. Getting almost 2 to 1 on my money, I felt I had to call, and I did. Mohamed flipped up ace–king offsuit. "Nice hand," I said. But the flop brought a jack and the turn brought another one. I said nothing, but just shook a heart-broken Mohamed's hand as he exited the tournament. I was back up over a million.

Not too much later I experienced Ricky Confrontation Number Two. Ricky opened in late position, and I called on the button with jack–ten of spades. The blinds folded, and the flop came queen–jack–nine, with one spade. Ricky led out for T150,000. "Raise," I said, sliding T500,000 into the pot. Ricky went into deep thought. I was actually pretty relaxed. I knew I would call for my last T600,000, if Ricky moved in on me, so what did I have to think about? "Call," Ricky finally said. Hmmm, that was a possibility I hadn't considered. The four of spades hit the turn, and Ricky instantly said, "I'm all-in." I threw my hands in the air. The pot had about T1.8 million in it, and I had to call T600,000. I had a pair, an open-ended straight draw, and a flush draw. "I have to call," I said. "I call." Ricky flipped over his hand—ace–jack offsuit. I had eighteen outs, and more than 40 percent equity in the T2.4 million pot. The dealer burned and turned . . . an eight of spades. I bolted from my chair before the card even hit the felt. "Yes," I screamed, not caring what anyone thought. It wasn't every day that I won a pot worth somewhere around half a million real dollars in equity. I soon sat back down, though, and counted out my chips so Ricky could pay me. To his credit, Ricky was a great sport. He didn't complain, he just went back to his business. About fifteen minutes later he said, "Nice hand, Matt." I just shook my head by way of apology.

Things moved fast after that. With ten players left in the tournament, I busted the Frenchman Patrick Bruel, with bottom two pair against a strong top pair in a blind-on-blind battle. Later, I called off T720,000 to Steve Brecher (yes, RGP's Steve Brecher) with ace–queen suited against his queen–queen (nice reraise, Steve). We got to dinner break eight-handed, and I had a strong feeling that I would fail to become one of the final six who got to play in front of the cameras. But when we got back to the action, T. J. Cloutier moved his chips in what turned out to be two bad spots, and he became the eighth-place finisher. We were one away from making Day Five.

After T.J. busted, the player to my immediate right became . . . Russell Rosenblum. Unfathomably, one of us was assured of making the WPT broadcast, and there was a decent chance we would both get there. There was still, however, some poker to be played.

First to act, I opened with king–ten offsuit. A tight player, Tom Jacobs, the same player who I had moved in on during the supersatellite and who might have ended my entire tournament run before it started if he'd called then, called me this time. The blinds folded, and Tom and I took a flop of jack–ten–seven with two diamonds. I checked, and Tom checked behind me. It was unlikely then that Tom had a big hand, given how dangerous that flop was for just about anything. The turn brought an offsuit queen. Once again I checked. Tom bet T300,000. Having practically begged him to bet by checking twice, I called with my pair plus open-ended straight draw. The river brought an ace, except it was the ace of diamonds. The board now read seven–ten–jack–queen–ace, with three diamonds. I only had the straight. I thought through my options. I could bet, but it would be almost impossible for Tom to call with a worse hand, and he would at least call with a better one. I could check, inducing a bluff—but what if the bluff I induced was a very large bet I didn't want to call? But if Tom had made a flush, why would he want to make a very large bet against a player who had checked on every street? He couldn't possibly expect to get paid. I decided I was not risking a large bet if I checked, and that furthermore the *only* way I could make any money if I had the best hand was to check. So I finally checked. Tom thought for a while . . . and then moved all-in for T1.3 million into the T900,000 pot. Ooops. Tom had made the huge bet after all. "How much is it? Does he cover me?" I asked. They counted him down, and it turned out I would have a paltry T300,000 left if I called and lost. I took off my PartyPoker.com hat, leaned back, and tried to make sense of Tom's bet. I realized there were many reasons to believe Tom did not have me beat. First, he would have had to call me preflop with two suited cards that didn't contain an ace. Tom was a tight player, and unlikely to show me six–five of diamonds, or eight–nine of diamonds. Second, if Tom did flop a flush draw with something like king–queen of diamonds, why did he check behind me on the flop? He would have been in an ideal semibluffing situation. Finally, and this goes back to the whole reason I checked in the first place, if Tom had a flush, why would he bet all his chips? He shouldn't be expecting a call from a player who had checked three times. No, I didn't think Tom had a flush. The only explanation I could come up with for his bet was that he *knew* I didn't have a flush, so he thought he would try to promote the straight in his hand from a chopping hand to a scooping hand. This was my analysis. I gritted my teeth. I clenched my stomach. I balled my hands into fists. "I call," I said, almost in anger. Tom turned up his palms and shook his head, and my eyes went wide. Was I getting this whole pot after all? Tom rolled over two black nines. And the celebration was on.

I flipped my hand up and screamed, yelled, hugged Russell, and did some kind of jumping. Again, I don't think I was out of line here. I was experiencing a once-in-a-lifetime thrill, and I wanted to enjoy the moment.

Five minutes later, a classy but deeply saddened Tom Jacobs shook my hand. "You made a great call," he said.

When the chatter with Russell, the fevered applause and hugs from strangers in the PartyPoker suite, and the interview scheduling with the WPT higher-ups had ended, Ivy and I walked down the quiet Bellagio hallway, finally with a moment to ourselves. We just started laughing. I had locked up $232,862, a mind-numbing sum for a graduate student like myself, and I was entering the final table in second chip position, and in a near-perfect seat (Russell and Ricky on my right, Steve Brecher and professional Hasan Habib, both of whom had been playing tight, on my left, and directly across from Martin de Knijff, a very tough, solid player). Even though I would be playing for $2.5 million more the next day, with the results broadcast to millions of people, I slept many hours that night.

The final table wasn't scheduled to begin until 8 P.M. That left much of the day to attend to preparatory crap. After ordering room service, Ivy and I went to the mall to buy a dress shirt, belt, slacks, socks, and boxers (I hadn't packed optimistically enough when I'd flown out a week earlier). When we finished, we had to rush back to the Bellagio for first a press conference in the PartyPoker suite, and then the WPT player interview that every final tableist does. The WPT gave me a .999 fine silver chip protector with the World Poker Tour symbol on the front, and "FINAL TABLE, WPT Championship, April 23, 2004" on the back. "Cool," I said, unable to think of another way to describe it. I have no interest in selling that silver for ten or twenty or fifty times its value.

With the interviews out of the way, Ivy and I went to dinner with Russell and Ed Pizzarello, another mutual friend who had flown out to Vegas on short notice. I had a turkey club sandwich (Ivy's suggestion) as my "last meal." A mere half an hour after dinner, it was time to report to the set.

My advice to any future WPT final table participants is to ignore as much of the hoopla as you can. Between getting fitted for a microphone, looking at the cameras while making an entrance, making sure your hole cards are positioned correctly, hearing Mike and Vince and even Shana prattle on about you in the background, and playing in front of a mob of people (not to mention the television audience), it's extremely easy to get distracted. I was distracted. I was nervous. All of us were, except, I think, for Martin. He seemed as relaxed as he'd been when we played together on Day Two (did I mention I logged about fifteen hours at the table with Martin during this tournament?).

There is little to report on the sixty-nine hands I played at the final table. The best pocket pair I saw was nine–nine (I raised preflop, Martin called in the big blind, and then he check-folded to my bet on an ace-high flop), and the best unpaired hand I saw was ace–queen (I reraised Martin before the flop and took down the pot). Aside from that, I had nothing. Sure, I raised preflop with five–two offsuit (I actually did this twice, winning once and losing once), check-raised an ace-high flop with two diamonds when holding the jack–five of diamonds (and won), but I never had a situation where I could accumulate a lot of chips. The good news was my bad run of cards allowed me to watch from the sidelines as first Steve, then Russell, and then Ricky lost all their chips. By doing little more than sitting at the table, I'd made almost half a million dollars in real money.

After sixty-eight hands of high-pressure final table poker, the producers of the WPT came out to the table and told the three remaining players that we needed to be more talkative. It made for better TV. There was a $2 million difference between third place and first place, and now I had to worry about how much I was talking? It was one distraction too many. I am not making excuses—but I was annoyed. I should have been more focused. But this directive from the producers made something in my brain snap.

I was the shortest stack with about T2.4 million in front of me, and the blinds had just been raised to T80,000 and T160,000. I looked down at ace–five offsuit on the button and, in my attempt to be better TV, said, "Five hundred straight." Hasan folded (as he'd been doing most every hand), but Martin called quickly in the big blind.

The flop came jack–ten–two rainbow. Martin checked. Having missed this flop completely, I checked behind him. The turn brought a nine, and Martin led out for T500,000, a small bet into this T1.1 million pot. Well, the nine gave me an open-ended straight draw with my ace–eight offsuit. I decided Martin would fold enough of the time here that I could semibluff all-in, falling back on my straight draw if called. So I moved in for T1.4 million more. Martin called instantly, and I threw up my hand as if to say, "You got me." I almost said out loud, "I have a straight draw." Good thing I didn't. Because it was then I turned my hand over and realized, as the reader surely does already, that I did not have ace–eight in my hand, but the same ace–five I'd started with. In the most high pressure moment of my poker career, something in my brain had failed me, and I had misremembered my hand.

Martin had king–jack, I didn't hit any of my three outs, and I was done. Even if I'd had ace–eight I would have been done, although if I'd realized I had ace–five I would have just folded, leaving myself the very short stack at T1.9 million. Of course, I was and am extremely disappointed at the way I busted from my first WPT final table. But I have many reasons to be happy about the outcome.

1. I played great for four and a half days, and am confident there are very few players who would've done better with the cards I had.
2. I made good poker decisions at the final table. It wasn't a bad decision that cost me but a malfunction under stress. I find that somewhat more palatable.
3. I wrote earlier in this book, "If I ever make a WPT final table broadcast, I will probably be nervous and possibly even make some hideous blunder, but I won't be changing my strategy." Well, that's pretty much exactly what happened. I made a big blunder but didn't change my style of play. That's fine. Now that I got the first final table out of the way, I'll be much more relaxed and less likely to blunder next time.
4. There was, I estimate, a 70 to 75 percent chance I would have finished third even if I'd folded.
5. (And this one is probably the most important.) I won $706,903.

Strangely, the money didn't change my life much. I'm still a writer and a poker player, same as I was before. Sure, there is much less worry about how to pay rent now (in fact, instead of rent, I'm making mortgage payments), and I play in some higher limit games than I used to, but the nuts and bolts of my day-to-day existence are pretty much the same. What I do have, however, that I didn't have before, is an experience I will be remembering, reliving, discussing, and rehashing probably for the rest of my life. It makes for quite a story, and I am grateful to the World Poker Tour Championship for providing me with the final, satisfying chapter to this book.

Glossary

Advance action checkboxes: In online poker, checkboxes that allow you to declare your action before the action gets to you.

Aggressive: Describes a player who often bets or raises.

All-in: Describes a player who has put all his chips in the pot.

Angle-shooter: A player who, while not technically cheating, engages in unethical behavior in an effort to gain an advantage at the table.

Backdoor draw: In Hold'em and Omaha, a draw that requires hitting cards on both the turn and the river (also called "runner–runner draw").

Bad beat: When a hand that was heavily favored to win ends up a loser after all the cards are dealt because another hand improved to beat it.

Bet: To put money in the pot that opponents must match if they want to stay in the hand.

Big bet: In games with structured betting rounds, the bet size used on later streets.

Big blind: The larger of the two forced bets in Hold'em and Omaha.

Big slick: Ace–king.

Blind: In Hold'em and Omaha, a bet players are forced to make before the cards are dealt; similar to an ante.

Bluff: A bet whose purpose is to get a better hand to fold.

Board: In Hold'em or Omaha, the five community cards placed faceup on the table.

Bot: A computer poker player.

Bubble: To finish just out of the money in the tournament.

Bunching: Refers to the increased likelihood that the remaining players have strong hands after the first several players have folded.

Burn: A card the dealer removes from play before dealing the flop.

Button: In Hold'em and Omaha, a white disk that identifies the last player to act after the flop.

Call down: To call an opponent all the way to the showdown.

Call: To match a bet that another player has made.

Calling station: A player who often calls but rarely raises or folds.

Change gears: To adjust one's style of play within the same tournament, or session.

Check behind: To check after another player has checked.

Check: A pass when it's your turn to bet; a bet of nothing.

Checked around: When all players have checked on the same betting round.

Check-raise: A raise of an opponent's bet after having checked earlier on the same betting round.

Cold-call: To call a raise without having previously put money in the pot.

Cutoff: In Hold'em and Omaha, the position to the right of the button.

Deposit bonus: Additional money a player might receive when he adds funds to his real money account at an online card room.

Domination: Refers to when two Hold'em hands share a common card; in other words, AK dominates AQ.

Drawing dead: This happens when a player has no chance to improve to the best hand.

Drawing live: Occurs when a player does not have the best hand but has some possibility of improving to the best hand.

Drawing: Playing a hand not because it is best, but because it might improve to the best hand.

Effective odds: The amount you stand to win, compared to the amount it will cost to see the hand to a showdown.

Expected value (EV): The amount of money a given play, or hand, will earn in the long run.

Exploit: To take advantage of mistakes in an opponent's strategy.

Fish: A weak player.

Flat-call: To call rather than raise, usually with a strong hand.

Flop: In Hold'em and Omaha, the first three community cards; they are dealt at the same time.

Flush draw: Four cards to a flush.

Fold: To surrender one's hand and forfeit any chance of winning the pot.

Game selection: The skill of choosing which games a player should and should not play in.

Game theory: A branch of mathematics developed to study decision-making in situations where two or more parties have competing interests.

Good game: A lineup of players that should be profitable for a good player.

Gutshot: Describes a straight draw that can only be filled with a card of one specific rank.

Hand for hand: In a tournament, when each table plays the same number of hands until a player is eliminated, only starting a new hand if the other tables have finished theirs.

Heads-up: One on one.

Heads-up match: A tournament between two players.

High limit: Describes games with stakes of $50–$100 or higher.

Ignorant end: In Hold'em and Omaha, the lowest straight that can be made when there is four to a straight on board.

Implied odds: The amount you stand to win if your hand improves, compared to the amount it costs to call a bet.

Kicker: In Hold'em, the unpaired hole card of a player that flops a pair.

Kill game: A ring-game in which the stakes are raised when a certain kill criteria is met (e.g., the pot of the previous hand was more than $100).

Lammer: A chip that can only be used to buy-in to a tournament.

Leak: Something a player does consistently that costs him money in the long run.

Limp: In Hold'em and Omaha, to just call the first bet before the flop.

Live six: In Omaha, a low hand made up of four low board cards (even though you don't use all four board cards), plus a six; similar definitions for "live seven" or "live eight".

Live: In Stud, a hand that has many cards left in the deck to improve it.

Lock up a seat: Have the poker room management reserve a seat for you at a table.

Loose: Describes a player who plays many hands, or a table in which most pots are contested between many players.

Low limit: Describes games with stakes of $5–$10 or less.

Made hand: A hand that doesn't need to improve to win the pot.

Major tournament: An annual event consisting of several large buy-in tournaments, usually capped off with a championship tournament.

Making it $X to go: Raising to a total of $X.

Micro limit: Describes games with stakes of $1–$2 or less.

Middle limit: Describes games with stakes between $10–$20 and $30–$60.

No Limit: Variant of poker where a player can bet all of his chips at any time.

Nosebleed: Describes games with extremely high stakes, $600–$1200 or higher.

Nut draw: A draw that, if it hits, will make the nuts.

Nut–nut: In Omaha, a hand that is the best possible high and best possible low.

Nuts: The best possible hand.

Odds: The number of times an event will happen compared to the number of times it won't, in the long run.

Offsuit: Describes a Hold'em hand containing two cards of different suits.

On tilt: Allowing emotions to influence betting decisions.

Open-ended: Describes a straight draw with four consecutive cards that can be completed with a fifth card on either end.

Optimal play: A strategy that cannot be exploited.

Option: In Hold'em and Omaha, the big blind gets the option to raise preflop in unraised pots.

Outs: The cards left in the deck that will improve a player's hand.

Overbet: A bet larger than the size of the pot.

Overcall: A call made after another player has already called (usually on the river).

Overcards: In Hold'em and Omaha, cards higher than any card on board.

Overpair: In Hold'em and Omaha, a pocket pair higher than any card on board.

Passive: Describes a player who rarely bets or raises, or a table where there is not much betting or raising.

Play back: To raise or reraise a player who has bet into or raised you.

Play money: In online poker, describes games that are not played for real money.

Play, Amount of: In a tournament, measure of how quickly or slowly the rising blinds will force players to be aggressive with less than premium hands.

Playing blind: To play a hand without looking at it (also called "playing dark").

Position: A player's seat relative to his opponents.

Post: To put up a blind before the cards are dealt.

Pot Limit: Variant of poker where the maximum bet size is the amount currently in the pot.

Pot odds: The amount of money in the pot compared to the amount it costs to call a bet.

Preflop: In Hold'em and Omaha, the round of betting before community cards are dealt.

Presto: Pocket fives.

Probability: The chance of an event occurring, expressed as a percentage or fraction.

Quads: Four of a kind.

Qualify: In hi–lo games, to hold a hand that is low enough to be eligible for half the pot.

Quartered: Winning only a quarter of the pot (usually only applies to hi–lo games).

Rags: Lousy cards.

Rainbow flop: A flop with cards of three different suits.

Raise: To put additional money in the pot after a player has bet.

Rake: Money the house takes out of the pot.

Range of hands: The set of all hands consistent with the actions a player has taken.

Read: An on-the-spot analysis of the strength of an opponent's hand based on betting patterns and/or body language.

Rebuy: Purchase more chips.

Result: The outcome of a given hand or session.

Results-oriented thinking: Evaluation of a strategy based on whether it made a player money during a particular hand or session.

Ring-game poker: Traditional poker, where chips are worth real money and players can cash out at any time.

River: The last card dealt.

Runner-runner: In Hold'em and Omaha, a draw that requires hitting cards on both the turn and the river (also called "backdoor draw").

Running bad: Catching bad cards and losing.

Running good: Catching good cards and winning.

Satellite: Single-table tournament whose prize is an entry into a larger tournament.

Save: In a tournament, a deal where each remaining player pockets a fixed sum of money and the players continue to play for whatever is left in the prize pool.

Scoop: To win an entire pot, not just half (usually only applies to hi–lo games).

Semibluff: A bet with a hand that figures to be behind if called but has a chance to improve to the best hand.

Set: In Hold'em and Omaha, a three of a kind made using two hole cards and one community card.

Slowplay: To check and call with a strong hand in the early betting rounds, waiting for the later rounds to bet and raise.

Small bet: In games with structured betting rounds, the bet size used on the earlier streets.

Small blind: The smaller of the two forced bets in Hold'em and Omaha.

Smooth-call: To call rather than raise, usually with a strong hand.

Spike: To catch a card that allows an underdog to improve to the best hand.

Stack size: The amount of chips a player has in front of him.

Steal: To bet or raise with a weak hand.

Steel wheel: A five-high straight flush.

Stop-loss: An amount of money that a player sets as a maximum loss for the night.

Straddle: In Hold'em and Omaha, to raise preflop UTG before the cards are dealt; the straddler has an option to reraise when the action gets back to him.

Street: A round of betting.

Stuck: Losing.

Suited: Describes a Hold'em hand containing two cards of the same suit.

Supersatellite: A multitable tournament whose prizes are entries into a larger tournament.

Sweat: To watch someone else play poker; usually the sweater gets to see the player's hole cards.

Teaser bet: A small bet intended to entice an opponent to call.

Tell: Something a player does that gives away the strength of his hand.

Texas Hold'em: Poker variant where each player gets two unique hole cards and the rest of his hand is made up of five community cards.

Tight: Describes a player who plays few hands, or a table in which most hands are contested heads-up.

Toke: Tip.

Top pair: In Hold'em and Omaha, a pair using the highest card on the board.

Top pair–top kicker: In Hold'em and Omaha, top pair with the highest possible off-card.

Tournament poker: A game where all players start with the same number of chips and play until one player has them all.

Trade: In a tournament, when two players agree in advance to exchange a certain percentage of whatever either of them might win.

Trap: To set up an opponent by playing weakly in the hopes that he will eventually commit a lot of chips with a less than premium hand.

Trips: Three of a kind.

Turn: In Hold'em and Omaha, the fourth community card dealt.

Under the gun (UTG): The position to the left of the big blind in Hold'em and Omaha.

Up front: In early position.

Value bet: A bet whose purpose is to get called by a worse hand.

Wheel: A five-high straight (A2345).

Wheel wrap: In Omaha, a draw to the wheel that will be completed by any wheel card that doesn't pair the board.

Acknowledgments

This project benefited greatly from the efforts of many people.

My first college roommate, Thomas Chi, graciously gave me the idea. Ben Lindsey, Siobhan Phillips, Jeremy Rissi, Mom (Barbara Matros), and the rec.gambling.poker community encouraged me to follow through and write the book. Noreen Wald helped immensely with the proposal. Kim Eisler got it looked at by relevant parties.

Greg Dinkin and Frank Scatoni at Venture Literary helped with just about everything, and were very patient with an author working on his first book.

Russell Rosenblum, my good friend and poker mentor, was the brains behind a lot of the theory, and the heart of a lot of the anecdotes.

Barry Kornspan, Molly Ball, Ivy Janet Blackman, Neal Bituin, Thomas Chi, Peter Sung, Jerrod Ankenman, Mom, Dad (William Matros), Chris Burke, Kevin Maurer, and Noreen Wald and her Writing Center class all provided helpful feedback during the writing process.

The Mohans—Neal, Rome, Ben, Fabian, A.J., Shri, Jeremy, Kevin, Justin, and Isaac—kept poker fun week after week.

Sarah Lawrence College, and especially the Student Affairs staff, made me feel welcome and supported at a time when I was unsure whether this project would fly.

Josh Henkin, my thesis advisor, not only improved my writing a ton, but turned a blind eye when I spent far too much time working on this book and almost no time working on my thesis.

Ivy, the best partner a poker player/writer could ask for, made smiling so much easier every day.

Finally, I'd like to thank my family: Mom, Dad, Nick, and Cathy. They were and are a constant source of support.

Index